There Are No Children Here

There Are

The Story
of Two Boys Growing Up
in the Other America

ALEX KOTLOWITZ

No Children Here

ANCHOR BOOKS

DOUBLEDAY

New York   London   Toronto   Sydney   Auckland

AN ANCHOR BOOK

PUBLISHED BY DOUBLEDAY

a division of Bantam Doubleday Dell Publishing Group, Inc.
1540 Broadway, New York, New York 10036

ANCHOR BOOKS, DOUBLEDAY, and the portrayal of an anchor
are trademarks of Doubleday, a division of Bantam Doubleday
Dell Publishing Group, Inc.

There Are No Children Here was originally published in hardcover by
Nan A. Talese/Doubleday in 1991.
The Anchor Books edition is published by arrangement with
Nan A. Talese/Doubleday.

All dates, place names, titles, and events in this account are factual. However, the
names of certain individuals have been changed in order to afford them a
measure of privacy.

Grateful acknowledgment is made to the following for permission to quote
from copyrighted material:
Lyrics from "I Need Love," by J. Todd Smith. Copyright © 1987 by
Def Jam Music Inc. (ASCAP). Used by permission.
Lyrics from "Make It Last Forever," by Keith Sweat and Teddy Riley.
Copyright © 1987 by Zomba Enterprises Inc./Donril Music (administered by
Zomba Enterprises Inc.). Copyright © 1982 by WB Music Corp.
All rights reserved. Used by permission.
Lyrics from "Superwoman," by Baby Face, L. A. Reid, and Daryl Simmons.
Copyright © 1988 by Kear Music, Green Skirt Music and Epic/Solar Songs, Inc.
All rights reserved. Used by permission.
The poem "Dream Deferred," reprinted from *The Panther and the Lash*
by Langston Hughes, by permission of Alfred A. Knopf, Inc. Copyright © 1951
by Langston Hughes.
The articles "How Young Pair Beat Odds in Public Housing" by
Leslie Baldacci and "Gang Member Killed" are reprinted with permission
from the Chicago *Sun-Times*.

Library of Congress Cataloging-in-Publication Data

Kotlowitz, Alex.
There are no children here / Alex Kotlowitz. — 1st Anchor Books ed.
p.   cm.
"Originally published in hardcover by Nan A. Talese/Doubleday in 1991"—
T.p. verso.
Includes bibliographical references (p.   ) and index.
1. Children—Illinois—Chicago—Social conditions—Case studies.   2. Family—
Illinois—Chicago—Case studies.   3. Inner cities—Illinois—Chicago—Case stud-
ies.   I. Title.
[HQ792.U5K683   1992]
305.23'09773'11—dc20
                                                                    91-28532
                                                                      CIP

ISBN 0-385-26556-5
Copyright © 1991 by Alex Kotlowitz

30   29   28   27   26   25   24   23   22   21

To my mother and father

What happens to a dream deferred?

Does it dry up
like a raisin in the sun?
Or fester like a sore—
And then run?
Does it stink like rotten meat?
Or crust and sugar over—
like a syrupy sweet?

Maybe it just sags
like a heavy load.

Or does it explode?

—Langston Hughes

Ah! What would the world be to us
    If the children were no more?
We should dread the desert behind us
    Worse than the dark before.

—Henry Wadsworth Longfellow

Preface

I FIRST MET Lafeyette and Pharoah Rivers during the summer of 1985. Lafeyette was then ten. Pharoah was seven. I was working as a free-lance journalist at the time and had been asked by a friend to write the text for a photo essay he was doing on children in poverty for *Chicago* magazine. He'd met the two boys and their mother through a local social services agency and had spent a number of days taking photographs of them at the Henry Horner Homes, a public housing complex.

Before I ever met Lafeyette and Pharoah, I had seen their

likenesses. One photograph in particular struck me: Lafeyette stood in a dark hallway of his building. He was wearing a striped tank top, baggy jeans, and a Kangol cap that was too big for him; his high-tops were untied. In his hands was what appeared to be a baseball. And yet, despite the youthful attire, he looked like an old man. There seemed bottled up inside him a lifetime's worth of horrors. His face revealed a restless loneliness.

When I went to meet him and his family, the interview didn't last long—maybe a few hours—because I was writing only a short essay to accompany my friend's photographs and had over a dozen families to interview in a couple of weeks' time. But even during my short stay with Lafeyette, I was unnerved by the relentless neighborhood violence he talked about. In fact, I had trouble believing it all. And then I asked Lafeyette what he wanted to be. "If I grow up, I'd like to be a bus driver," he told me. *If*, not *when*. At the age of ten, Lafeyette wasn't sure he'd make it to adulthood.

Two years later, I returned to the Henry Horner Homes to write a story for *The Wall Street Journal* on the toll inner-city violence takes on the children who live there. I spent the summer at Henry Horner, playing basketball with the kids, going to lunch with them, talking with their parents, and just hanging out. Over those weeks, I became good friends with Lafeyette and his brother Pharoah, and our friendship lasted long after the *Journal* story appeared and, I'm sure, will continue well beyond the publication of this book. We have spent time together nearly every weekend. We visit museums, play video games, take walks in the country, go to the movies, and browse in bookstores. Each summer we take a fishing trip to northern Michigan. And we keep talking. I've been encouraged by their resilience, inspired by their laughter, and angered by their stories.

In 1988, I suggested to their mother, LaJoe, the possibility of my writing a book about Lafeyette, Pharoah, and the other children of the neighborhood. She liked the idea, although she hesitated, and then said, "But you know, there are no children here. They've seen too much to be children."

One of every five children in the United States lives in poverty—an estimated twelve million children, according to the Children's Defense Fund. In cities like Chicago, the rate is considerably higher: one of every three children. Many grow up in neighborhoods similar to Lafeyette and Pharoah's. By the time they enter adolescence, they have contended with more terror than most of us confront in a lifetime. They have had to make choices that most experienced and educated adults would find difficult. They have lived with fear and witnessed death. Some of them have lashed out. They have joined gangs, sold drugs, and, in some cases, inflicted pain on others. But they have also played baseball and gone on dates and shot marbles and kept diaries. For, despite all they have seen and done, they are—and we must constantly remind ourselves of this—still children.

LaJoe was not only agreeable to the project, she felt it important that their stories be told. She had once said to me that she occasionally wished she were deaf. The shooting. The screaming. Babies crying. Children shrieking. Sometimes she thought it would all drive her insane. So maybe it would be best if she couldn't hear at all. Her hope—and mine—was that a book about the children would make us all hear, that it would make us all stop and listen.

This book follows Lafeyette and Pharoah over a two-year period as they struggle with school, attempt to resist the lure of the gangs, and mourn the death of friends, all the while searching for some inner peace. During this time, both boys undergo profound changes. They are at an age when, through discovery of themselves and their world, they begin to form their unique identities. Consequently, it is a story that doesn't have a neat and tidy ending. It is, instead, about a beginning, the dawning of two lives. Most of all, it is a story about two friends.

_____ Summer 1987 _____

One

NINE-YEAR-OLD Pharoah Rivers stumbled to his knees. "Give me your hand," ordered his older brother, Lafeyette, who was almost twelve. "Give me your hand." Pharoah reached upward and grabbed hold of his brother's slender fingers, which guided him up a slippery, narrow trail of dirt and brush.

"C'mon, man," Lafeyette urged, as his stick-thin body whirled around with a sense of urgency. "Let's go." He paused to watch Pharoah struggle through a thicket of vines. "Man, you slow." He had little patience for the smaller boy's clumsiness. Their friends had already reached the top of the railroad overpass.

It was a warm Saturday afternoon in early June, and this was the children's first visit to these railroad tracks. The trains passed by at roof level above a corridor of small factories on the city's near west side. To reach the tracks the children had to scale a steep mound of earth shoved against one side of the aging concrete viaduct. Bushes and small trees grew in the soil alongside the tracks; in some places the brush was ten to fifteen feet thick.

Pharoah clambered to the top, moving quickly to please his brother, so quickly that he scraped his knee on the crumbling cement. As he stood to test his bruised leg, his head turned from west to east, following the railroad tracks, five in all, leading from the western suburbs to Chicago's downtown. His wide eyes and his buck teeth, which had earned him the sobriquet Beaver and kept his lips pushed apart, made him seem in awe of the world.

Looking east, Pharoah marveled at the downtown skyline. With the late afternoon sun reflecting off the glass and steel skyscrapers, downtown Chicago glowed in the distance. As he looked south a few blocks, he glimpsed the top floors of his home, a red brick, seven-story building. It appeared dull and dirty even in the brilliant sun. Farther south, he could just make out his elementary school and the towering spire of the First Congregational Baptist Church, a 118-year-old building that he'd been told had been a stop on the Underground Railroad. The view, he thought, was pretty great.

But he soon was distracted by more immediate matters. A black-and-yellow butterfly wove effortlessly through the wind. Fixed on its dance, Pharoah stared silently for minutes, until a rising summer breeze carried it away. The abundant clumps of white and lavender wildflowers that grew along the rails soon won his attention, so he bent down to touch the soft petals, to finger the vines as if to measure their growth. He breathed in the scent of the blossoming wood anemones, then licked a salty drop of perspiration that had dropped from his brow. The humidity had already begun to tire him.

Lafeyette jostled his brother from behind. "Stop it," Pharoah screeched, swatting at his brother as if he were an annoying pest. Lafeyette reached for Pharoah, but the younger one scampered away. Lafeyette laughed. He could be rough in his play, which annoyed Pharoah. Sometimes, their mother called Lafeyette "Aggravatin'," as in "Aggravatin', get over here," or "Aggravatin', stop aggravatin' your brother." Lafeyette took the ribbing good-naturedly.

He thrust a crowbar into Pharoah's hands, one of four they and their six friends had dragged to the top of the viaduct. They had ventured onto these railroad tracks only once before, and then just to explore. Back then, though, they hadn't had a mission.

The eight boys split into pairs, trying to be soft afoot, but in the excitement their whispers quickly turned to muffled shouts as their arms hacked away at the high weeds. One boy walked tightrope along a rail, his young limbs bending and twisting with each gust of wind. His companions ordered him down.

Pharoah glued himself to his cousin Leonard Anderson, whom everyone called Porkchop. A couple of years younger than Pharoah, Porkchop was unusually quiet and shy, though filled with a nervous energy that kept him in constant motion. He grinned rather than talked. The cousins were inseparable; when they met after school—each attended a different one—they frequently greeted each other with a warm embrace.

Lafeyette wandered off with James Howard, a close friend, who lived in the same building. They had grown up together and knew each other well, though James, a wiry, athletic boy, was a year older than Lafeyette and was much more agile. He also was a more easygoing boy than Lafeyette; his mischievous grin spanned the width of his face in the shape of a crescent moon.

Lafeyette and James found what they thought might be a good spot, a small bare patch in the brown dirt. Lafeyette plunged the short end of the crowbar into the ground. He did it again. And again. The soil gave way only a couple of inches with each plunge of the makeshift shovel. James fell to his knees. His small hands unearthed a few more inches, taking over for Lafeyette and the crowbar. Nothing.

"Daaag," muttered James, clearly disappointed. "There ain't nothing up here." Again, they noisily plowed through the weeds.

The boys were looking for snakes. For another hour, they dug hole after hole in the hard soil, determined not to go home empty-handed. They figured that a garter snake would do well at home as a pet; after all, they thought, the snake neither bites nor grows to a great length. The boys had got the idea for this urban safari when last year an older friend named William had nabbed a garter snake and showed it off to all the kids. William let them touch it and hold it and watch it slither across the brown linoleum tiles of their building's breezeway. Lafeyette had never touched such an animal before, and he and the others had eagerly crowded around William's pet, admiring its yellow-and-black coat and its darting orange tongue. William died a few months later when a friend, fooling around with a revolver he thought was unloaded, shot William in the back of the head. Lafeyette never learned what happened to the snake.

The boys' search turned up little, though that might have been expected; they had never seen a snake in the wild and didn't really know where to look. But they did find three small white eggs resting on the ground, and debated whether they held baby reptiles or birds. James spotted the only animal of the afternoon, a foot-long rat. It had scampered alongside the tracks, sniffing for a treasure of its own.

Bored by the fruitless search, Pharoah and Porkchop had long ago wandered to a stretch along the tracks where there was a ten-foot-high stack of worn automobile tires. The cousins scrambled in and out of the shallow rubber tunnels created by the tires. Porkchop, the more daring of the two, climbed to the top of the pile, bouncing off the tires with abandon. Pharoah stood to the side, watching his cousin's antics, until a sparrow began to fly over his head in what seemed like threatening loops. Pharoah screamed with a mixture of fear and delight as he tried to avoid the dive-bombing playmate.

James, who had also given up the hunt, hoisted himself into an empty boxcar on one of the sidetracks. As Lafeyette tried to follow, a friend sighted a commuter train approaching from downtown. "There's a train!" he yelled. James frantically helped Lafeyette climb into the open boxcar, where they found refuge in a dark corner. Others hid behind the boxcar's huge wheels. Pharoah and Porkchop threw themselves headlong into the weeds, where they lay motionless on their bellies. "Keep quiet," came a voice from the thick bushes. "Shut up," another barked.

The youngsters had heard that the suburb-bound commuters, from behind the tinted train windows, would shoot at them for trespassing on the tracks. One of the boys, certain that the commuters were crack shots, burst into tears as the train whisked by. Some of the commuters had heard similar rumors about the neighborhood children and worried that, like the cardboard lions in a carnival shooting gallery, they might be the target of talented snipers. Indeed, some sat away from the windows as the train passed through Chicago's blighted core. For both the boys and the commuters, the unknown was the enemy.

The train passed without incident, and soon most of the boys had joined James and Lafeyette in the boxcar, sitting in the doorway, their rangy legs dangling over the side. Lafeyette and James giggled at a private joke, their thin bodies shivering with laughter.

Pharoah was too small to climb into the car, so he crouched in the weeds nearby, his legs tucked underneath him, and picked at the vegetation, which now reached his neck. He was lost in his thoughts, thoughts so private and fanciful that he would have had trouble articulating them to others. He didn't want to leave this place, the sweet smell of the wildflowers and the diving sparrow. There was a certain tranquillity here, a peacefulness that extended into the horizon like the straight, silvery rails. In later months, with the memory of the place made that much gentler by the passage of time, Pharoah would come to savor this sanctuary even more.

None of the boys was quite ready to call it a day, but the sun had descended in the sky, and nighttime here was dangerous. Reluctantly, they gathered the crowbars, slid down the embankment, and, as Lafeyette took Pharoah's hand to cross the one busy street, began the short trek home.

Two

THE CHILDREN called home "Hornets" or, more frequently, "the projects" or, simply, the "jects" (pronounced *jets*). Pharoah called it "the graveyard." But they never referred to it by its full name: the Governor Henry Horner Homes.

Nothing here, the children would tell you, was as it should be. Lafeyette and Pharoah lived at 1920 West Washington Boulevard, even though their high-rise sat on Lake Street. Their building had no enclosed lobby; a dark tunnel cut through the middle of the building, and the wind and strangers passed freely along it. Those tenants who received public aid had their checks sent to the local currency exchange, since the building's first-floor mailboxes had all been broken into. And since darkness engulfed the building's corridors, even in the daytime, the residents always carried flashlights, some of which had been handed out by a local politician during her campaign.

Summer, too, was never as it should be. It had become a season of duplicity.

On June 13, a couple of weeks after their peaceful afternoon on the railroad tracks, Lafeyette celebrated his twelfth birthday. Under the gentle afternoon sun, yellow daisies poked through the cracks in the sidewalk as children's bright faces peered out from behind their windows. Green leaves clothed the cottonwoods, and pastel cotton shirts and shorts, which had sat for months in layaway, clothed the children. And like the fresh buds on the crabapple trees, the children's spirits blossomed with the onset of summer.

Lafeyette and his nine-year-old cousin Dede danced across the worn lawn outside their building, singing the lyrics of an L. L. Cool J rap, their small hips and spindly legs moving in rhythm. The boy and girl were on their way to a nearby shopping strip, where Lafeyette planned to buy radio headphones with $8.00 he had received as a birthday gift.

Suddenly, gunfire erupted. The frightened children fell to the ground. "Hold your head down!" Lafeyette snapped, as he covered Dede's head with her pink nylon jacket. If he hadn't physically restrained her, she might have sprinted for home, a dangerous action when the gangs started warring. "Stay down," he ordered the trembling girl.

The two lay pressed to the beaten grass for half a minute, until the shooting subsided. Lafeyette held Dede's hand as they cautiously crawled through the dirt toward home. When they finally made it inside, all but fifty cents of Lafeyette's birthday money had trickled from his pockets.

Lafeyette's summer opened the way it would close, with gunshots. For Lafeyette and Pharoah, these few months were to be a rickety bridge to adolescence.

If the brothers had one guidepost in their young lives these few months, though, it was their mother, LaJoe. They depended on her; she depended on them. The boys would do anything for their mother.

A shy, soft-spoken woman, LaJoe was known for her warmth and generosity, not only to her own children but to her children's friends. Though she received Aid to Families with Dependent Children, neighbors frequently knocked on her door to borrow a can of soup or a cup of flour. She always obliged. LaJoe had often mothered children who needed advice or comforting. Many young men and women still called her "Mom." She let so many people through her apartment, sometimes just to use the bathroom, that she hid the toilet paper in the kitchen because it had often been stolen.

But the neighborhood, which hungrily devoured its children, had taken its toll of LaJoe as well. In recent years, she had become more tired as she questioned her ability to raise her children here. She no longer fixed her kids' breakfasts every day —and there were times when the children had to wash their own clothes in the bathtub. Many of the adults had aged with the neighborhood, looking as worn and empty as the abandoned stores that lined the once-thriving Madison Street. By their mid-thirties many women had become grandmothers; by their mid-forties, great-grandmothers. They nurtured and cared for their boyfriends and former boyfriends and sons and grandsons and great-grandsons.

LaJoe, in her youth, had been stunning, her smooth, light brown complexion highlighted by an open smile. When she pulled her hair back in a ponytail, she appeared almost Asian, her almond-shaped eyes gazing out from a heart-shaped face. She had been so pretty in her mid-twenties that she briefly tried a modeling career. Now she was thirty-five, and men still whistled and smiled at her on the street. Unlike many other women her age, she hadn't put on much weight, and her high-cheekboned face still had a sculptured look. But the confidence of her youth had left her. Her shoulders were often hunched. She occasionally awoke with dark circles under her eyes. And her smile was less frequent now.

LaJoe had watched and held on as the neighborhood slowly decayed, as had many urban communities like Horner over the past two decades. First, the middle-class whites fled to the suburbs. Then the middle-class blacks left for safer neighborhoods.

Then businesses moved, some to the suburbs, others to the South. Over the past ten years, the city had lost a third of its manufacturing jobs, and there were few jobs left for those who lived in Henry Horner. Unemployment was officially estimated at 19 percent; unofficially, it was probably much higher. There were neighborhoods in Chicago worse off than Horner, but the demise of this particular community was often noted because it had once been among the city's wealthiest areas.

Ashland Avenue, a six-lane boulevard just east of Henry Horner, was named for the Kentucky estate of Henry Clay. By the mid-nineteenth century, it had become one of the city's smartest thoroughfares, lined with dwellings constructed of elegant Attic marble, fashionable churches, and exclusive clubs. "People would parade along the sidewalk to ogle at the notables and to be seen themselves; to watch the fine carriages spin along the macadam boulevard, to see the latest manifestation of changing fashion," read one newspaper account. But the neighborhood slowly changed. As immigrants, primarily German, Irish, and Eastern European Jews, settled on the west side, the city's glitter moved eastward to the lake, just north of the Loop, a strip now known as the Magnificent Mile and the Gold Coast.

The Ashland Avenue area quickly lost its luster. Jane Addams's founding of the renowned Hull House in 1889 signaled the west side's growing decline. It was one of the nation's first settlement houses, delivering various services to the poor of the area and acting as their advocate in housing, health care, and children's rights. Soon, the mansions on Ashland were transformed into headquarters for local unions or rooming houses for the transients of Skid Row. By 1906, the neighborhood had deteriorated still further, and tuberculosis claimed 5 percent of the west side's population. The Chicago Lung Association, then called the Chicago Tuberculosis Institute, opened its office on the west side, where it is still located.

The blight has continued and is particularly evident today west of Horner, a section of the city that, along with the south side, during the 1930s, 1940s, and 1950s became home to over a half-million blacks who migrated from the South, displacing the earlier immigrants. Western Avenue, now a strip of fast-food outlets, car washes, and family-run stores, borders Henry Horner to the west, though it is not a boundary of much significance, since on the other side the rubble continues. The two-and three-family tenements sag and lean like drunkards. Many of the buildings are vacant, their contents lying on the sidewalk. To LaJoe, the neighborhood had become a black hole. She could more easily recite what wasn't there than what was. There were no banks, only currency exchanges, which charged customers up to $8.00 for every welfare check cashed. There were no public libraries, movie theaters, skating rinks, or bowling alleys to entertain the neighborhood's children. For the infirm, there were two neighborhood clinics, the Mary Thompson Hospital and the Miles Square Health Center, both of which teetered on the edge of bankruptcy and would close by the end of 1989. Yet the death rate of newborn babies exceeded infant mortality rates in a number of Third World countries, including Chile, Costa Rica, Cuba, and Turkey. And there was no rehabilitation center, though drug abuse was rampant.

According to a 1980 profile of the Twenty-seventh Ward—a political configuration drawn, ironically, in the shape of a gun and including both Henry Horner and Rockwell Gardens, a smaller but no less forbidding public housing complex—60,110 people lived here, 88 percent of them black, 46 percent of them below the poverty level. It was an area so impoverished that when Mother Teresa visited it in 1982, she assigned nuns from her Missionaries of Charity to work at Henry Horner. They had set up a soup kitchen, a shelter for women and children, and an afterschool program. Where there used to be thirteen social service agencies there were now only three: the Missionaries of Charity, the Boys Club, and the Chicago Commons Association. The latter two provided recreational activities as well as tutoring, counseling, and day care, but they had limited funds. A Chicago Commons' program called Better Days for Youth targeted children under thirteen who were having problems in school or with the police, but there was money to serve only twenty-eight children at a time.

LaJoe sometimes believed that the city had all but given up here. A local billboard warned NEEDLES KILL. There was a time when such a message read DRUGS KILL.

And despite Horner's proximity—one mile—to the city's booming downtown, LaJoe and her neighbors felt abandoned. Horner sat so close to the city's business district that from the

Sears Tower observation deck tourists could have watched La-feyette duck gunfire on his birthday. But city residents never had reason to pass the housing complex unless they attended a basketball or hockey game at the Chicago Stadium, just a block away.

Exacerbating the isolation was the fact that nearly half of the families in Henry Horner, including the Riverses, had no tele-phone. Residents also felt disconnected from one another; there was little sense of community at Horner, and there was even less trust. Some residents who didn't have a phone, for instance, didn't know any others in their building who would let them use theirs. Some neighbors wouldn't allow their children to go outside to play. One mother moved aside her living room furni-ture to make an open and safe place where her children could frolic.

But though the isolation and the physical ruin of the area's stores and homes had discouraged LaJoe, it was her family that had most let her down. Not that she could separate the two. Sometimes she blamed her children's problems on the neigh-borhood; at other times, she attributed the neighborhood's de-cline to the change in people, to the influx of drugs and vio-lence.

Her three oldest children, to whom she felt she'd given every-thing she could, had all disappointed her. All had dropped out of school. All had been in jail at least once. All had been in-volved with drugs. The oldest, LaShawn, a slender twenty-year-old, was so delicately featured some called her "China Doll." She worked as a prostitute from time to time to support her drug habit. The next oldest, nineteen-year-old Paul, named af-ter his father, had served time in an Indiana prison for bur-glary. Terence, now seventeen, had been the most troublesome problem for LaJoe and, because of their extraordinary close-ness, her biggest disappointment. He began selling drugs at the age of eleven and had been in and out, usually in, trouble with the law ever since.

LaJoe also had a set of four-year-old triplets: Timothy, Tif-fany, and Tammie. The two girls so resembled each other that not even their father could tell them apart.

All eight children had the same father, Paul, to whom LaJoe

had been married for seventeen years. But the two had long ago fallen out of love. He lived at home only sporadically.

LaJoe wanted it to be different for Lafeyette and Pharoah, different from the way it had been for her three oldest children and different from the way it had been for her.

In her husband's absence, Lafeyette had become LaJoe's confidant. She relied on him. So did the younger children. Lafeyette watched after Pharoah and the triplets. He wouldn't let anything happen to them. He had been a carefree child, a bit of a ham, in fact. For a photograph taken when he was about four, he shoved a big cigar in his mouth and plopped a blue floppy hat on his small head. It was Christmastime, and Lafeyette's cousins, who in the photo were all crowded behind him, seemed amused by his antics. When he got older, around eight or nine, he'd hop on the Madison Street bus by himself to visit his grandmother, who lived in an apartment farther west. And he loved to draw, mostly pictures of superheroes. He boasted that his name appeared on all seven floors of his building. He was a boy bubbling with energy and verve.

But over the past year Lafeyette had begun to change, LaJoe thought. The past spring, he'd been caught stealing candy from a Walgreen's downtown. It was the first time he'd gotten into any kind of trouble. He had been hanging out with a youngster, Keith, who was known among the neighborhood kids for his ability to swipe expensive bottles of cologne from the display cases at downtown department stores. Lafeyette was placed in the Chicago Commons' Better Days for Youth. One of the first children in the new six-month program, Lafeyette received help with his school work as well as counseling. Keith moved out of town, and Lafeyette made friends with Chicago Commons' staff members, whom he'd periodically visit after his completion of the program.

Lafeyette still laughed and played with Pharoah and friends, but he could be bossy, ordering around his younger brother and the triplets with cockiness and the fury of a temperamental adult. He had inherited his mother's temper and could turn on the younger ones in an instant. It wasn't that Lafeyette and they didn't get along; it was that he worried about them, like a father worrying about his children. He admonished them for hanging out with the wrong people or straying too far from his sight. He cared almost too much about everything and everybody. Sometimes the strain of responsibility showed in his thin, handsome face; it would tighten, like a fist, and it seemed as if he would never smile again. He'd purse his lips and clench his jaw; his deep-set, heavy-lidded eyes would stare straight ahead. His face revealed so little, his mother thought, and yet so much.

Pharoah was different, not only from Lafeyette but from the other children, too. He didn't have many friends, except for Porkchop, who was always by his side. LaJoe had given him his name but, like his brother's name, spelled it in an unusual way. At the time, LaJoe hadn't known the story of Moses and the Pharaoh, but in later years when she found out she laughed. Pharoah was anything but a king.

Pharoah clutched his childhood with the vigor of a tiger gripping his meat. He wouldn't let go. Nobody, nothing would take it away from him. When he was two, Pharoah would run around the apartment naked; sometimes he'd be wearing just small white shoes. When he was four or five, he told LaJoe that he wanted to live on a lake so that he could always feel the wind on his back. At the age of five, he had an imaginary friend, Buddy, whom he'd talk to and play with in his bedroom. Frequently, Pharoah got so lost in his daydreams that LaJoe had to shake him to bring him back from his flights of fancy. Those forays into distant lands and with other people seemed to help Pharoah fend off the ugliness around him.

Now, at the age of nine, he giggled at the slightest joke; he cried at the smallest of tragedies. He had recently developed a slight stutter, which made him seem even more vulnerable. And he listened to classical music on the radio because, he said, it relaxed him. He sensed that his playfulness delighted the adults, so he would tease them and they him. He wanted to be recognized, to know that he was wanted. At the age of eight he wrote a short letter to his Aunt LaVerne, one of LaJoe's sisters.

Jan. 1986
Pharoah Rivers

I love you do you love me. You are my best aunt verny. I love you very much. The people I love.

Verny
Grandmother

Linda
Randy
Moma
Dad
Brothers
Sisters
Cousins
Aunt

"Oh, that Pharoah," family and neighbors would say to LaJoe, recounting some enchanting incident involving the nine-year-old. They adored him.

Pharoah liked to tell people he was big-boned "like my mama," though she was, in fact, a small woman. He had LaJoe's open and generous smile, and, like his mother, who was only five feet two, he was short, so that LaJoe could, until he was nine or ten, pass him off as a five-year-old to get him on the bus without paying fare.

Where the adults found Lafeyette handsome, they found Pharoah cute. The women would josh both of them, saying that someday they'd be lady killers. The local Boys Club used a photograph of Pharoah in one of its fund-raising brochures. In the picture, Pharoah, along with four other young boys, was dressed in marching cap and cape with a drum set, almost as large as Pharoah himself, slung around his neck. As he often did, he had cocked his head to one side for the camera and grinned cheerfully, a pose he must have known made him look even cuter.

The boys got along, and for that LaJoe was grateful. The two shared a room and, on most mornings, walked to school together. Occasionally, Lafeyette played rough with Pharoah or told him off, but LaJoe knew that if Pharoah ever needed his older brother, he'd be there. Older and bigger, he offered Pharoah some protection from the tougher kids in the neighborhood.

LaJoe knew that Lafeyette and Pharoah were like millions of other children living in the nation's inner cities. She knew that she was not alone in her struggles, that other women in other cities were watching their children grow old quickly, too. She had heard of some mothers who moved their families to Milwaukee or to the suburbs, some of which were poorer than Henry Horner, in an effort to escape the neighborhood's brutality. In the end, LaJoe would almost always learn, these families were up against the same ruthless forces they had faced in Chicago.

It wouldn't happen to Lafeyette and Pharoah, she had vowed to herself. It just wouldn't happen. They would have a childhood. They would have a chance to enjoy the innocence and playfulness of youth and to appreciate the rewards of school and family. They would bring home high school diplomas. They would move out of the neighborhood. They would get jobs and raise families. She had made mistakes with the older children that she was determined not to repeat with her younger ones.

But during the summer of 1987, when drugs and the accompanying violence swept through the neighborhood, she lived in daily fear that something might happen to her young ones. Though she would never say as much, she worried that they might not make it to their eighteenth birthday. Too many hadn't. Already that year, fifty-seven children had been killed in the city. Five had died in the Horner area, including two, aged eight and six, who died from smoke inhalation when firefighters had to climb the fourteen stories to their apartment. Both of the building's elevators were broken. Lafeyette and Pharoah knew of more funerals than weddings.

So that summer LaJoe wanted to be prepared for the worst. She started paying $80 a month for burial insurance for Lafeyette, Pharoah, and the four-year-old triplets.

Lafeyette had promised his mother he wouldn't let anything happen to Pharoah. But for a brief moment, he thought he had lost him.

Three days after Lafeyette's birthday, gunfire once again filled the air. It was two-thirty in the afternoon; school had just let out. As Lafeyette and his mother hustled the triplets onto the floor of the apartment's narrow hallway, a drill they now followed almost instinctually, they caught glimpses through the windows of young gunmen waving their pistols about. One youth toted a submachine gun.

The dispute had started when two rival drug gangs fired at each other from one high-rise to another.

From his first-floor apartment, Lafeyette, who had left his fifth-grade class early that day, watched hopefully for Pharoah as the children poured out of the Henry Suder Elementary School, just a block away. Panicking, many of the youngsters ran directly toward the gunfire. Lafeyette and his mother screamed at the children to turn back. But they kept coming, clamoring for the shelter of their homes.

Lafeyette finally spotted his brother, first running, then walking, taking cover behind trees and fences. But then he lost sight of him. "Mama, lemme go get him. Lemme go," Lafeyette begged. He was afraid that Pharoah would run straight through the gunfire. Pharoah would later say he had learned to look both ways and that's why he'd started walking. "My mama told me when you hear the shooting, first to walk because you don't know where the bullets are coming," he explained. LaJoe refused Lafeyette's request to let him go after his brother. She couldn't even go herself. The guns kept crackling.

Lafeyette's friend James, who was cowering behind a nearby tree, sprinted for the Riverses' apartment. Pharoah saw him and ran, too. The two frantically pounded with their fists on the metal door. "Let us in!" James wailed. "Let us in! It's James and Pharoah!" James's heart was beating so hard that he could hear it above the commotion. But with all the noise, no one heard their frenzied pleas, and the two ran to a friend's apartment upstairs.

Meanwhile, the police, who at first thought they were the targets of the shooting, had taken cover in their cars and in the building's breezeway. Passersby lay motionless on the ground, protected by parked vehicles and a snow-cone vending stand. Then, as suddenly as it began, the battle ended. No one, amazingly, had been hurt. Lafeyette learned later that one errant bullet pierced a friend's third-floor window with such force that it cut through a closet door and lodged in the cinder-block wall.

The police made no arrests. And when a reporter called the police department's central headquarters the next day, he was told that there was no record of the shoot-out.

But Lafeyette knew. So did Pharoah.

Three

THOUGH ONLY four years old at the time, LaJoe forever remembered the day she and her family moved into the Henry Horner Homes. It was October 15, 1956, a Monday.

The complex was so new that some of the buildings had yet to be completed. Thick paths of mud ran where the sidewalks should have been. A thin, warped plank of wood substituted for the unbuilt steps.

But to LaJoe and her brothers and sisters, it all looked dazzling. The building's brand-new bricks were a deep and luscious red, and they were smooth and solid to the touch. The clean windows reflected the day's movements with a shimmering clarity that gave the building an almost magical quality. Even the two unfinished buildings, one to the west and one to the south, their concrete frames still exposed, appeared stately.

It was quiet and peaceful; there were not even any passersby. On this unusually warm fall day—the temperature topped 70 degrees by noon—LaJoe could even hear the shrill songs of the sparrows. The building, 1920 West Washington, stood empty. They were to be the first family to occupy one of its sixty-five apartments.

LaJoe's father, Roy Anderson, pulled the car and its trailer up to the building's back entrance. He was a ruggedly handsome man whose steely stare belied his affable nature and his affection for children. He and his wife, Lelia Mae, had been eagerly awaiting this move. They and their thirteen children, including three sets of twins, had been living in a spacious five-bedroom apartment, but the coal-heated flat got so cold in the winter that the pipes frequently froze. On those days they fetched their water from a fire hydrant. The apartment was above a Baptist church, and there were times when the rooms overflowed with the wailings of funerals or the joyful songs accompanying baptisms. And the building canted to the east, so whenever a truck passed, the floors and walls shook vigorously, sometimes scaring the children into thinking the entire structure might collapse.

For Lelia Mae and Roy their south side apartment seemed adequate enough. Both had come from the shacks and the shanties of the South. Lelia Mae had left Charleston, West Virginia, at the age of twenty in 1937. Her father had been a coal miner and a part-time preacher for the Ebenezer Baptist Church. She headed for Chicago, where she'd been told she could make good money. Her older sister, who had moved to Chicago a few years earlier, promised Lelia Mae to get her a job in the laundry where she worked. Once in Chicago, Lelia Mae, already divorced and with one child, met her second husband, Roy, who worked in one of the city's numerous steel mills. Roy hailed from Camden, Arkansas, where his father had been the deacon of a Baptist church. Roy was a spiffy dresser whose trademark was a small Stetson; it balanced with astounding ease on his large, dignified head.

The two had raised their family in the second-floor Chicago apartment above the church, but their home was to be demolished to make way for a university building, part of the new Illinois Institute of Technology, and they had to move. They were given the opportunity to move into public housing, the grand castles being built for the nation's urban poor.

In the middle and late 1950s, publicly financed high-rise complexes sprang up across the country like dandelions in a rainy spring. In 1949, Congress, in addressing a postwar housing crisis, had authorized loans and subsidies to construct 810,000 units of low-rent housing units nationwide. At the time, it was viewed as an impressive effort to provide shelter for the less fortunate.

But the program's controversial beginnings were an ominous sign of what lay ahead. White politicians wanted neither poor nor black families in their communities, and they resisted the publicly financed housing. In over seventy communities, public housing opponents brought the issue before the electorate in referenda. In California, voters amended the state constitution so that all public housing projects required their approval. In Detroit, a 14,350-unit public housing program was reduced when a public housing opponent was elected mayor. In Chicago, the opposition was fierce. The city's aldermen first bullied the state legislature into giving them the power of selecting public housing sites, a prerogative that had previously belonged to the local housing authority.

Then a group of leading aldermen, who were not above petty vindictiveness, chartered a bus to tour the city in search of potential sites. On the bus ride, they told reporters that they were out to seek vengeance against the Chicago Housing Authority and the seven aldermen who supported public housing, and they chose sites in neighborhoods represented by these aldermen. Like prankish teenagers, they selected the most outrageous of possibilities, including the tennis courts at the University of Chicago and a parcel of land that sat smack in the middle of a major local highway. The message was clear: the CHA and its liberal backers could build public housing but not in their back yards.

The complexes were not, in the end, built at these sites. Instead, they were constructed on the edges of the city's black ghettoes. Rather than providing alternatives to what had become decrepit living conditions, public housing became anchors for existing slums. And because there were few sites available, the housing authority had no alternative but to build up rather than out. So the ghettoes grew toward the heavens, and public housing became a bulwark of urban segregation.

On the city's near west side, on the periphery of one of the city's black ghettoes, was built the Henry Horner Homes. The complex of sixteen high-rises bore the name of an Illinois governor best known for his obsession with Abraham Lincoln and his penchant for bucking the Chicago Democratic machine.

The buildings were constructed on the cheap. There were no lobbies to speak of, only the open breezeways. There was no communication system from the breezeways to the tenants. During the city's harsh winters, elevator cables froze; in one year alone the housing authority in Chicago needed to make over fifteen-hundred elevator repairs. And that was in just one development.

The trash chutes within each building were too narrow to handle the garbage of all its tenants. The boiler systems continually broke down. There were insufficient overhead lighting installations and wall outlets in each unit. And the medicine cabinet in each apartment's bathroom was not only easily removed, but was connected to the medicine chest in the adjoining apartment. Over the years, residents had been robbed, assaulted, and even murdered by people crawling through their medicine cabinet.

When a group of Soviet housing officials visited Henry Horner in October of 1955, while it was still under construction, they were appalled that the walls in the apartments were of cinder block. Why not build plastered walls, they suggested. "We would be thrown off our jobs in Moscow if we left unfinished walls like this," I. K. Kozvilia, minister of city and urban construction in the Soviet Union, told local reporters.

"In the American way of doing things," huffed *The Chicago Daily News* in an editorial the next day, "there is little use for luxury in building subsidized low-cost housing." It was no surprise, then, that thirteen years later a federal report on public housing would describe Henry Horner and the city's other developments as "remindful of gigantic filing cabinets with separate cubicles for each human household."

But on this day, LaJoe and her siblings were bubbling over with joy at the sight of their new home. It was, after all, considerably prettier and sturdier and warmer than the flat they'd left behind. Before their father could unload the rented trailer and hand his children the picnic table, which he planned to use in the kitchen, and the cots, which he hoped to replace soon with bunk beds, they ran into the newly finished building. He and his wife could only smile at the children's excitement.

LaJoe's older sister, LaGreta, then seven, urged the others into the apartment. As LaJoe scurried through the open doorway, they counted off the five bedrooms in delighted giggles. They were struck by the apartment's immensity; the hallway seemed to go on forever, one room following another and another and another. What's more, the freshly painted walls shone a glistening white; even the brown linoleum floors had a luster to them. The youngest children found the coziness of the doorless closets inviting; LaJoe's infant twin brothers spent much of the first day playing in one. And because of the apartment's first-floor location, the older children quickly learned, they could exit through the windows, a route they would use in their teens when they wanted to leave unseen by their mother.

In those early years, the children of Horner thrived. LaJoe and LaGreta joined the Girl Scouts. They attended dances and roller-skating parties in their building's basement. They delighted in the new playground, which boasted swings, sliding boards, and a jungle gym. Their brothers frequented the project's grass baseball diamond, which was regularly mowed.

All of them spent time at the spanking new Boys Club, which had a gym and in later years an indoor Olympic-size swimming pool. On Friday nights, the family attended fish fries. LaJoe joined the 250-member Drum and Bugle Corps, a group so popular among the area's youth that some came from two miles away to participate. The marching teenagers, attired in white shirts, thin black ties, and black jackets, were a common sight in city parades.

The Anderson children were exposed to politics as well. Their mother was active in the local Democratic Party, and politicians, from aldermen to United States senators, would visit the complex and on occasion stop by the Andersons' home. Elected officials paid attention to the people's concerns. They had to. People were well organized. In the 1960s, area residents formed the Miles Square Federation, which vigorously fought for better schools and health clinics. The Black Panthers' city headquarters was only a few blocks from Horner. Martin Luther King, Jr., on his visits to the city would preach at the First Congregational Baptist Church.

Nurtured by a strong sense of community as well as the programs at the Boys Club and other social agencies, Henry Horner boasted numerous success stories: an executive at a *Fortune* 500 company, a principal of one of the city's top parochial schools, the medical director of a nearby hospital, and a professor at a local university.

On that first day at Horner, the Anderson family knew only hope and pride. The future seemed bright. The moment, particularly for the children, was nearly blissful. Lelia Mae made doughnuts to celebrate and played Sam Cooke and Nat King Cole albums on her hi-fi through the evening. That night, in one of the back bedrooms, the sisters lay on their narrow cots and stared out the windows. Because there was no one yet living in the building and few streetlights, they could clearly see the moon and the stars. They had their very own window on the universe.

LaJoe held on tightly to those early memories because so much had since gone sour. By the 1970s, the housing authority ran out of money to paint the apartments. The cinder-block walls became permanently smudged and dirty. The building's bricks faded. The windows had collected too heavy a coat of grime to reflect much of anything. In 1975, someone, to this day unknown, strangled one of LaJoe's grown sisters in her bathtub. The oldest brother, home on leave from the Marines, died of a heart attack that day on hearing the news. LaJoe's parents moved out of Horner because of the murder. Roy died of bone cancer in 1982.

LaJoe hadn't moved far since that fall day in 1956; she was just down the hall, where she now lived with Lafeyette, Pharoah, her two oldest sons, Paul and Terence, and the triplets.

"When I got my apartment I thought this is what it was meant to be," she said thirty-one years later. "I never looked any further than here. It wasn't like it is now. The grass was greener. We had light poles on the front of the building. We had little yellow flowers. We had it all. I really thought this was it. And I never knew, until I lost it all, that it wasn't."

By 1987, the thirty-four acre Henry Horner complex wasn't the largest of the city's nineteen public housing developments. That title went to the two-mile long Robert Taylor Homes, which was home to fifteen thousand people. Nor was Henry Horner the most dangerous. That distinction alternately went to Rockwell Gardens, a neighboring complex, and Cabrini-Green, which in 1981 was the site of so many shootings—eleven killed and thirty-seven wounded in the first two months—that the city's mayor, Jane Byrne, chose to move in. Along with a contingent of police and bodyguards, she stayed for three weeks to help restore order. Some, including LaJoe, viewed the move as gutsy and brave. But that single act by Byrne, more than any murder or plea for help, highlighted the isolation and alienation of these poor, mostly black inner-city islands. It was as if the mayor, with her entourage of police, advisers, and reporters, had deigned to visit some distant and perilous Third World country—except that Cabrini-Green sat barely eight blocks from the mayor's posh Gold Coast apartment.

Henry Horner's buildings range from seven to fifteen stories and cover eight blocks. The architect surely had an easy time designing the development, for it is only one block wide, leaving little room for experimentation with the placement of the high-rises. The buildings, with a few exceptions, line each side of the block, leaving the corridor in between for playground equipment, basketball courts, and parking lots. A narrow street once cut through the development's midsection, but that has long since been displaced and is now part of the concrete play area. At first that pleased the parents, who worried about their children getting hit by speeding cars, but later it served to isolate parts of the complex even more, making it easier for criminals to operate with impunity.

In the summer of 1987, six thousand people lived at Horner, four thousand of them children. They would quickly tell you that they dared not venture out at night. At Horner, for every one thousand residents there were approximately forty violent crimes reported, a rate nearly twice that of Chicago's average.

Inside their apartment's hallway, Lafeyette and Pharoah huddled on the floor, sweating in the early July heat. Pharoah shook with each gun pop, his big eyes darting nervously from one end of the long hallway to the other. He clutched a garbage bag filled with aluminum cans he'd collected; his small body was curled up against the security of the cool concrete wall.

The muscles in Lafeyette's face tensed. He had his hands full, watching over Pharoah and the triplets. The young ones knew enough to stay in the windowless corridor away from possible stray bullets, but they chattered and fought until Tiffany, too restless to sit still for long, stood up. Lafeyette shoved her back down.

"We wanna go," whined Tiffany.

"Be quiet," admonished her brother. "You crazy?"

The narrow hall of their four-bedroom apartment had become their fallout shelter. Stray bullets had zipped through their apartment before, once leaving two holes the size of nickels in the olive-green living room curtains. Another time a bullet found its way into the hallway; it had traveled through a bedroom window and the bedroom door, missing Terence by inches. The children now knew enough to sit away from the doorways.

The five children squatted on the musty floor long after the shooting subsided. LaJoe, who huddled with them, could sit still no longer. Wearing a T-shirt that read WIPE OUT GRAFFITI, she walked into the kitchen and began to sweep the floors. Cleaning house was the only way she could clear her mind, to avoid thinking about what might happen or what might have been. It was cathartic in demanding focus and concentration. She scrubbed and washed and rearranged furniture, particularly when things got tense—with family problems, shootings, and deaths. The kids knew to stay out of her way, except for Lafeyette, who, like his mother, also found cleaning a useful distraction.

"Lemme help you," he begged, still sitting by the wall. "You figuring to start cleaning up 'cause you upset. You figuring to start cleaning up." LaJoe didn't hear him. "Mama, let me help you. Ain't nobody gonna get killed out there today."

"Stay there, Lafie. Someone's gotta watch the triplets," LaJoe said.

Lafeyette shrugged, but resigned to his duties, he slithered down the wall, resting on the floor as he kept the triplets in check and watched his mother work.

For LaJoe, cleaning the apartment seemed nearly hopeless. The apartment never looked perfectly neat and orderly: a chair always faced in the wrong direction or a rug's edge curled up or under itself. Eight people lived in the apartment—LaJoe, her five youngest children, and the two older brothers, Terence and Paul. It swelled to nine if the children's father stayed over. He would sleep on the couch or, on occasion, in the double bed with the triplets. A stack of food-caked dishes, waiting to be washed, often filled the kitchen sink, or the plastic garbage container overflowed with leftovers and paper. Roaches were everywhere. Even when the housing authority sprayed, the roaches came back. Once a small colony of them took refuge from the pesticides in a small portable radio that belonged to one of the older children. The insects were discovered days later, thriving. Maggots nested in the building, mostly by the undersized incinerator, which overflowed with garbage.

Even had LaJoe been able to catch up with the dirty dishes and misplaced furniture and overflowing garbage, the apartment itself defied cleanliness. In keeping with the developers' tight-fisted policies in building these high-rises, the housing authority continued its miserly regard for their upkeep. Maintenance was a bare minimum.

The walls inside the home were what the Soviets first saw, white cinder block. Along with the encrusted, brown linoleum-tiled floor, which was worn through in many places, and the exposed heating pipes, which snaked through the apartment, the home at night resembled a dark, dank cave. The bedrooms were particularly drab. Not much bigger than some prison cells —they were ten by eleven feet—they got little sunlight.

Because the bedrooms' shallow closets had no doors, they were an invitation to messiness. Clothes spilled into the rooms. For all practical purposes, there was no distinction between the closets and the rest of the rooms; the closets looked like two-foot

indentations in the walls. They were constructed to accommodate curtains, but the curtain rods had long been missing.

The kitchen and living room blurred together. They were
essentially one large room partly divided by a cinder-block wall
that ran halfway down the middle.

The thirty-year-old kitchen cabinets, constructed of thin
sheet metal, had rusted through. They were pockmarked with
holes. LaJoe organized her dishes and cookware so as to avoid
having them fall through these ragged openings. She usually
piled them in the corners of the cupboards.

The housing authority used to paint the apartments once every five years, but with the perennial shortage of money, in the
1970s it had stopped painting altogether. LaJoe couldn't remember when her apartment was last painted. No matter how hard
she scrubbed, the smudged walls never looked clean.

But the apartment's two bathrooms were in the worst shape
of all. Neither had a window, and the fans atop the building,
which had provided much needed air circulation, had been
stolen. In the first bathroom, a horrible stench, suggesting raw,
spoiled meat, periodically rose from the toilet. On such days,
LaJoe and the family simply avoided using that bathroom.
Sometimes she would pour ammonia in the toilet to mitigate
the smell. LaJoe had heard rumors that the previous tenants had
performed abortions there, and she attributed the smell to dead
fetuses.

The second bathroom housed the family's one bathtub. There
was no shower, a luxury the children had never experienced.
The tub doubled as a clothes washer, since the building's laundry was long ago abandoned, and the closest one was now a
mile away. The tub's faucet couldn't be turned off. A steady
stream of scalding hot water cascaded into the tub day and
night. The boys had learned to sleep through the noise, but the
constant splashing drove LaJoe batty. She had considered muf-
fling it by placing a towel under the faucet, but then she realized that the bath would overflow. Instead, she used the towel to
wedge shut the bathroom door, which was missing a knob.

In the winter, the building's heating system stormed out of
control. The apartment could get like a furnace, considerably
hotter and drier than in the warmest days of summer. These

summer months were a welcome relief from the dog days of winter.

LaJoe had done what she could to spruce up the place, to brighten it. By the television, which she left on nearly twenty-four hours a day to discourage prowlers, she placed artificial logs. If they had been hooked up to gas, the imitation logs would have lit up, but the family had no such source of fuel. On the living room wall she had hung two identical drawings of a red rose, a portrait of Jesus (though she was no longer religious), and a rendering of a waterfall and a country home on black velvet.

*"You grow up 'round it,"
Lafeyette told a friend. "There are a
lot of people in the projects who say
they're not gonna do drugs, that
they're not gonna drop out, that they
won't be on the streets. But they're
doing it now. Never say never." He
paused. "But I say never. My
brothers ain't set no good example
for me, but I'll set a good example
for them."*

The apartment was cluttered. In the kitchen, in addition to the stove and refrigerator, there was a broken six-foot-high freezer and an old wooden hutch, which housed plates and glassware and, like the freezer, served to stop stray bullets that might come through the kitchen windows. Living on the first floor required such ingenuity. One woman placed big stuffed animals in her windows in the hope that gang members would mistake them for people.

"Mama, lemme help," Lafeyette pleaded again. His words were lost in the roar of the elevated train, which passed just a hundred feet from their building. Lafeyette waited for it to pass. "Mama. Mama. I'm gonna take out the garbage."

"No, you ain't." LaJoe looked at Lafeyette and the others. They had had enough sitting. The shooting had stopped fifteen minutes ago. "Okay, Lafie, tie up the garbage. Don't take it out. Just tie it up."

Lafeyette jumped to his feet and walked quickly into the kitchen, where he nimbly snatched the broom to sweep up a pile of paper. The triplets wandered into the living room, continuing their chatter, beseeching their mother to let them go outside. Pharoah lazily strolled to the couch, where he balled up, lost in his private thoughts. He clutched the bag of aluminum cans, oblivious of the activity around him. He too wanted to go outside. But there wasn't much to do out there.

The Riverses' building and three other high-rises were laid out roughly in the shape of a diamond so that they all opened up on a concrete park. The two swing sets, which boasted only one swing between them, and the three sliding boards were, as far as anyone could tell, the same equipment that had originally been installed thirty-one years before, when the development first opened.

Across the street sat the baseball diamond, long since paved over, for reasons residents couldn't recall. Nearby, a rusted orange basketball rim was shoved and twisted against the leaning metal backboard. The court's opposite rim and backboard were gone entirely. Local management had stopped replacing the rims, so they got installed only when a resident could muster the energy and the money.

On this early summer day six of Horner's four thousand children vied to use one of the neighborhood's few good courts. They arched jump shots into the opening created by the crossbars of a faded yellow-and-blue jungle gym. It, too, was over three decades old. Lafeyette could dunk on this makeshift rim; Pharoah, not quite yet.

"Hey, Laf, let's play," James urged his friend. James loved basketball. Frequently, he sneaked into the Chicago Stadium to convince players, from both the Bulls and visiting teams, to donate their sneakers to his collection. On his bedroom shelves sat an impressive array of boat-size basketball sneakers, including a pair from the Detroit Pistons' Isiah Thomas and from Charles Oakley, then a Chicago Bull. James, who was short for his age, dreamed of playing professional basketball.

"I don't wanna play ball with them," Lafeyette said, referring to the children by the jungle gym. "They might try to make me join a gang."

About a week earlier, members of one of the local gangs had asked Lafeyette to stand security, and it had made him skittish. His mother told the teenage members she would call the police if they kept after Lafeyette. "I'd die first before I let them take one of my sons," she said.

Gangs often recruit young children to do their dirty work. Recently, a fourteen-year-old friend of Lafeyette's allegedly shot and killed an older man in an alley half a block north of Lafeyette's building. Residents and police said the killing was drug-related. "I wish he hadn't done it," Lafeyette had told James.

Lafeyette and James constantly worried that they might be pulled into the gangs. Lafeyette knew what might happen: "When you first join you think it's good. They'll buy you what you want. You have to do anything they tell you to do. If they tell you to kill somebody, you have to do that." James figured the only way to make it out of Horner was "to try to make as little friends as possible."

So while a group of young boys shrieked in delight as the basketball ricocheted through the jungle gym's opening, Lafeyette, James, and a few other boys perched idly on the metal benches in front of their building. Like the swing sets, the benches resembled an ancient archeological find. The entire back of one was gone; only two of four metal slats remained on another, thus making it impossible for anyone other than a small child to sit there. Nearby, Pharoah and Porkchop pitched pennies.

"I'm gonna have my own condominium in Calumet Park," James told the others, referring to a Chicago suburb. "It's nice out there. You could sit outside all night and nothing would happen."

"They have flowers this tall," said Lafeyette, holding his hand four feet off the ground.

James laughed and hurled an empty bottle of Canadian Mist onto the playground's concrete, where it shattered, adding to the hundreds of shards of glass already on the ground. "If I had one wish I'd wish to separate all the good from the bad and send them to another planet so they could battle it out and no innocent people would get hurt," James mused.

"That's two wishes," asserted Lafeyette. "I wish to go to heaven."

"I'd wish there be no gangbangers," piped up Pharoah, wishing out of existence those who fought for the gangs.

"Wherever you go there be gangbangers," replied Lafeyette.

"Not in Mississippi," Pharoah assured him. An argument ensued as to whether there was, in fact, any state or city or neighborhood that didn't have gangs. It was on their minds a lot these days.

By season's end, the police would record that one person every three days had been beaten, shot at, or stabbed at Horner. In just one week, they confiscated twenty-two guns and 330 grams of cocaine. Most of the violence here that summer was related to drugs.

Four

ON A WARM DAY in mid-July, a caravan of three cars pulled up to the sidewalk at the two high-rises just across the street from the Riverses'. Two young bodyguards stepped out of the first and last sedans. Then from the middle emerged Jimmie Lee, a barrel-chested, square-jawed man who was no more than five-feet-seven. A bulletproof vest sometimes made him look even bulkier. He held his cellular telephone at his side as a band of worshiping teenagers mobbed him.

A commotion caught Lee's attention. In the entranceway of

one of the buildings, a drunken man berated his young daughter. "You bitch. What did I tell you?" the father screamed at the cowering girl. Lee walked toward the building and, with a suddenness that left the father defenseless, slugged him in the jaw, knocking him to the ground. Lee stared at the crumpled drunk.

"You don't give no kid disrespect," he told the man.

"But that's my daughter," the fallen man explained.

"I don't care if she is your daughter. She's thirteen years old and you're calling her a bitch. Don't do it again." Lee walked into the building, where he had a meeting with some of his workers.

Lafeyette, Pharoah, and the other children knew to keep their distance from Jimmie Lee. But they also knew that he and no one else—not the mayor, the police, or the housing authority—ruled Henry Horner. The boys never had reason to speak to Lee or to meet him, but his very presence and activities ruled their lives.

When he pulled up in his caravan, they knew enough to go inside. When nighttime fell and Lee's business swung into action, they knew enough to stay away. And when something happened to Lee or one of his workers, they knew enough not to talk about it. Jimmie Lee, it was said, was everywhere. He knew who was talking about him, who was finking, who was flipping to the other side. And when he knew, someone would pay.

Jimmie Lee headed a drug gang called the Conservative Vice Lords. Its name had nothing to do with its political affiliation. The members controlled Henry Horner. No one could sell drugs without their approval. Their arsenal included pistols, Uzis, and even grenades. Some of its members were well schooled in torture techniques, and once allegedly threatened to shove a hot nail up an opposing gang member's penis. Lee even had an "enforcer," according to the police, a young man whose job it was to maim and kill and who kept a two-shot derringer for such a purpose.

Residents so feared and respected the gang's control that they refused to call 911. In Chicago, the caller's address automatically flashes at police headquarters, and police will sometimes then appear at the caller's home, seeking more information. Snitching could get you killed. The police installed a hot-line number and promised confidentiality, but in all of 1986, public housing residents called the number twenty-one times. One woman so feared the long tentacles of the gang that after she drew a rough diagram of a recent gun battle for a friend, she ripped it into small shreds for fear that the Vice Lords would find it.

By 1987, Lee's notoriety had grown to such an extent that his photo, taken with five other high-ranking Vice Lords, hung on the walls of every police station on the city's west side. Next to the others, all of whom glared menacingly at the camera, Lee looked calm, even pensive. He sported a full beard and aviator glasses. His red sweatshirt had BULLS emblazoned on the front; he also wore blue jogging pants and high-tops and a thick gold necklace. Lee worked out with weights, and that showed even in his baggy jogging suit. His upper torso and neck were thick and wide; his closely cropped hair made him look that much heavier. The information under the photo identified him as weighing 210 pounds.

The rest of the text warned: "They are known to be involved in drug traffic, home invasions of dope flats, extortion (especially of narcotics operations), and other crimes. They have been known to employ fully automatic weapons, travel in car caravans, usually with tail cars for protection."

But Lee ruled by more than fear. To neighborhood residents, he could sometimes be a positive force. He reportedly didn't take drugs himself and, if he drank, did so in moderation. He occasionally bought food for families who needed it. Because of his love for children, he refused to let "peewees," those around thirteen or fourteen, gangbang for the Conservative Vice Lords. In fact, young boys periodically received lectures from Lee to stay away from drugs and the gangs. On occasion, Lee gave children dollar bills or, if their shoes were torn, bought them new ones.

Lee's efforts paid off. To the residents of Horner, he became a figure of contradictions. To some, he was a model. In a neighborhood of runaway fathers, Lee had been married to the same woman for nearly twenty years. And adults and children alike pointed to his generosity.

"The thing I liked about him was that he gave kids and

women respect. He really wasn't a bad person," said one resident. "I have a lot of respect for Jimmie Lee," said another.

Even Charlie Toussas, a plainclothes officer known for his tough manner, conceded, "He was a real gentleman."

Jimmie Lee might be considered by some the hero of a Horatio Alger story. As a child, he didn't have much going for him. He grew up in Horner. His father was a construction worker, his mother an assembler at a plating company. He had a child by the time he was eighteen; he dropped out of school in the eleventh grade with only a sixth-grade reading level. Later, while in prison, he received his high school equivalency.

The police speculate that Lee had been associated with the Vice Lords, which has over twenty factions, for possibly as long as twenty years. One of his first tussles with the authorities was when he was seventeen, charged with killing a fourteen-year-old boy who was found in the gangway of a building, shot through the heart. A jury found Lee not guilty. Two years later, Lee and some buddies robbed three men at gunpoint. A letter to the court from Lee's counselor at the American Institute of Engineering and Technology, where he had received drafting instruction, noted: "While he was with us, Mr. Lee was quiet and passive. He lacked self-confidence and disparaged himself. He handled his conflicts by retreating." But Lee went on to serve a little over four years in one of the Illinois prisons, which are notorious for their large and strong gang populations and where most gang leaders earn their rank.

After his release, in July 1974, Lee was in and out of trouble with the law, including a conviction of unlawful use of a weapon. The preceding November, in 1986, the police caught Lee with fifty-six grams of heroin. He met the $50,000 bond and continued about his business. To the residents of Henry Horner, he seemed to operate with impunity.

A taciturn man, Lee, who was sometimes known as General Lee or by his middle name, Oswald, came from a long Chicago tradition of smart, sophisticated gang leaders. He was no youngster; he was thirty-eight years old.

The city's black street gangs, of which there are three main ones—the Vice Lords, the Disciples, and the El Rukns (formerly known as the Blackstone Rangers)—originated in the early 1960s mostly as young kids duking it out over turf rights.

At Henry Horner, the Vice Lords and Black Souls, a faction of the Disciples, fought fist to fist with white gangs whose turf lay just north of the complex. As the whites moved out, the Vice Lords and Black Souls fought among themselves. Eventually, the city's gangs split into two main groupings known as the Nation and the Folks. The Vice Lords and El Rukns belonged to the Nation; the Disciples to the Folks.

By the late 1960s, the gangs had won some standing among the establishment, particularly with liberals who felt that these young hoodlums, given proper guidance, might turn their energies and enviable organizing and leadership abilities to bettering their neighborhoods. The gang leader who served as a prototype for others, Jeff Fort, the El Rukns' head, managed to pull in over $300,000 in funds from federal agencies for ostensible job-training programs. During the riots following the death of Martin Luther King, Jr., the El Rukns took to the streets to calm the neighborhoods. Businessmen whose windows had DO NOT TOUCH posters signed by the El Rukns' leadership later held a press conference to commend the El Rukns for helping protect their property. The gang had won such legitimacy that Fort was invited, at the behest of a United States senator, to President Nixon's inauguration.

At Henry Horner, the Vice Lords gained a similar standing when a local hospital bequeathed a former Catholic boys' school it owned, coupled with a grant of over $20,000, to local gang leaders in the hope that they would open a neighborhood center. The three-story, nine-year-old structure had oak floors, oriental rugs, chandeliers, and silver place settings.

Efforts, though, to convert the bad to the good failed miserably, some quicker than others. Within months, the gangs had gutted the Catholic school. The chandeliers and place settings were gone. The gang used much of the grant money to buy an old fire-engine-red ambulance, which they used to transport friends around the neighborhood, as well as new clothes, mostly army fatigues and jump boots.

The El Rukns' good intentions unraveled, too, though not as quickly. In the early 1970s, a judge sentenced Jeff Fort to five years in Leavenworth for conspiring to misapply federal funds. He was released in 1976, but went back to prison again in 1983 for drug trafficking. And then, while in prison, he was sentenced to an additional eighty years as the first United States citizen to be convicted for conspiring to commit terrorist acts on behalf of a foreign government. Prosecutors contended that Fort had made a deal with Moammar Ghadhafi in which the El Rukns were to receive $2.5 million to bomb buildings and airplanes in the United States for the Libyan leader.

By the late 1970s, the city's gangs, once organizations of neighborhood pride and turf rights, had turned to big business: the marketing and selling of narcotics. Ironically, the well-intentioned efforts of the late 1960s left the gangs with strong organizational structures, which they needed to have in place when applying for federal and local funding.

The gangs became so powerful in Chicago that they have managed to do what no big city police force has done: they kept crack out of the city. Not until 1988, long after the crack scourge had devoured entire neighborhoods in cities like New York and Washington, D.C., were there any crack-related arrests in Chicago. Even then, crack made up only 5 percent of all drugs seized. The police knew of only one extensive crack operation, which they swiftly closed down. If crack found its way to Chicago, the inexpensive, highly addictive drug would open the market to small entrepreneurs, and possibly break the gangs' oligopoly over the drug trade.*

The gangs also became an institutional force in many of the

---

* It should be mentioned that certain high-ranking officials of the Chicago Police Department dispute the theory that the gangs kept crack out of Chicago, though it is supported by, among others, the Drug Enforcement Agency and the U.S. Attorney's Office. In a 1989 interview, Raymond Risley, then the commander of the police department's narcotics unit, listed a number of reasons that crack had not enveloped Chicago. The reasons seem so naïve that one suspects the police want to diminish the impression that the city's gangs are, in fact, very powerful. Commander Risley suggested that people in Chicago said no to crack after watching the devastation wreaked in other cities, including the much publicized death of the basketball star Len Bias. He also surmised that crack was easier to introduce in cities like Detroit and New York because, he contended, they had more abandoned buildings that could be used as crack houses. Chicago, needless to say, boasts a plethora of vacant buildings. What's more, crack has become the drug of choice in a number of poor suburbs just south of the city, towns that certainly don't contain more abandoned buildings than Chicago. The one plausible explanation proposed by Commander Risley is that cocaine prices have dropped so significantly in recent years that there has been little demand for cheaper drugs. A kilo of cocaine cost $55,000 in 1980; it dropped to between $17,000 and $19,000 nine years later. With such low prices, street dealers could sell bags of cocaine for as little as $10, enough for one snort. As a result, crack may not be as prized a drug.

city's neighborhoods, so that even in recent years they have been used for seemingly legitimate political purposes. In 1983, a state representative, Larry Bullock, allegedly paid the El Rukns $10,000 to campaign for Jane Byrne in her quest for the mayoralty. Police say they pocketed the money and never worked for Byrne.

At Henry Horner, a young local politician recruited gang members from playgrounds to pass out leaflets and accompany campaign workers in his successful 1987 bid for Democratic ward committeeman. He paid each gang member $20 a day. Because of two threats on his life and because his campaign van had been riddled with bullets, he needed the protection.

Residents and police tell the story of one former west side alderman who announced that he would move into a public housing project for a few nights, à la former Mayor Byrne. He wanted to draw attention to the awful conditions there. The housing authority found him a vacant apartment in a high-rise, but it happened to be controlled by the Vice Lords. The gang eagerly awaited his arrival. The alderman, it seems, had previously aligned himself with the rival Disciples. He never moved in.

The city's top gang leaders and drug lords have such standing in the community that every summer they throw a huge bash for friends at the Dan Ryan Woods on the south side. One summer, residents of many of the city's poor black neighborhoods received mimeographed invitations to the "Players' Picnic." Fliers promised free food and drink, softball for the children, and a car show and wet T-shirt contest for the adults. The flier brazenly identified some of the sponsors of the party by their nicknames: Highsmith, Fat Cat, Bub, and Disco. About two thousand Chicagoans attended the get-together, dancing to the funk rock of a live band and grilling hot dogs and ribs. Cars were so backed up going into the park that the police had to assign extra traffic details. The kingpins showed off their glistening new Mercedes-Benzes, Rolls-Royces, and Jaguars. They danced and drank until ten P.M., when the police broke up the festivities.

At the age of ten, Lafeyette had his first encounter with death; he saw someone killed. It was the beginning of Henry Horner's brutal drug wars, when Jimmie Lee and the Conserva-

tive Vice Lords made their move to take control of Henry
Horner. By 1985, drugs had swept through Chicago's west side.
Big money was involved. And Lee began his efforts to establish
his part of the trade.

The Vice Lords, with the aid of another gang, pushed to oust
the Disciples from the east end of Horner, the more populated
section of the complex and thus the more lucrative. They even
brought in thugs from other parts of the city. The first victim
was a young Disciple nicknamed Baby Al, who was shot with a
.357 Magnum not far from the Riverses' building. Wounded, he
ran into the high-rise, where, while trying to climb the stairs,
he fell backward and lost consciousness. Lafeyette came running out of his apartment to see what all the commotion was
about. He watched as Baby Al bled to death. Two years later,
his blood still stained the stairwell.

A couple of weeks later, as Lafeyette and Pharoah played on
the jungle gym in midafternoon, shooting broke out. A young
girl jumping rope crumpled to the ground. Lafeyette ran into
his building, dragging behind him one of the triplets. Pharoah,
then seven, panicked. He ran blindly until he bumped into one
of the huge green trash containers that dot the landscape. He
pulled himself up and over, landing in a foot of garbage.
Porkchop followed. For half an hour, the two huddled in the
foul-smelling meat scraps and empty pizza boxes, waiting for
the shooting to stop, arguing about when they should make a
break for their respective homes. Finally, the shooting subsided
and they climbed out, smelling like dirty dishes. They watched
as paramedics attended to the girl, who luckily had been shot
only in the leg. Her frightened mother, who had fainted, was
being revived. It was at that point that Pharoah first told his
mother, "I didn't wanna know what was happening."

By late 1986, the Conservative Vice Lords occupied two of
Horner's high-rises just across the street from the Riverses'.
Lee's soldiers used the buildings' four stairwells to escape from
the police. They found refuge in several of the vacant apartments, some of which were connected by large holes knocked in
the cinder-block walls, through which they could make their
getaways. The gang also controlled three apartments. The tenants were young single women who in exchange for money or
drugs rented out the entire unit or just a bedroom to Vice

Lords. In these so-called safe houses, the gang's lieutenants stored their drugs, guns, and money. In the underbelly of a refrigerator in one of the apartments, they hid a disassembled machine gun. The gang had also outfitted an eighth-floor vacant apartment with a sofa, lounge chair, and a television set; it was a sanctuary for members who needed a place to stay. No guns or drugs were allowed. Jimmie Lee lived farther west, outside Horner, with his wife and three children.

The Vice Lords added to the natural defenses—most notably the stairwells and the vacant apartments—the buildings provided. They knocked out all the lights in the open breezeways so that even during the day it was difficult if not impossible to see in. Wandering sentries warned of approaching unmarked squad cars, which even young children could identify on sight. They communicated through walkie-talkies, the kind used by football coaches. Their code word for police was "boppers."

Most wore baseball caps with the bill turned to the left, an indication that they were Vice Lords. Many wore earrings in the left ear, and some hung such heavy gold jewelry from their necks that it seemed a wonder they could hold their heads upright. Also, the Playboy bunny had become a Vice Lord symbol, so a member might sport a gold one around his neck. The five-pointed star, the gang's insignia, decorated the entrances to the two buildings, as did other items identifying the area as belonging to the Vice Lords. The top hat signified shelter, the cane stood for strength, the glove meant purity, and the champagne glass symbolized conservatism or propriety. Members often learned the meaning of these symbols while in prison, where the gangs did much of their recruiting.

Much of the business was with people in the neighborhood, but the bulk of it was with outsiders, who drove their cars up Wolcott Avenue and parked in front of the Vice Lords' two buildings. Usually they didn't have to get out of their cars; the young runners took their orders. The "soldiers" sold the cocaine and heroin and then returned a certain percentage of the proceeds to the bosses and kept the rest. Both the police and former gang members estimated that Lee's business grossed $50,000 to $100,000 a week.

On December 13, 1986, there began a frenzy that would last through the summer. Four top Vice Lords chose to show their force against a rival drug gang, the Gangster Stones, that was encroaching on their turf. They had already successfully moved the Disciples farther west.

The four waited until after midnight to launch their attack. They knew that was when the tough plainclothes cops of the city's gang crimes and public housing units went off duty. They had no third shift. The Vice Lords strolled into the breezeway of a nearby building, carrying with them an Uzi, two sawed-off shotguns, and a .25 caliber automatic handgun.

The first rival gang member they came on in the dark lobby was Larry Wallace, or Wild Child, a thirty-one-year-old heavy drinker who had recently moved from Horner but was back visiting friends. People in the neighborhood continue to dispute whether he was an active gang member at the time. The gunfire lasted maybe thirty seconds. Wallace was shot five times; one bullet pierced his chest and exited from the back, and another entered through the upper back and lodged in his left cheek. Buckshot pellets littered his buttocks. The Vice Lords had fired at him from just about every conceivable angle. Even at Horner, the viciousness of this slaying unnerved people. By summer's end, as the Vice Lords established their dominance, the war had touched the lives of almost everyone living in Henry Horner. Lafeyette and Pharoah, as well as the adults, began talking of the "death train" that drove smack through their community.

Five

BIRD LEG LOVED DOGS. And for that reason, Lafeyette loved Bird Leg. His real name was Calvin Robinson, and though he was three years older than Lafeyette, he let the younger boy tag along with him, in part because he had few friends. The older boys made fun of his obsession with dogs; the younger ones seemed to understand it.

Bird Leg and Lafeyette hunted for German shepherds, mutts, and even pit bulls in the small, fenced-in back yards of the Hispanic and white neighborhoods just north of the housing project. Ordinarily, the dogs growled and fought with Lafeyette and other strangers, but Bird Leg could communicate with them in ways the other children found uncanny. As he climbed into the back yards, he talked to them, consoled them, cajoled them, lured them, until they sidled up to him, drooling on their newfound friend. Then he unchained them, lifted them over the yard fence, and brought them home.

"The dogs would always come with him," recalls one boy, with a combination of amazement and respect. "He had more dogs than he did friends."

With Lafeyette's assistance, Bird Leg kept his assortment of canines—some stolen, some strays, some raised from birth—in an abandoned garage catty-corner from Lafeyette's building. Bird Leg often got down on his hands and knees to speak to his companions. Sometimes he kissed them on their sloppy chops, a practice the other children shook their heads at in disbelief. A few nights a week, Bird Leg scrounged through the trash bins behind the nearby Kentucky Fried Chicken, and collected half-finished meals to feed his pets. Lafeyette often helped.

Bird Leg occasionally spent the night with his animals in the worn, leaning garage, huddling among them for warmth. On one unusually cold fall night, Bird Leg, only twelve at the time, built a fire by the garage door, fueling it with cardboard and rags. The heat, he hoped, would warm his shivering friends. Instead, the old wooden building, without much coaxing, quickly caught fire and burned to the ground. The police brought Bird Leg to his mother, who, though angry, couldn't help laughing at her son's misguided intentions. It was the first of what were to be many brushes with the law.

As Bird Leg got older, he became involved with the Vice Lords, and he and Lafeyette grew apart. Lafeyette was too young and too wary to join the gangs, but he cherished all that Bird Leg had taught him about dogs. And he missed him.

Bird Leg, his mother suspects, sought protection from the gang in the same way he sought love from his dogs. Jimmie Lee, said his mother, had become like a big brother, though Bird Leg didn't run drugs for him. In fact, many of Lee's older workers didn't even know Bird Leg. Also, a close relative was a Vice Lord, which meant that Bird Leg, who lived on the western edge of Horner, Disciples' territory, frequently had to withstand a beating just to enter his building. Uncles' and cousins' associations with a particular gang can mark children too young to have chosen their own affiliation.

As a teenager, Bird Leg became increasingly reckless and hard-headed. By the age of fourteen, he had for all intents and purposes dropped out of school. Friends say he would sometimes borrow a shotgun from a friend and randomly shoot at Disciples, a practice not uncommon among the very young gang members. He also started raising his pit bulls to fight. His favorite was a light brown muscular terrier named Red. "I was scared of that dog," Alberta Robinson said later. "I once went to hit Bird Leg for something he did and that dog just about bit me." The police eventually confiscated the starving and scarred terrier; Bird Leg had used it to threaten an officer.

Bird Leg had always lived on the edge and, indeed, earned his nickname when at the age of four he chased a tennis ball into a busy street and was struck by a speeding, drunk driver. The doctors had to insert pins in one knee and ankle. When the chest-high cast came off after many weeks, his leg was so thin and fragile-looking that his grandmother started calling him Bird Leg.

In the summer of 1986, while shooting dice with some friends, he was approached by a man with a shotgun demanding his money, and Bird Leg, in his youthful defiance, ran. The man emptied a cartridge of buckshot into Bird Leg's shoulder. That incident, added to the intensifying war between the gangs, caused his mother to move her family into an apartment on the city's far north side. But, as is often the case when families move, Bird Leg and his brothers kept returning to Horner to visit friends.

Sometimes at Henry Horner you can almost smell the arrival of death. It is the odor of foot-deep pools of water that, formed from draining fire hydrants, become fetid in the summer sun. It is the stink of urine puddles in the stairwell corners and of soiled diapers dumped in the grass. It is the stench of a maggot-infested cat carcass lying in a vacant apartment and the rotting food in the overturned trash bins. It is, in short, the collected scents of summer.

In mid-August of the summer of 1987, the Vice Lords and

their rivals reached a temporary truce. Because of the season's violence, the police had increased their presence at Horner. The gangs knew that more police would only disrupt their drug transactions, so they agreed among themselves to stop, in their own word, "clowning." But for young members like Bird Leg, such business acumen seemed at odds with what had become almost instinctual for young gang members: Vice Lords got along with neither Gangster Stones nor Disciples. Truce or no truce.

On a Thursday night late in August, a rival gang member shot Bird Leg in the arm with buckshot. After being treated at the hospital, he joked with his older brother and cousin that if he were to die he wanted to be buried in his white jogging suit. They laughed and told him they would oblige him.

The next evening, August 21, Bird Leg, despite his mother's protestations, left his north side apartment to visit friends at Horner. As he sat in the late day's heat and watched two friends play basketball, a group of young Disciples started taunting him, tossing bricks and bottles at his feet. His thirteen-year-old sister, who also was at Horner visiting friends, pleaded with Bird Leg to come inside the building to their cousins' apartment. "Get your ass upstairs," Bird Leg ordered her. "I'm gonna kill some of these punks today or they're gonna kill me." It was tough talk for a fifteen-year-old; his sister ran inside, crying. By the time she climbed the six floors to her cousins' apartment, a single pistol shot had echoed from below.

Twenty-four-year-old Willie Elliott had stepped from between two parked cars and aimed a pistol at Bird Leg. Only two feet away, the boy froze like a deer caught in the glare of a car's headlights. The bullet tore through Bird Leg's chest. He clutched his wound and ran through the breezeway of one highrise. "Man, I've been shot!" he hollered in disbelief. He appeared to be heading for the safety of a busy street. He didn't make it. The bullet, which had hit him at point-blank range, entered his chest and spiraled through his body like an out-of-control drill, lacerating his heart, lungs, spleen, and stomach. Bird Leg, struggling to breathe, collapsed beneath an old cottonwood, where, cooled by its shade, he died.

Word of death spreads fast in Henry Horner. Sometimes the killing happens late at night when most people are asleep.

Then, since few witnesses are around, the incident can take on mythic proportions. A stabbing becomes a butchering. A shooting becomes an execution. Sometimes it can take days for the correct name of the victim to surface. But a daytime killing here draws a crowd, and as Bird Leg lay against the tree, a young boy mounted his bike to deliver the news.

From a friend's second-floor window, Lafeyette heard the boy's breathless rendering of the fight, but he decided not to join the other children who ran across Damen Avenue to the crime scene. "I just didn't want to go," he said later. He had already seen enough.

James, however, more adventurous, sprinted across Damen and snaked through the crowd that had already gathered around Bird Leg. He later told Lafeyette what he saw. On the grass, only ten feet from a small playground filled with young children, lay Bird Leg, his white jogging suit stained with blood. Wrapped around one of his closed fists was his only weapon, his belt.

"I was just shocked," James told Lafeyette. "The eyes just rolled to the back of his head and he was gone."

Within minutes after Bird Leg died, Jimmie Lee stepped through the crowd. It was, said one, like Moses parting the waters. People stepped back to let him through. He looked down at Bird Leg's limp body, said nothing, and then walked back through the crowd, where he assembled a band of thirty teenagers. With Lee at their flank, the young militia marched west, looking for revenge. James and the rest of the crowd scattered.

Charlie Toussas, the plainclothes officer who knew Lee well, confronted Lee and his army. "Jimmie, this isn't a good time for this." Lee, according to Toussas, silently turned to his followers, lifted his hand, and pointed to the other side of Damen; and the contingent of Vice Lords, as if manipulated by puppeteers, turned and marched back to their own turf. In the weeks to come, Disciples were the targets of gunfire.

When someone at Henry Horner is killed, mimeographed sheets usually go up in the buildings' hallways, giving details of the funeral. Bird Leg's family, though, avoided this procedure. Having heard that the Disciples planned to storm the funeral home and turn over the casket, they didn't want to publicize the funeral's location. They not only moved it from a nearby mortuary to a distant south side church, they also called the police, who assigned two plainclothesmen to sit through the service and, in effect, keep watch over the dead.

Bird Leg's swollen face made him look twice his age. But the new red-trimmed white jogging suit, which his mother had bought to honor his wishes, and a small gold friendship pin bearing his initials were reminders that Bird Leg had been only fifteen.

Lafeyette, Pharoah, and James were the first to file up to the open casket, where Lafeyette ran his fingers along Bird Leg's jogging suit. At first hesitantly and then with great affection, he caressed the boy's puffy face. James also gently touched the body, pulling back before his fingers reached his friend's rounded cheeks. Pharoah, barely tall enough to see into the casket, stood on tiptoe but kept his hands to his side. He had hardly known Bird Leg; he was here to be with his big brother.

"It looks like he's breathing," James whispered to Lafeyette, desperately wanting to be told he was wrong.

"He ain't breathing," Lafeyette assured him.

James glanced at Bird Leg again and, to no one in particular, muttered, "I'm figuring to cry." He wiped the tears from his face with the back of his hand.

Except for its plush red-cushioned pews, the one-story Zion Grove Baptist church, formerly a barbershop and before that a grocery store, seemed tired and worn. It adjoined an abandoned hamburger stand and faced a vacant lot. Inside, the church was sparsely decorated. A nearly lifesize rendering of *The Last Supper* covered the back wall; an American flag, wrapped around its pole, was draped in clear plastic.

The low ceiling and cinder-block walls did little to discourage the late August heat. The two bright floral arrangements, one at each end of the casket, struggled to retain their beauty through the hour-long service. Friends and relatives and fellow gang members, about 150 in all, shifted uncomfortably in the pews, fanning themselves with the mimeographed programs in a futile attempt to keep from perspiring.

The humidity put everyone on edge. Bird Leg's sister, in her grief, wailed in a pained, high-pitched voice that echoed through the small church like a stiff wind through a canyon. "I wanna kiss him. He ain't dead. HE AIN'T DEAD," she cried. Months later, her protestations would echo in Pharoah's head; it was the one moment he would vividly recall from the funeral.

The three boys found seats off to the side, positioned so that one of the numerous thin pillars wouldn't obstruct their view of the lectern. Lafeyette wore faded gray corduroy pants and a shimmery silver-colored nylon jacket; Pharoah wore matching navy blue corduroy pants and sweatshirt. Both outfits were in sharp contrast to the tight suits and carefully cocked fedoras of most of the men. James himself looked like a young man, in his own purple high-waisted suit and black fedora. Three of Bird Leg's relatives, including a brother, wore T-shirts that read I ♡ BIRD LEG. Jimmie Lee, dressed in a charcoal-black sport coat, sat unobtrusively in the crowd. He had been asked to be a pallbearer.

To the deep, sorrowful spirituals played on the church's organ, the Reverend C. H. Stimage, an elderly minister who had been preaching here for over thirty years, climbed to the lectern. "God needs some young soldiers among the old soldiers," he consoled the gathered mourners. His message in funerals for the young was usually the same: he warned of the evils of drinking and drugs, and sometimes, when he felt comfortable about it, cautioned them against the lure of the gangs. When young gang members die, other youngsters attend church; it was, reasoned the minister, the only time he could preach to them about the love of God.

Carla Palmore, a sturdy, self-assured seventeen-year-old who had been a friend of Bird Leg's, followed the minister to the lectern. Carla wanted to be upbeat, to be hopeful, and, as if to proclaim her intent, sported a matching pink skirt and blouse that, amid the mourners' somber suits and dark dresses, seemed all the more cheerful. Despite her efforts, though, her speech underlined the general feeling among her peers that many of them, like Bird Leg, might not make it to adulthood. During her impromptu sermon, Lafeyette and James and the others in the church nodded in assent.

"Tomorrow is not promised for us. So let's take advantage of today," she urged them. "Sometimes we take tomorrow for granted. Oh, I'll do this tomorrow or tomorrow this will happen. And we forget that tomorrow's not promised to us and we never get a chance to tell those people that we love them or how we feel about them and then, when they're gone, there's so much pain that you feel because you didn't get to do that." Carla caught her breath; her audience remained silent and attentive.

"Bird Leg wasn't a perfect person, but he wasn't a terrible person, and people are going to say that he was a great person or some people are going to say he deserved it, that he was a terrible person. We can't pass judgment on him, because whatever he's doing, there's somebody who's doing more or somebody who's doing less. He cared about his family and I don't think he was deep into it as much as people thought. All of you are here to pay your tribute to him as Bird Leg or as a gang member and maybe you're here for both or either one of them, but it could be you. You take tomorrow for granted and it could be you tomorrow. We just never know what's going to happen. You all need to get your lives together before it's too late."

Jimmie Lee hugged her as she stepped down. "You did a good job," he told her. "I appreciate what you said. I heard you." Meanwhile, another family friend led the congregation in a spirited rendition of the pop song "Lean on Me," a song that always stirred Pharoah's emotions. Here, in the company of other sobbing children and adults, large tears slid down his plump cheeks. He clutched his rolled-up sweatshirt to his chest for security, and, as often happened to him in tense situations, he found himself battling a piercing headache.

James cried too. It looked to some as if he might be doubled over in pain, but he hid his teary face in his black felt hat, which he held between his legs so that others wouldn't see him cry. Lafeyette stared hard at the whirling blades of the long-stemmed electric fan behind the lectern, his eyes sad and vacant, his right arm slung over the pew in front of him so that he could hold the hand of his two-year-old nephew, Terence's child, Snuggles. "Look," Snuggles said to his young uncle, "Bird Leg's asleep." Lafeyette shushed him, his chin buried in his free hand. "I cried on the inside," he said later. "I didn't have enough in me to cry."

As the service closed and the mourners moved forward to pass the casket for one last look at the body, Pharoah, still gripping his balled-up sweatshirt, asked of Lafeyette, "What's up in heaven? Do they have stores?"

"Shut up," Lafeyette said. "You don't know what you talking 'bout."

As the boys waited to file out of their aisle, they heard a mother, two rows back, scold her son: "That could have been you if I'd let you go over there. They would have killed you, too." When gang members passed the casket for the last time, they flashed the hand signal of the Conservative Vice Lords at Bird Leg's stiff body, their thumbs and index fingers forming the letter C. The boys didn't speak until they were outside the church.

"We're gonna die one way or the other by killing or plain out," James said to Lafeyette. "I just wanna die plain out."

Lafeyette nodded. "Me too."

Six

LAFEYETTE FROZE, then stabbed at a fly resting on the stove. "Got it." He shook his fist a couple of times and threw the startled insect into the hot, stagnant air. "C-c-c-c'mon, Lafie, let's . . . let's . . . let's go," Pharoah pleaded. Lafeyette reached out again, this time swatting the back of his brother's head. "Shut up, punk. I ain't going."

Pharoah begged his brother to take him back to the railroad tracks. He wanted to get away from his suffocating home, from Horner, from the Vice Lords, from the summer. It was the only place that offered him a respite. He thought a lot about the fun they had had there hunting for snakes, the momentary peace of mind it had given him.

The summer's violence had woefully unnerved Pharoah, and his stutter, which only a few months before had been nearly imperceptible, had become a real impediment to communicating. Words tangled in his throat. Once, unable to speak, he had to write a question to a friend on a napkin. Sometimes he would struggle so hard to get a sentence out that LaJoe could see his neck muscles constricting; it was as if he were trying to physically push the words up and out. It was painful for LaJoe to hear Pharoah stumble over his thoughts. When he was younger, he had talked so proper, she thought. Friends used to joke that he talked like a white person. Embarrassed by his stammer, Pharoah kept to himself, hanging out mostly with Porkchop, who followed his cousin everywhere, silently, like a shadow.

Pharoah now trembled at any loud noise. LaJoe worried about his vulnerability. And then a few weeks ago, while bullets tore past the living room window, Pharoah had pleaded with her, "M-m-m-mama, M-m-m-m-mamma, make'em, make'em stop!" As the gunfire continued, he fainted.

Earlier in the summer, Lafeyette, along with James, had given in to Pharoah's pleadings and agreed to go back to the railroad tracks. But on a Saturday afternoon, as the boys gathered in the breezeway, a band of teenagers from across the street ran wildly through the corridor, pummeling the three youngsters. Mimicking the behavior of some of the older gang members, they pulled Lafeyette's and James's jackets over their heads and hit them in their stomachs. Pharoah refused to fight back and ran into the apartment before "the shorties," as these young gang members were called, could grab hold of him. James and Lafeyette followed when they realized they were hopelessly outnumbered and outsized. No one was hurt, just shook up.

The next day, the three heard that someone had got trapped under a train and lost his legs while hunting for snakes. Rumor here is often taken for truth. Given the brutality of Horner, almost everything is believable. So the boys, particularly the older ones, decided not to take any chances with their own limbs.

"Man, you . . . you lied," Pharoah whined, as he ducked yet another blow from his brother.

"I ain't lied. Don't tell no stories," Lafeyette countered.

"Let's . . . let's . . ."

Pharoah pushed his head forward as if that might help the words travel up his throat and out his mouth. But Lafeyette grew impatient and walked away without letting Pharoah finish his thought. He just wasn't going. That was it. It wasn't safe.

"Mama," Lafeyette said to LaJoe, "I ain't going back there. Tell Pharoah that. I ain't going."

The summer—and particularly Bird Leg's death—had begun to change Lafeyette. He kept his worries to himself now. LaJoe couldn't remember the last time she'd seen him cry. She scolded Lafeyette for being cruel or too hard on Pharoah, but she knew it was only because he felt protective of the younger boy. For a twelve-year-old, he felt too responsible. She remembered one afternoon when Lafeyette, braving gunfire, tried to get a young friend to take cover. Nine-year-old Diante was the younger brother of William, the successful snake hunter who had been killed last spring. When the gunfire erupted, Diante had remained glued to the swing, repeating over and over, "I wanna die. I wanna die." Lafeyette wouldn't leave him there alone.

And then in early September, Lafeyette witnessed a firebombing, or "cocktailing," as it's called, but he refused to talk about it. He knew better. Lafeyette watched as three teenagers hurled three Molotov cocktails through the windows of the apartment next door. The people who lived there ran a makeshift candy store, selling candy and soda pop through the first-floor window. Lafeyette wouldn't discuss the cocktailing until two years after it happened, and even then with much circumspection. That evening he had desperately wanted to get away from the commotion. To witness such acts is upsetting, but to talk about them, or even to acknowledge that they happened, can only bring trouble, possibly injury to yourself or a member of your family. Denial is simply a means of survival here. So as he walked onto the stoop and passed the shattered windows where earlier in the day he had bought a soda pop, he turned his head away from the burning apartment. "I didn't wanna be nosy," Lafeyette later explained. Luckily, the family, who apparently expected such an attack, had moved in with some friends, so nobody was hurt. The newspapers reported nothing. The apartment remained boarded up for over two years.

(Pharoah didn't learn of the firebombing until the next morning when he walked out onto the stoop. He had apparently slept through it and the efforts by the fire department to douse the flames. "It was stanky in there. Everything was burned," recalled Pharoah, who stuck his head through the opening where the windows once had been. "I saw a Teddy bear busted open with all the cotton on the floor. The couch was turned upside down. It was black on the walls, like burned black stuff on the walls. Their windows were knocked out. The floor tiles was torn up. The sink, I don't know where that was. It was gone. It was a disgrace, a plain disgrace. They shouldn't of done it. People wouldn't want their house to be done like that.")

Through all the turbulence, LaJoe thought, Lafeyette still looked for reason and order. She found it reassuring that he hadn't given up. When a police bomb squad removed a World War II grenade from a fourth-floor apartment, Lafeyette looked on from the playground and matter-of-factly told a friend that the gangs "were figuring to blow up my building." But, he explained, "there be a whole lot of old people and little kids in the building, so they said, 'Don't throw the bomb.' "

Bird Leg's funeral haunted him. He believed he had seen Bird Leg's spirit at a friend's apartment. "He was trying to tell us something," he told his mother, though he wasn't sure what. Lafeyette confided to LaJoe, who tried vainly to get him to verbalize his grief, that talking wasn't going to help him, that everything that "goes wrong keeps going on and everything that's right doesn't stay right."

His face masked his troubles. It was a face without affect, without emotion. Sometimes he appeared stoic or unamused. In an adult, the hollowness of his face might have been construed as a look of judgment. But in Lafeyette it conveyed wariness. Even in its emptiness, it was an unforgiving face. He was an unforgiving child.

"I don't have friends," he told his mother. "Just associates. Friends you trust."

To look into Lafeyette's rust-colored eyes that summer was to look into a chasm of loneliness and fear. Yet those darting eyes missed little.

And so, despite Pharoah's repeated requests, he refused to return to the railroad tracks. It would, he believed, only invite trouble.

—————— Fall 1987–Spring 1988 ——————

Seven

A NARROW PARKING LOT cut between the back of the Riverses' building and a squat, one-story paint factory, Professional Coatings, Incorporated. Few concerned themselves with the factory. Even when operating at maximum levels, it was virtually noiseless and employed only twenty-five people, five of whom, at most, came from Horner.

Among the parked cars, LaJoe leaned against a rusted sedan, its windows and front tires long gone. Though it was a few weeks into September, summer still lingered. A warm breeze swirled through the development, cutting through the breeze-ways and the parking lot.

LaJoe, like the others here, clung to her summer clothes; she wore cut-off blue jeans and a baby-blue, short-sleeved hospital shirt, which she had bought secondhand for forty cents. Her closest friend, Rochelle, grinned and chatted as she rested on the car's hood, her long legs crossed at the knees.

Rochelle was six years younger than LaJoe. They had met as children; their mothers had been best of friends. Rochelle's mother baby-sat for LaJoe's three oldest when the younger woman worked at a health clinic in the 1970s. LaJoe and Rochelle, like their mothers, eventually became best of friends, the only real friends, they would say, each one had. Rochelle had no children of her own, though for five years she had raised two children who had been abandoned by their drug-addicted mother. LaJoe would say that Rochelle had become "like a sec-ond mother" to Lafeyette, Pharoah, and the others; Rochelle occasionally bought them clothes or toys or gave them a dollar for candy. Though she didn't have a job or an income—she had worked for eight and a half years at a printing company, until it closed and moved south—she ran a monthly card game, which sometimes netted her as much as $700 a month. She and her parents lived a couple of blocks from LaJoe in Horner; her fa-ther was retired from a metal-plating factory. LaJoe often vis-ited them. And Rochelle, as on this day, often came by to see LaJoe.

Whenever the gangs entered into a peace treaty—they actu-ally called it that—the edge of this narrow parking lot became a meeting ground for neighbors. This was such a day, and the children took advantage of the reprieve. "You're it," one tall, ungainly girl yelled as she went sprawling on the pavement, just missing tagging her friend. She had tripped over a metal chain that ran the length of the sidewalk, just a few inches off the ground; it often entangled ankles. Presumably it had been installed to keep people off the grass; in fact, many years ago the housing authority fined adults and children who trod on the lawns. But now the chains had become more a nuisance than a barrier. Besides, the lawns were so trampled that the grass grew only in patches, and there was little left to preserve.

While the adults watched in concern, the girl, who couldn't

have been older than eight, picked herself up, brushed off her skinny legs, and continued to give chase.

As the young children pursued each other from one end of the parking lot to the other, Pharoah stood by himself on the building's back stoop. He leaned on the black metal bannister, chin in hand, and stared into space, paying little attention to the shrieking children just a few yards away.

"He's daydreaming lots," LaJoe said to Rochelle. "He's getting more forgetful. I asked him to take the garbage out. He didn't. I said, 'Pharoah, how 'bout that garbage?' He covered his mouth, you know how he do, and told me he forgot. Just done forgot. You know, he probably did. He's forgetting lots.

"Pharoah!" she called. "Pharoah, come here."

The boy's head jerked up as if he had awakened from a deep sleep. He smiled and ran over to his mother's side, and she ran her fingers through his hair, which had grown to cover much of his neck. Rochelle gave Pharoah a smile.

"What you thinking?" LaJoe asked. Pharoah looked up at her.

"Mama, w-w-when . . . when . . . w-w-when . . ." The words tangled in his throat as he strained to answer her. LaJoe continued to stroke his hair and his head.

"W-w-w-when . . . when . . ."

LaJoe didn't let him finish. "Soon, Pharoah. Once they get off strike."

The city's teachers were into the second week of their fourth strike in five years; as in the other walkouts, the main dispute centered on money. The teachers wanted a pay raise and a reduction in the size of their classes. A beginning teacher with a bachelor's degree didn't earn much, $17,651. The school board, on the other hand, proposed trimming the school year by three days in an effort to save money, which would result in an effective 1.7 percent pay cut.

Pharoah loved school. Unlike the streets, where his stammer and small size made him the object of ridicule, he stood tall in school. He read at the level of third grade and six months, as measured by the Iowa Tests of Basic Skills, two months below where he should have been. Nonetheless, that placed him near the top of his upcoming fourth-grade class, whose average was 2.6, a year and two months below grade level.

When school was in session, Pharoah was the first to leave

home each morning. While Lafeyette was still dressing, Pharoah would race out the door, urging his brother to hurry up, warning him that he might miss the nine o'clock bell. The school sat a block away. During all of third grade, Pharoah had been late only four times. Lafeyette's tardiness record the preceding year was eighteen.

At night, Pharoah frequently read until his eyes hurt. Because he had no lamp or working overhead light in his bedroom, he would lie on his belly on the brown floor with his head poking out the door to take advantage of the hallway light. The naked, sixty-watt light bulb did little to brighten the narrow hallway, so Pharoah's eyes quickly grew weary. He was sure he needed glasses. In fact, he desperately wanted a pair. They might help him read longer, he felt, and certainly would make him stand out in school. Maybe, he suggested, if he wore glasses, his teachers would choose him more often to run errands or to answer questions. They would, at the very least, he insisted, make him look smarter. Though a later eye examination showed him to have perfect vision, he continued to ask for a pair, even if their lenses were just clear glass.

When he got bored or had nothing better to do, he practiced his penmanship. His teachers noted that he had an unusually neat and delicate handwriting for someone so young. But Pharoah worked at it, usually writing his name over and over on a piece of paper, so that by the time he had finished, his name appeared maybe two dozen times, leaping in all directions. The P's would stand out in their grace and dominance over the other letters; he would even loop the letter's stem to give it a more pronounced presence. Sometimes, if he got carried away, his name would angle upward, with curls adorning the other letters, too, as if his name were a fanciful spaceship about to rocket off the edge of the paper.

This summer he had had a lot of time to practice his handwriting. For him, the strike-extended vacation had dragged on far too long. During the long summer, another friend of the family's, a man in his early twenties, had been shot and killed. The circumstances were never clear. Both boys refused to attend the burial; they still hadn't gotten over Bird Leg's death.

Concerned about the safety of her children, LaJoe sent Lafeyette and Pharoah to stay with her mother until school opened.

Lelia Mae Anderson lived with a granddaughter on the first floor of a two-family home about two miles farther west. Though it is one of the poorest areas of the city, the gang violence and drug dealing were not as prevalent as at Horner.

When school finally did open—on October 4, four weeks after it had been scheduled to (the teachers won a 4 percent pay boost for each of two years after a record-long walkout)—Pharoah approached it with fervor. It was to be an important school year for him.

The Henry Suder Elementary School, named after a turn-of-the-century physical education director, is an unimposing, two-story, red brick building whose architecture is more utilitarian than esthetic. The building is horseshoe-shaped; the three sides surround a concrete courtyard where the children can play football and tag and other games under the faculty's watchful eye. The courtyard butts up against Horner, separated only by a waist-high fence.

Suder was one of three area elementary schools built between 1952 and 1963, the period of largest influx of families into Henry Horner. Some five thousand children moved in. In the area's heyday, years before Horner was built, the neighborhood schools educated such future luminaries as Lillian Russell, Edgar Rice Burroughs, and Florenz Ziegfeld. But that was when the public schools were strong and respected institutions.

While there has been a lot of focus in recent years on the sad state of the nation's inner-city schools, residents in communities like Horner have always found the schools inadequate. In the early and mid-1960s, the schools, in fact, were a rallying point for blacks in Chicago, who charged that education was both separate and unequal for their children. In 1964, 90 percent of black children of elementary school age attended schools that were 90 percent black. A Chicago Urban League study found that in the predominantly minority schools, the budget for teacher salaries was only 85 percent of that for predominantly white schools, and operating expenses per pupil were only 66 percent as high. Moreover, the school board discouraged paren-, tal involvement. It didn't list the telephone numbers of individual schools in the city's phone book, so parents couldn't reach their children's school by phone.

The School board president, Benjamin Willis, became the center of the controversy and, to the burgeoning civil rights movement, a symbol of the inequity in the schools. In 1961, Willis announced that no black child could transfer unless his or her school averaged more than forty to a classroom, and no white school could accept transfers unless it had an average of fewer than thirty to a room. To accommodate the overcrowding in the predominantly black schools, he introduced mobile units, which derisively became known as Willis Wagons. The schools near Henry Horner, including Suder, were so crowded that they ran two half-day sessions.

In 1963, 225,000 children, or half the city's enrollment, stayed home from school in protest of Willis's clearly discriminatory overcrowding policy. Nearly ten thousand parents and children picketed City Hall, demanding his resignation. Under pressure from community leaders, Willis eventually resigned, in 1966, but the schools continued their slide. It came as no surprise, then, to those living in neighborhoods like Horner when, twenty years later, William Bennett, President Reagan's Secretary of Education, tagged Chicago as the nation's worst school system. It had always been lousy. Why should it be any different today? In 1963, the citywide dropout rate was 38 percent; twenty-five years later it was 40 percent. The citywide reading scores were about the same as they had been twenty years earlier.

Suder, though, is somewhat unusual for an inner-city school. While its children test below grade level—on average, its eighth-graders graduate a year behind in reading—its halls are well monitored, its children, for the most part, well behaved. Moreover, the reading and math scores of its students show steady improvement by the time they graduate from eighth grade. Much of the good record is due to its dynamic, if sometimes imperious, principal, Brenda Daigre, who has been the school's head since 1975. Ms. Daigre won't tolerate hats or earrings in the school, both of which signify affiliation with a gang. The school is free of graffiti and violence.

A three-foot-high sign hangs from the school's second-floor windows: PROJECT AFRICA. It is, perhaps, Ms. Daigre's finest contribution to Suder, and has earned her praise throughout the city. Nineteen eighty-seven was the program's first year. Ms.

Daigre was raising money to travel to Africa over the summer with about a dozen students. In later months, she would display African artifacts in the first-floor hallway, including wood carvings, a handmade straw bowl given as a gift by an African tribal chief, money from various west African nations, and a T-shirt advertising Project Africa. The trips, now an annual institution, continue to garner wide attention; a local television station ran a special program on one of them.

Ms. Daigre, though, is not universally loved. Some mothers complain that she is too quick to judge their children, that she often plays favorites. Some have even transferred their children to other neighborhood schools, where, they hope, their children won't be written off as "bad students." On occasion, teachers have protected children from Ms. Daigre. At least one teacher thinks twice before sending a particular student to the principal's office for fear that Ms. Daigre's punishment will far exceed the crime.

There are also elements beyond Ms. Daigre's control. Like other big-city schools, Suder has experienced financial constraints. Its art and music classes were cut in 1980. Its one counselor must administer the Iowa Tests, maintain the students' medical records, and set up career day for the eighth-graders, leaving little time for counseling the school's seven hundred students. Also, Suder must share a nurse and psychologist with three other schools and a social worker with four others.

Suder has another problem common to most urban elementary schools. Of its thirty-eight teachers, only a handful are men. In a community where positive male role models are scarce, school is one of the few places where children could come into regular contact with an employed man who is not a police officer. (An estimated 85 percent of the households at Horner are headed by women.) The lack of male teachers was felt so acutely at Suder that when the school was awarded extra funds by the city, teachers suggested they be used to hire more male teachers.

It was the first day back from school after the strike, and Diana F. Barone, forty, strode into her fourth-grade classroom. Her students fluttered around her like baby robins angling for a worm.

"Where you been?"

"D'you get your money?"

"Sure happy you back."

The questions and comments came at her fast and furious. They made her feel good. Everyone, students and teachers alike, were glad the strike was finally over.

Ms. Barone, who had recently gotten married and was still known to her students by her maiden name, Ms. Fecarotta (some students combined the two and called her Ms. Fecarone), had begun teaching at Suder sixteen years earlier, and, while she hadn't lost her enthusiasm for teaching, she had become a bit leery of investing as much energy and time as she once did. In her early years, it wasn't unusual for her to spend $500 of her own money to buy books and supplies for her students. She had since become more frugal. Each year, she decorated her four bulletin boards with posters on reading and with essays written by students. One board, she devoted to phonics and displayed large punctuation marks. She dressed them in sneakers and hats. To conserve money, though, she had the characters laminated so that she could use them year after year. She also retained various other bulletin board material, some of which dated back sixteen years.

Ms. Barone tired of the large classes, which at one point swelled to as many as thirty-four students—they now numbered around twenty-five—and of the funding cutbacks. And she worried so much about her children, many of whom came in tired or sad or distracted, that she eventually developed an ulcerated colon.

The relentless violence of the neighborhood also wore her down. The parking lot behind the school had been the site of numerous gang battles. When the powerful sounds of .357 Magnums and sawed-off shotguns echoed off the school walls, the streetwise students slid off their chairs and huddled under their desks. The children had had no "duck and cover" drills, as in the early 1960s, when the prospect of a nuclear war with Cuba and the Soviet Union threatened the nation. This was merely their sensible reaction to the possibility of bullets flying through the window. Ms. Barone, along with other teachers, placed the back of her chair against a pillar so that there would be a solid object between herself and the window.

She dreaded the walk each morning and afternoon from and to her car. She no longer wore jewelry or carried her leather purse. Instead, she used a cheap plastic handbag. She regularly slipped her paycheck into her bra before making the short trek to her car.

But none of this had depleted Ms. Barone's tremendous energy. A short, spunky woman, she spoke so rapidly that it sometimes sounded as if someone had turned up the rpm. She was always in motion. In the previous year's school talent show, she and three other teachers had dressed up as the California Raisins, in costumes of black garbage bags, black pants, white gloves, and enormous sunglasses. They entered the auditorium boogying to the tune "I Heard It Through the Grapevine." Ms. Barone always looked as if she were boogying.

As if to compensate for her free-spirited personality, Ms. Barone turned to her military training—two years in the Marines and three years in the Air Force reserve—to help maintain order in the classroom. And on this first day of school, she explained to her students that they had to follow a set procedure for getting to their desks. They must, she informed them, march single file to the back of the room and then down the appropriate aisle. If a student took home a book, the next morning he or she had to place it on the upper right-hand corner of the desk. Children could go to the bathroom no more than twice a day, and then only as an entire class; they could dispose of garbage only on the way out of the classroom.

"The kids want this orderliness," Ms. Barone reasoned. "They appreciate it. They like it. It gives them a sense of being in an environment that is safe and comfortable."

On the first day of school, Ms. Barone had the students introduce themselves. When it was Pharoah's turn, she noticed his stammering. "M-m-mymy name . . . m-m-my name is Pharoah Rivers," he told the class. She was struck by his determination. The words came hard sometimes, but that didn't stop him. Ms. Barone urged Pharoah to slow down, to take his time talking. But Pharoah's stutter that year, as his family ran into a series of problems, would only worsen.

Ms. Barone had an unusually talented fourth-grade class this year. Her top student was Clarise Gates, one of seven sisters attending Suder. The girls were well known at the school for their collective smarts; the seven of them had already won over a hundred awards. Clarise was the third oldest. Ms. Barone was taken with Clarise's maturity; she seemed much older than the others. Ms. Barone had her tutor other students.

And then there was Pharoah. He flourished under Ms. Barone's rigid discipline and high energy—and Ms. Barone, despite promises to herself to treat all students alike, quickly came to treasure Pharoah. "You try to treat everyone the same, no matter how partial you feel," Ms. Barone would say in explaining her philosophy about teaching. "But Pharoah's special. I'll always have a little soft spot for Pharoah."

Ms. Barone quickly learned that Pharoah, despite his stuttering, liked to talk in class. Sometimes he would answer questions out of turn; at other times he would simply start up conversation with his neighbor, often smack in the middle of a lesson. In all likelihood, Pharoah talked and moved freely at school because he felt protected there. With a sense of security comes comfort, and Pharoah, who in the streets often seemed withdrawn and flighty, livened up at school. There he gossiped and played with a freeness he rarely exhibited outside. Later in the year, his classroom chatter got so out of hand that Ms. Barone had to call in LaJoe to talk with her about it.

Ms. Barone insisted that Pharoah sit in the front row next to her desk so that she could keep an eye on him. Pharoah relished the idea. He would be sitting at the head of the class, next to the teacher and the blackboard.

Because of his size, Pharoah was often picked on by the other children. Once, in the middle of a test, a girl sitting next to him hit him on the neck with a spitball. Pharoah screeched, and then, to the delight of his classmates, hollered, "Old girl be hitting me! Old girl stop it." Everyone in the class broke out in laughter. Pharoah was always referring to others as "old girl" and "old boy," even the adults, and it never failed, though he couldn't fathom why, to tickle everyone who heard him.

Pharoah often asked Ms. Barone to let him help collect papers in the class or to run errands to the principal's office, anything that might give him some responsibility. He was earnest about everything, from talking to his neighbors to finishing his schoolwork.

But Pharoah most endeared himself to his teacher and his classmates by his imagination and writing. He loved words. He'd remember names of places like Ontonagon River and Agate Falls because he liked the way they sounded. When he could, he'd play Scrabble with friends, spelling out words like *motel* and *quake*. He was so proficient at spelling that later in the year, Ms. Barone would choose him to compete in the annual spelling bee, one of the school's biggest honors.

The class was once asked to write an essay entitled "My Pet Monster," and Pharoah's composition won him classroom raves. He wrote about a monster who, like himself, had an uncontrollable sweet tooth. Pharoah knew that candy and cakes and soda pop were bad for him, but he couldn't help himself. Sometimes his face would break out. If he couldn't stop, at least he could laugh at himself—and that's what he did in his essay. Ms. Barone asked Pharoah to read it to the class. He stuttered only occasionally, racing through parts of it, thinking that if he did so he wouldn't trip over any words. It also helped that he was reading and didn't have to think about what he was going to say.

Once I had a pet and his name was "My Pet Monster" and he loved sugar milk more than any other thing. He always was getting into trouble, and every time he get into trouble I'll lock him up with some hand cups and then he'll try to con me to let him out but I wouldn't until a certain time.

One day the stores had closed down for a week. Then "My Pet Monster" found out the stores were closed down and started thinking, he started thinking about his sugar milk. He started running around everywhere to find out if a store was open in the town. He found out there was no store open in the town. "My Pet Monster" was unhappy and he didn't talk to nobody. That's how unhappy he was.

The week passed and the stores were now open and "My Pet Monster" was the first to enter the store. He got two gallons of milk and two quarts of sugar, and "My Pet Monster" said "the only reason I got two of each so if the stores closed I will have an extra gallon and wouldn't have to worry."

The kids laughed uproariously at the tale, and Ms. Barone brought it home that evening to read to her husband. She then tacked it to one of the bulletin boards, where all the students and passing teachers could see it. It was a treasured moment for Pharoah, who had often been teased about his studiousness. Some students called him a nerd; others made fun of his buck teeth. The taunting upset Pharoah—and he knew he wouldn't always be able to deflect it with humorous stories. Early that school year, though, he found a friend who helped keep his tormentors at bay.

Eight

PHAROAH FIRST MET RICKEY at school, where they were classmates. Rickey asked Pharoah for a favor. Rickey had developed a crush on Pharoah's cousin Dede. "Pharoah," he said one day at school, "ask Dede if she'd go out with me." Pharoah giggled, delighted to be entrusted with such a task. When he delivered the message to Dede, she told him, "No way."

"Ask her again," Rickey implored. Pharoah did, and this time Dede said she would date Rickey, at least give it a try. Before too long, graffiti began appearing in Pharoah's building: RICKEY LS DEDE. Rickey and Pharoah became friends after that.

Rickey, whom the adults called Richard, lived in Henry Horner with his mother, Gloria, and a younger brother and two older sisters. His father had left when Rickey was three, and the boy last saw him two years ago.

Rickey lived just two buildings west of Pharoah, but his house seemed much farther away, because it was on the other side of Damen Avenue. Damen acts as the dividing line between the Vice Lords' and the Disciples' turfs. It also divides the housing complex in half. Although younger children freely cross the four-lane street, teenagers and even adults take considerable care in crossing the gang boundary. Most children living west of Damen, in what is called the "new projects" because the buildings were a second stage of Horner, don't hang out at the Boys Club, which is in Vice Lords' territory. Rickey lived one building west of Damen; Pharoah, two buildings east of the line.

So, for starters, it seemed strange that a boy from the new projects would befriend a boy from the old projects. But more surprising was that Rickey and Pharoah would find some bond despite the startling differences between them. Not even Ms. Barone suspected that her two students spent time together.

Where Pharoah was slight, Rickey, in the words of one local policeman, was "built like a pit bull." For an eleven-year-old, he had unusually solid muscles; he looked far older than his age.

Where Pharoah adored school, Rickey shunned it. He could barely read, and had already been held back a year. He was a year and a half older than Pharoah. Moreover, he had been written up so many times for bad behavior that his anecdotal history at Suder, a compilation of past incidents, was nearly the thickness of a phone book. Once, the police had to be called in to handle him. He frequently got into fistfights, and because he was stronger than most of the other boys, he could do them considerable harm. When he got angry, he used foul language, even with the adults. He once told Ms. Barone to "fuck off." Ms. Barone sometimes took a nap after school just to recover from her encounters with the class bully.

And where Pharoah tried to keep a distance from the neighborhood's violence, Rickey was in the thick of it. Rickey had been with Bird Leg when he died. The two were second cousins. Rickey was one of the younger children whom Bird Leg had befriended, and, like Lafeyette, he had loved being around Bird Leg's dogs. On the day of the shooting, Bird Leg asked Rickey to hold his radio while he gave chase to the bottle-throwing Disciples. Rickey, though, wanting to help in the chase, put the radio down and joined the battle, hurling bricks at Bird Leg's assailants. He had heard the lone gunshot and watched his cousin stumble and fall by the cottonwood and die. He then sat on a nearby bench and wept. For the next two days, Rickey stayed in his apartment, refusing to talk or eat. He vomited throughout the weekend. His mother worried that he was ill, but by Monday he started eating again and venturing back outside. The anger about Bird Leg's death, though, didn't subside; instead, it simmered and stewed within him. It was two years before he talked to anyone about watching his cousin die.

"I felt like I lost a big brother. I used to think they should of shot him in the leg," Rickey said later. "Seem like I don't care no more. I don't feel sorry for people no more 'cause when they killed Bird Leg, the peoples who shot him mustn't of felt sorry for him. Like I be playing basketball or something, it seems like I can't sometimes get it off my mind. It just stay on my mind."

Often, when Rickey became embroiled in a fight, he began to relive Bird Leg's last minutes, and as he did so, his anger turned to rage. In class, he once choked another child so long and hard that, in the words of Pharoah, "he put him to sleep." These flashbacks, which were not unlike those of a traumatized war veteran, haunted Rickey for well over a year after Bird Leg's death.

"Now, it seems like if I get in a fight, I don't care if I kill or something. I don't even care. It be like, we be fighting, we be fighting other people. Someone be telling me in my mind, 'Hurt him, just don't worry about it.' Shhh. I just be thinking about hurting him. It just be pressure on my mind. Things that I be seeing, flashbacks. I just see when Bird Leg just bent down and almost tripped over the chain, then just lay down. I just catch myself right there. If I kill someone, it seems like I'm taking them on for the person who killed Bird Leg."

Pharoah and others were unaware of the effect that Bird

Leg's death had had on Rickey. Beneath the raw exterior lay a tender child who addressed many adults as "sir" and "ma'am" and who took the hands of younger children to help them cross the street. LaJoe thought his eyes were filled with sweetness. But it was a guarded softness. When he smiled, he seemed uncomfortable, as if he might be judged as being fragile or accused of being a sissy. There were times, later on, after numerous entanglements with the law and flirtations with the gangs, that Rickey would be standing with older friends on the back stoop of Pharoah's building, and he couldn't bring himself to say hello to passing adults or to young children. He would act distant and tough. But at eleven, Rickey didn't try to—perhaps he couldn't —hide his kindness.

What cemented Pharoah and Rickey's friendship was an incident that took place during gym class one day, shortly after Rickey started dating Dede. Another boy, Cortez, had snatched a basketball from Pharoah's hands. Pharoah was furious. "Give . . . give . . . give . . . it to me!" he demanded. Cortez smiled and dribbled the basketball, taunting Pharoah. Pharoah, who didn't like to fight, did nothing. Rickey, bigger and stronger than the other fourth-graders, had been watching the dispute from a distance.

"I don't know, they was arguing in the room. I didn't pay no attention," he later recalled. "I was just shooting basketball. Then I looked. He tried to hit Pharoah." Rickey grabbed the basketball from Cortez and gave it to Pharoah. All seemed settled until a few minutes later, when Cortez went over to Pharoah as he shot baskets and threw him to the ground.

"Cortez, man, why you do that?" Rickey demanded. He walked slowly up to Cortez and, before he could resist, put him in a headlock until he begged Rickey to let him go. Rickey then pummeled him. "Poom! Poom! Poom! Then I stopped," he recalled. "Everybody picks on Pharoah 'cause he's so short and he doesn't like to fight. It just feel like he's a little brother to me." Cortez left Pharoah alone after that.

To the adults of the neighborhood, Rickey's friendship with Pharoah seemed odd. Perhaps Rickey considered Pharoah family, since he was now dating his cousin. Or maybe, torn between his desire to bully and to embrace, Rickey felt he had found someone with whom he had no choice but to be friends.

Pharoah, after all, would have been no match for Rickey in a fight. Most likely, both reasons explain Rickey's attraction to Pharoah.

From Pharoah's perspective, the friendship was easier to understand. Rickey offered Pharoah protection; he was a trusted friend. When Rickey had money, he would give some to Pharoah. Though he never said as much to Pharoah, it was understood that he wouldn't let anything happen to him.

Lafeyette was wary of his brother's new friend. "I worry about Pharoah a lot," Lafeyette explained. "I don't want anything to happen to him, because he's my little brother. I'm supposed to watch after him. He makes me mad at times but I still love him."

He was proud of how well Pharoah did at school. A smart child himself, Lafeyette never took school as seriously as Pharoah did. He had already been held back a year. His attendance record at times was woeful: in 1986, he missed thirty-five days and received a D average. The excuses varied: flu, stomachache, chicken pox, no clean clothes to wear. Sometimes he missed days because of suspensions resulting from fights in school. He secretly wished his mother would push him more, make him go to sleep early, make him do his homework. LaJoe conceded that she could be too soft on her children, though she wanted nothing more than to see Lafeyette and Pharoah graduate from high school.

Despite his poor attendance record, however, Lafeyette tested particularly well in his favorite subject, math. When he did attend school with some regularity, as in fourth grade, he earned a B— average. And when he reached seventh grade, he would earn A's in math and science. His teacher this fall, in sixth grade, Ruby Everage, liked him. She found that when Lafeyette came to school, he wanted to learn and was earnest about his work. Lafeyette grew fond of Mrs. Everage and, toward the second half of the year, attended school with greater regularity and helped throw a surprise party for her. She was about to leave to have a child.

On occasion, Lafeyette skipped gym class to talk privately with Mrs. Everage about problems at home or in the neighborhood. Lafeyette told her how he sometimes found himself daydreaming in class, worrying about his brothers and sisters. He struck her as a sensitive child, as someone who had a lot on his mind. She told him, as she would others, that there was hope, that indeed there was a life outside Horner. She'd take her students on numerous field trips to places like the Museum of Science and Industry and the Robert Crown Center for Performing Arts to prove her point.

It especially frustrated Lafeyette that his younger brother refused to fight. He worried that if Pharoah couldn't stand up for himself, he'd get mauled by the older boys. So Lafeyette believed he had an obligation to toughen him up. He'd badger Pharoah—sometimes calling him "fag" and "punk"—and slap him until he could take it no longer and would begin to flail back.

"You gotta fight," Lafeyette would tell him. "I ain't gonna be there all the time to fight for you. C'mon. C'mon. Hit me."

Pharoah would beg his brother to let him be and, if that didn't succeed, would appeal to their mother for help. He didn't want to fight.

"It ain't right," Pharoah said to Lafeyette. "Why's people fighting people?"

"That's stupid," Lafeyette countered.

Lafeyette talked to his mother. Wasn't there something she could do to keep Pharoah away from Rickey, who undoubtedly would get Pharoah into trouble? It was, to be sure, a peculiar match: the bully and the bookworm. And so it came as no surprise to Pharoah that his brother would disapprove of his friendship with Rickey.

"Hey, man, he only gonna get you in trouble," Lafeyette warned Pharoah.

"You . . . you . . . you ain't my father," Pharoah retorted, walking away from his brother.

"He too old for you to be with," Lafeyette yelled after him.

But the friendship persisted despite Lafeyette's efforts to keep the two boys apart—and, ironically, in the end it was Lafeyette who would be more influenced by Rickey than Pharoah was.

Nine

THE JANUARY SUN had barely risen above the Loop's glass skyscrapers when Pharoah, who had just awakened, picked the two dead goldfish from their bowl and dropped them into a plastic bag. As he walked through the building's breezeway into the early morning quiet, he stopped to look around for an appropriate resting place. He chose a spot just to the left of the breezeway, a piece of lawn that edged right up to the building. Few people walk here, he figured; the grave, might remain untrampled.

With an ice cream stick in hand, Pharoah dug into the frozen ground. The stick cracked a little, but Pharoah reinforced it with his thumb and index finger, and kept digging until he had made a hole a couple of inches deep. He removed the once orange fish—in death, they had turned a cloudy gray—and gently lowered them into the ground.

"God bless these fish," he recited solemnly. "Don't let them go up to hell. Let them go to heaven."

He had already cried for three hours when he found his pets floating belly up in their bowl the night before. ("I fed 'em too much," he concluded.) They had been a Christmas present from his mother, and he had named them Abraham and Goldberg after characters on the television series *Diff'rent Strokes*. He wasn't going to cry again. He silently covered the fish with the crusty soil.

With all that swirled about Pharoah this winter, the death of his two fish seemed incidental. But it was, at least, one crisis he could deal with himself, one that he could comprehend.

The apartment was too crowded, LaJoe knew, but she didn't have the heart to kick anyone out. Her children had no place to go.

Shortly before Christmas, LaShawn, the oldest, had moved back home. She brought with her a small entourage: her boyfriend, her boyfriend's brother, and her two children, Tyisha, who was seven, and Darrell, who had just turned one. Everyone called him Baldheaded except Pharoah, who insisted on calling him Sir Baldheaded.

LaShawn and her children had been renting a room in a tenement with friends, but they ended up not getting along. LaJoe worried that LaShawn might be harmed when her boyfriend, Brian, went to work. Brian sold fake gold jewelry to unsuspecting tourists at O'Hare Airport, where he worked every day. LaJoe had also been concerned about her daughter's ability to take care of her two children, given her drug habit. She smoked Karachi, a potent mixture of Pakistini heroin and amphetamines. The drug was rarely injected, but rather smoked. It was particularly popular on the city's west side.

Like many other public housing apartments, the Riverses' overflowed with people, as many as thirteen if the boys' father, Paul, stayed over. LaShawn, Brian, and Sir Baldheaded slept in one room, Terence and Paul, whom everyone called Weasel, in another. The triplets and Tyisha bedded down in the front bedroom. Lafeyette and Pharoah shared the back room with Brian's teenage brother, Larry. Pharoah couldn't adjust to the crowded apartment, and had trouble concentrating on his schoolwork. But he conceded that having all those people living there made him feel safer. "If someone snatch you, you'll have a witness," he explained. LaJoe usually slept on the couch or with the children.

It isn't uncommon for a large number of people to pack into a public housing apartment. The Chicago Housing Authority estimated that in its nineteen developments, it has 200,000 tenants, 60,000 of whom aren't listed on the leases. Another 60,000 families are on the housing authority's waiting list, because there is such a shortage of low-rent housing in the city.

If LaJoe fretted too long about the jammed apartment, she had only to look around her to see what might happen if she didn't give her grown children shelter. Three weeks before Christmas, a group of homeless men and women sledgehammered their way into Horner's vacant apartments. Many tenants welcomed them. Better the homeless than the gangs, they reasoned. Also, it didn't make sense to LaJoe and others to let heated apartments stand empty. Most of the units also had running water, though some were missing toilets and sinks, items stolen and then sold for scrap. The city's fifty shelters were packed every night.

The Chicago Housing Authority said it was concerned about liability. In a game of cat and mouse that made the national evening news, private security guards searched out the squatters and physically removed them. As the guards flushed the homeless from one building, they would sneak into another, frequently with the aid of tenants, who directed them to the most habitable of the vacant units. This went on for weeks, until the housing authority and the press tired of the chase. The homeless, as they had done in previous winters (but with less brouhaha and publicity), continued to take refuge in Horner's empty quarters. Tenants often prepared hot meals for their new neighbors.

LaJoe felt pressured that winter. On occasion and without much provocation, she would explode in anger, ordering her young ones to shut up or telling Lafeyette and Pharoah to clean their room. She rarely felt that she could sail through a day and enjoy such simple moments as the coming of spring or Pharoah's smile or Lafeyette's playful teasing. There was no time to reflect on the past or to plan for the future. If it wasn't the shooting outside, it was her daughter's drug habit or Lafeyette's troubles at school or Pharoah's stammer.

Sometimes, in addition to these constant concerns, LaJoe had prolonged episodes in her life that were sufficiently grave to affect her physically. She couldn't sleep and battled persistent colds and headaches. Her temper grew shorter. She felt, she said, as if her insides were being shredded. During these times, she considered giving up or starting out on her own again. She once said that had she known all that her younger children, Lafeyette on down, would have to endure, she would have returned them to the womb.

She felt that way this winter. First, the police arrested Terence, charging him with armed robbery. Then, the Department of Public Aid informed her that it had proof that her husband stayed with the family, and it planned to cut off her benefits, leaving her and her children without any income. She began to feel that the only people she could count on were Lafeyette and Pharoah and, indeed, she leaned on the two boys, particularly Lafeyette, to get her through this time.

The problems started with Terence. He had been LaJoe's closest child—and his failure was her biggest disappointment. For LaJoe, Terence became a kind of measuring stick for Lafeyette and Pharoah. She worried that they, like him, might let her down.

Born on January 31, 1970, Terence grew up during a difficult time for LaJoe and Paul. The two had met four years earlier at Swingville, a local dance hall. They still dispute who first asked the other to dance. But there's a lot now they disagree about. When the two first met, LaJoe lied about her age. She told Paul she was sixteen. She was actually three years younger.

Paul, then seventeen, was—and still is—a handsome man. Like LaJoe, he was shy and small in stature, but because he boxed as an amateur bantamweight, he had a rugged, wiry build. What first caught LaJoe's eye, though, was Paul's natty

dress. In his shiny leather shoes and freshly pressed pinstripe
suit, he stood out from the other men, most of whom wore jeans
and leather jackets. Paul's trademark became a steel-gray Stetson with two dimples punched neatly in the crown.

Despite his pugilistic hobby, Paul was of a gentle nature and
quick mind. He didn't like to fight outside the ring and, indeed,
had a nervous stomach disorder that incapacitated him at times.
He read a lot, magazines and newspapers mostly, which he carried around in his hip pocket. He was also a connoisseur of jazz,
and eventually collected over a hundred albums. Among his
favorites were the recordings of Thelonious Monk and Miles
Davis. He also loved to debate politics. He became involved
peripherally with the Black Panthers, whose city headquarters
was just two blocks from Horner, and then with the local Democratic Party machine. Major Adams, the leader of the Boys
Club Drum and Bugle Corps and a kind of father figure for the
neighborhood's youth, thought Paul one of the smartest young
men he'd ever met at Horner.

In their first few years together, Paul loved to listen to LaJoe
dream aloud of the two of them growing old together. She
would spin out soothing images of them raising a large family
in a quiet neighborhood with back yards and picket fences.
They would live in a wood-frame house where, in old age, they
could pass the time in rocking chairs on the front porch.

Paul and LaJoe wasted little time in starting their family.
Within a year of their meeting, LaJoe, only fourteen, gave birth
to LaShawn and then, a year later, to Weasel. Soon after, they
decided to get married. But on the day of the planned church
wedding, Paul backed out and, instead, got stone drunk. LaJoe's
mother, furious at the backpedaling groom, barred him from
visiting LaJoe. The two continued to date surreptitiously and
eventually moved in together. Their third child, Terence, soon
arrived, and that's when the dream began to fall apart.

Paul had already fathered a boy by another woman; the child
was born within a few days of Terence. LaJoe says she learned
of Paul's philandering when she was in the hospital. She was
admiring the day-old Terence through the glass when a woman
came along and pointed out her new arrival. "Who's the father?" LaJoe asked. "Paul Rivers," the woman responded. Paul
says LaJoe found out about his cheating later, weeks after she

returned home with Terence. However LaJoe learned of it, she never quite forgave Paul. (In later years, LaJoe, unable to turn anyone away, became like a second mother to Ivan, Paul's son by the other woman.)

At the time, though, LaJoe, in her youthful determination to make things right, got Paul to marry her. LaJoe wanted her children to have a father. She didn't want to bring them up alone. "I didn't have a corner I could run to," she said later. Paul too wanted the children to grow up with a man around the house. On August 22, almost seven months after Terence was born, they took the bus down to City Hall, where they were wed.

In a neighborhood where men fathered children and then disappeared into the gangs and the street corners and death, Terence and his siblings had an unusual family situation. Their mother remained married to the same man, and he fathered all eight children. They began to fall out of love, though, when LaJoe learned of Paul's drug habit.

Paul, unbeknown to LaJoe, began to dabble with drugs in the early 1970s, shortly after they were married. He already drank and, in fact, avoided being sent to Vietnam by purposely arriving at his draft board inebriated. He had downed Robitussin, a cough syrup that was a popular quick high at the time. He also began popping pills, mostly barbiturates called Red Devils and Christmas Trees. By the age of twenty-two, when a poolroom friend introduced Paul to heroin, he started shooting up the drug; the habit, which he has bucked at times, has stayed with him for the better part of twenty years.

LaJoe first learned for certain of Paul's habit—she had earlier suspected it—around 1978, when Terence was eight. She was sitting in the front bedroom when she heard Paul collapse in the bathroom. He had wedged himself between the door and the bathtub. Finally, after minutes of pushing and shoving the door, trying not to injure her husband, LaJoe managed to squeeze into the bathroom. Paul lay there unconscious; blood filled the syringe bulging from his forearm. He had overdosed and, in falling, had cracked his head against the steam pipe. LaJoe yanked the needle out of his arm and called for an ambulance. After he had been taken to the hospital, she cried for hours.

Paul survived and a couple of years later made it through yet another overdose. LaJoe hated him for it. Although she knew he drank and dabbled with drugs, she never thought he'd become dependent on them. Most of the money he spent on heroin was financed by his good-paying jobs with the city. After working eight years as an upholsterer, Paul was rewarded for his work with the local Democratic machine by a job in the city's sewer department. There, he earned $350 to $450 every two weeks. He then went to work as a garbage collector and, more recently, as a city bus driver.

LaJoe wanted to kick him out for good. But she also strongly wanted her children to have a father—and, as she readily admitted, she had trouble saying no to people. So she let him come around and even allowed him to stay over, though they rarely slept together. Nonetheless, Paul fathered the triplets. LaJoe, who had gone back to school to earn her high school equivalency, worked off and on for five years as a clerk for the Miles Square Health Center. She also flirted briefly with a modeling career, which quickly foundered. For a while she displayed pictures of herself in flowing gowns and stylish African turbans, but in time she threw them away. The disappointment lingered, and it was one of the few things LaJoe refused to discuss with anyone. During the times she was unemployed, she received welfare.

As LaJoe became more distressed by Paul's drug habit, they talked less, sometimes not at all, and the strain led to awkward moments when Paul came around. If he came into the house high, the children scattered to the bedrooms.

In Paul's absence, LaJoe found comfort in her children. Particularly Terence. As a young boy, Terence was built almost exactly like Lafeyette, rail-thin and gangly. When he was sixteen, he weighed only 110 pounds and was five-feet-five. He wasn't a gifted athlete, nor was he much of a fighter. If anything, he was an anxious child; the corner of his mouth sometimes twitched nervously.

Terence wanted to fit in, to be accepted by his peers. Once, a group of children climbed to the second floor of a two-story building and dared each other to jump onto a pile of mattresses. None would jump until, to the surprise of all, Terence volunteered. Eleven at the time and the youngest among them, he leaped out the window onto the mattresses a good thirty feet below.

Always by LaJoe's side, Terence seemed to some a mama's boy. LaJoe did pamper the child—and at times, she concedes, she acted more like a big sister than a parent. Terence received a weekly allowance, and once a month LaJoe treated him and his older brother and sister to a dinner at the South Pacific, a downtown restaurant. She so adored Terence that she even promised him she would have no more children, that he would be the last.

"Anything I asked my mama for, I got it," recalled Terence. "Out of all, I got it. My mama loved all of us the same, but it seemed to me that I was the favorite one out of all."

But when she later gave birth to Lafeyette, then Pharoah, and then the triplets, Terence became jealous of the new arrivals and withdrew from the family. His mother had let him down. The attention once directed toward him slowly turned to the younger children, and LaJoe grew impatient with Terence's clinging.

"Terence was the one maybe I should have paid more attention to. He always wanted to be under me," LaJoe recalls. "This is how Terence went: it was always me and Terence. Wherever I went, Terence went. He was my baby then. And I don't think Terence never wanted to turn me loose. As the other kids came, Terence never wanted that 'cause he used to tell me all the time, 'You should of just had me.' And then I would tell him, I shouldn't of just had him. I had Shawnie and Weasel before I had him and I love you and I love Shawnie and Weasel.

"I would always have to repeat myself with Terence. Over and over, too. All the time. But Terence just left one day. He was about nine. No, he was about ten. He left one day. I couldn't find him. The police were looking for Terence. When I saw him, it was three months later. I couldn't do nothing 'cause I didn't know."

What LaJoe didn't know was that a local drug dealer, Charles, had taken Terence under his wing. Charles used the youngster, who had not yet entered sixth grade, to sell what were called T's and Blues, a mixture of Talwin and antihistamines, at the time a popular substitute for heroin.

It was 1981, about the time drug prices began to drop and the trade blossomed. Terence would stand on Madison Street among the liquor stores and pawnshops, just two blocks south of the projects. He hid his wares in the steel pillars that supported the El tracks. Using juveniles is popular among drug dealers, since children tend to be treated less harshly than adults by the courts. What's more, once found guilty, they can't be held past their twenty-first birthday. Most are rarely held beyond twenty days.

Terence was not only earning as much as $200 a day, but Charles virtually adopted him, setting him up with his own room, complete with bed and television. Sometimes, Charles entrusted Terence with as much as $10,000 in cash, which he had him hold, knowing that neither the police nor extortionists would suspect an eleven-year-old of carrying that kind of money. Charles also taught Terence to shoot a .45 caliber revolver. They took target practice at night in the back alleys of the neighborhood. Terence was so small that he had to hold the gun with both hands; he eventually traded it for a smaller gun, which he could handle more easily. Though Terence carried the revolver with him, stuffing it in the waistband of his pants, he pulled it out only once, when he and Charles threatened to shoot some men who planned to rob them. Terence had little need for school. He dropped out in the seventh grade and was recorded as "lost" by the school system. Because he left before the legal age of sixteen, he wasn't considered a dropout.*

By the time LaJoe learned what had become of Terence, she couldn't win him back. Friends would inform her if they sighted her son, but when she got to the specified location, Terence was long gone. Once, she confronted Charles.

"I want my son," she told him.

"Terence is my son. He belongs to me," Charles replied.

LaJoe tried everything. She even went to the police. If they could find him, they would bring him home; there he stayed for a few weeks before taking off again. She asked a friend of hers who was a social worker and from the neighborhood whether she'd talk with Terence. But LaJoe couldn't get Terence to visit the friend.

Paul also tried. Despite his estrangement from LaJoe and his habit, he never stopped caring about the children. For a short

---

* The Chicago school system has since changed the way it computes its dropout rate, so a child who leaves school before sixteen is now considered a dropout and not "lost."

period, he owned a car and took the children on a Saturday or Sunday outing to a nearby park. He didn't think Terence or the others knew about his involvement with drugs—Terence didn't —and, more than anything, he didn't want his children to repeat his mistakes.

One afternoon, early during the time of Terence's wanderlust, Paul grabbed his son by the collar. "C'mon, Terence, we're going up there and I'm going to talk to this son of a bitch. He ain't going to put nothing else in your hands when I get through with him." A friend offered Paul a pistol for protection. He turned it down and dragged Terence to the diner where he had heard Charles hung out.

In the parking lot, Terence stood silent, his eyes riveted to the pavement. "Is this Charles?" Paul asked. "That him? He the one that give you the drugs and what-not?"

"Yeah," Terence muttered. He couldn't lie to his father.

Charles sauntered up. He tried to explain to Paul that if this was what Terence wanted to do, Paul should let him do it.

Paul felt his temper rising, and he began to shake. His stomach churned. "What you mean, this what he want to do? You're taking advantage of him. The boy can't think for himself. He's only twelve years old. He don't know what to do for hisself." Paul paused. "Man, if you put some more drugs in my son's hands, I'm going to do something to you."

Charles just stood there. People began to surround the two men. To Paul they seemed to appear out of nowhere. From the barbershop. From a nearby fish market. From the diner. And from across the street. One had a hand buried in a brown paper bag. "Hey, bro," he asked Charles, "you want me to pop him?" Charles waved him away. He didn't say anything more. He just cleared a path and let Paul leave with a sullen and scared Terence. Paul felt so weak, his knees nearly gave out. As for Terence, "he slowed down for a long time after that," recalled Paul, "but then Terence, he at times would disappear. He would just disappear and stay with friends."

LaJoe and Paul lost Terence to the neighborhood. It is not unusual for parents to lose out to the lure of the gangs and drug dealers. And the reasons aren't always clear. In one Horner family, a son has become a big drug dealer, a daughter a social worker. In another, one boy is in jail on a gang-related murder, another has set up a neighborhood youth program. Some parents simply won't let their children leave the apartment even to play in the playground. A common expression among the mothers at Horner is "He ain't my child no more." Micki, James Howard's mother, would tell LaJoe, "Thank God I got a thirteen-year-old child who's still mine."

Lafeyette, who was six at the time, knew only that his brother sold T's and Blues, though he didn't understand until later years what that meant. Lafeyette considered Terence his favorite brother, and remembers Terence giving him $5.00 to $10.00 whenever he saw him. Lafeyette would see Terence in the street and, in full run, throw his arms around him.

"C'mon, Terry, let's go home."

"Naw, man, I gotta take care of my business," Terence would reply.

"C'mon, brother."

"Here's five dollars. Now go on. Tell Mama and them I say hi."

"Okay, I'm gonna tell Mama and them what you said." Lafeyette would pause again, still hopeful. "You gonna come home tomorrow?"

"Yeah, I'll come to see how they be doing."

"You gonna come?"

"Yeah, I'm gonna come."

Sometimes Terence would feel guilty and return home for a night or two. But mostly he kept on about his business, selling drugs. Sometimes when he ran into Lafeyette, he would treat him to a hot dog and french fries at a local diner. Lafeyette would be perched on one of the diner's stools, his legs dangling, while Terence went outside to sell his drugs. Pharoah, who was only three at the time, was too young to remember Terence's wanderings.

Terence missed his family. The first Christmas away, he heard from friends that his father had been robbed of several hundred dollars. A few days later, a young boy showed up at LaJoe's doorstep and asked for LaJoe Rivers. "That's me," she told him. The boy, who couldn't have been more than ten, thrust an envelope into her hand and then dashed out of the building. LaJoe, sensing that he might be a friend of Terence's, gave chase but quickly lost him. When she opened the envelope, she found $500 and a note from Terence, telling her that he'd heard of the robbery. The note asked her not to come looking for him.

Terence eventually grew tired of belonging to Charles; he wanted to be with his family again. What finally brought him home was an incident that at the time seemed minor to LaJoe but that Terence would talk about in later years as if it had happened the day before.

"My mom, she give me anything I want," he recalled. "She wasn't doing that no more. She stopped giving me anything. She just got fed up. There was one particular day, I didn't have no money. I just had all drugs on me, and I told her to give me ten dollars. She was at the bus stop, getting ready to go shopping, I'll never forget, on Damen and Lake Street. She told me no. She just said, 'I ain't got no money.' I said, 'Okay, okay, Mama.' She got on the bus. I sat there, you know, like, man, my mama just forgot about me. It was just she was fed up with me.

"Yeah, I'll never forget it 'cause I caught her coming back. She had some grocery bags with her. I helped her carry the bags. That's when I got to slacking up. I started staying home. My mama started talking to me. That was just a little lesson there. My mama was giving me everything I wanted. I was getting everything I wanted. Then she told me no. She was real aggravated, real angry at me, frustrated. She said, 'You don't listen to me no more.' And that hurted me. That was the first time she ever turned me down."

Terence returned home. But the troubles didn't end. He ran with a fast crowd. He and his friends shoplifted and broke into video games. He became the one who would jimmy open the machines. Some of the money went to drugs. Terence had started dabbling first with marijuana and then Karachi, the smokable heroin mixture.

He briefly joined the Disciples, who at that point oversaw his end of Horner. He got caught up in a few gun fights and had at least one friend killed. But he abandoned the gang because, while he was serving one month-long stint in detention, the members didn't visit him. He still has tattooed on his right arm the gang's insignia: a six-pointed star and a pitchfork.

Also, like many of his teenage friends, he became a father; he had three children in all, a boy and two girls. Like his mother, he had his first child when he was fourteen. As tradition dictated, the child was named after his dad, Terence, though everyone called him Snuggles.

There were times when Terence tried to slow down, and, for a while, he shined shoes at the airport or just hung around at home. But by the time he turned eighteen, he had been arrested forty-six times for crimes ranging from disorderly conduct to purse snatching.

For six months, from the summer of 1987 through January of 1988, fifteen taverns in the Nineteenth Police District on the city's mostly white north side reported robberies, sometimes as many as two a month. Two to four black males would pry open video games and run off with the change. In one instance, it amounted to $1500 from one machine, though usually it came to somewhere between $200 and $500 per game. The police say that in that same time period as many as thirty other taverns in adjacent districts reported similar crimes.

The robbers almost always worked the same way. Two teenagers would find a working-class neighborhood tavern where, early in the day—they never worked at night so as to avoid crowds—the clientele would be older and less likely to resist. The thieves concentrated on video poker games, a popular sport in many a bar even though it was played only for the thrill; the game returned winners no money. Since these machines took one-dollar and five-dollar bills, they tended to hold more money than other video games. While one of the youths would dance and shout in false excitement to allay any fears that they were in the bar for a purpose other than to play the game, his cohort would insert a long screwdriver into a narrow crack that ran down the front of the machine, and, using it as a lever, jimmy open the coin box. They would empty the coins into their pockets—they wore oversize overcoats for the purpose—and then race for the door, escaping by car or bus or the El. When four teenagers instead of two pulled off the theft, one sat down at the bar for a drink—usually a soda pop, since he was under age—and distracted the bartender with conversation while the others pried open the machines.

The police considered these "nuisance" crimes, because no one was hurt or, for that matter, even threatened. Also, the robberies didn't involve huge amounts of money. Nor was any other property taken. But north side barkeepers had been complaining regularly to the police, at one point even calling a community meeting. The police said to alert them if any suspicious people came into the taverns.

On January 15, the police received such a call from Lawry's Tavern on Lincoln Avenue, a street that had had four thefts over the previous two days. Two young black males had come in, one of whom ordered a Coca-Cola. Neither looked old enough to order a drink. Three plainclothesmen hurriedly drove to Lawry's, entering separately so as not to arouse suspicion. A few minutes later, as the three men watched from different ends of the bar, the two boys walked over to the video poker machine and began to play it. Then, suspecting that the three new customers might be police, they surreptitiously stashed their screwdriver behind a nearby radiator. They played two games, but as they started to leave, the police stopped them at the door and placed them under arrest. From one of the boys, they recovered a set of keys to other video machines; they also found the screwdriver. The police drove the boys to the precinct house, charged them with a misdemeanor, and took pictures of them in the hope that if they continued their robberies, bartenders would be able to identify them. The younger of the two, Terence Rivers, was the more easily identifiable: he wore his long hair combed straight back and down to his shoulders, at the time an unusual hairstyle. Moreover, Terence was slightly built, rangy and short.

When, two weeks later, four black males robbed Ann's Longhorn Saloon and one of them was identified as Terence, it was reasonable to conclude that, in fact, he had broken into yet another video poker game. Only now he was an adult, which meant that the penalty would be much stiffer than a month or two in the juvenile home.

Ann's Longhorn Saloon fit the profile: a working-class tavern in a sleepy, north side residential section of the city. The bar sits on a two-block commercial strip with another tavern and assorted small businesses; the El tracks cross at street level with automatic barriers that rise and fall with the coming of each train; they give the area the feeling of a small town.

Rebecca Mitchell, or Ann, as she preferred to be called, the bar's tender and owner of eight years, was a large, buxom red-head who retained her Alabama drawl. She had decorated the walls with life-size posters of scantily clad, busty women, an American flag, and, above the cash register, a Confederate flag. Beneath the Southern emblem and above the register protruded the bar's trademark: a set of longhorns measuring about seven feet from tip to tip.

The storefront was deeper than it was wide. The counter, almost twenty feet in length, extended from the door to the rear. It was to the right, just as patrons walked in. On the opposite wall sat the jukebox, which played mostly country and western music, and two video poker games. They had been burglarized five times in the past two years.

On the afternoon of January 28, Johnny Adams, a youth not much older than Terence, walked into Ann's Longhorn Saloon, sat down at the bar, and ordered a 7-Up and a bag of potato chips. He had been in once before, just briefly, a few days earlier, so he knew the layout of the tavern. A few minutes later, another black youth walked in.

"Hey, man, what's up. You still standing around here?" he asked Johnny. They pretended they hadn't seen each other in a while. Johnny "lent" him some quarters to play the video game. Two more friends entered the bar and joined him.

Ann Mitchell knew what they were planning. She had seen them nervously walk by the tavern just a few minutes earlier. They had been whispering to each other, most likely detailing how they would pull off the heist. As Johnny's friends started playing the poker game, Ann told him she had called the police. He ran to his friends, who had already cut open the padlock with bolt cutters and taken $200 from the machine. (Ann, like some of the other bar owners, had padlocked the machines to make them more difficult to pry open.) They emptied the change into their pockets, and as they raced out the door, one of the two patrons jumped off his bar stool.

"Get your ass back!" Johnny yelled at him. Ann says Johnny brandished a knife and nearly stabbed the patron in the back. Johnny denies having a weapon. The four youths sprinted out of the tavern into a waiting car, returning to their home, Henry Horner.

Three days later, on January 31, someone knocked on LaJoe's door. "It's the police," a voice said. LaJoe let them in. "We're looking for a Bobby Anderson. He here?" one of the officers asked. Terence used an alias; Anderson was LaJoe's maiden name.

Terence sauntered out of a back room. He told LaJoe he hadn't done anything. She asked the officers not to handcuff her son in front of Lafeyette and Pharoah, but they did so anyway. When the cuffs clicked behind his back, Terence's head dropped as if it had been held up by a string. "They ain't gonna bring you back," Lafeyette muttered. Pharoah said nothing. And as Terence was led out of the building, Snuggles, then two, yelled from a second-floor window where he lived with his mother, "Chumps, let my daddy go! Let my daddy go!"

The charge was armed robbery. Ann Mitchell had identified him from the Polaroid photograph taken earlier. He was also charged with theft of a video game at another tavern, a less serious offense than the armed robbery.

Ten

WELFARE RECIPIENTS call it "the interrogation room." It is tucked away on the second floor of the local welfare office, an expansive brick building on Western Avenue, directly across the street from Henry Horner. In 1987, this Department of Public Aid office paid out $31,720,194 in benefits to 23,247 west side recipients of such grants as Aid to Families with Dependent Children, General Assistance, and Medicaid.

To reach the room, one must walk through the building's front entrance, past the security guard, and up a flight of stairs.

Then, a quick right turn places you in the waiting area. It's filled with plastic chairs—red, yellow, green, and brown—and decorated with posters on child abuse, nutrition, and teenage pregnancy. One announces the celebration of Illinois Arts Week for 1985, three years previous.

On this windy April day, when it alternately snowed and rained, the waiting area was half filled. LaJoe, dressed neatly in jeans and a blue denim coat, waited nervously. She eyed a poster in a nearby cubicle. As if to mock the poverty of the clients, it advertised a Bermuda vacation, portraying a smiling, wet couple reclining on a beach, the tide lapping at their feet.

"Jesse Thomas," a caseworker announced. No one answered. "Jessseeee Thomas." With each appeal, the caseworker drew out the name more, her voice rising with a growing impatience. "Jesssseeee Thomas?"

LaJoe began to think that if Jesse Thomas was, in fact, there, slumped in one of the plastic chairs, he would do well to keep his identity to himself. Finally, the caseworker shouted the name so loud that other caseworkers chuckled at their clearly frazzled colleague. A middle-aged, unkempt man, wearing a red wool cap, snapped up from his sleep.

"Who's that?" the startled man asked.

"Jesse Thomas?" she curtly asked.

"Yeah, that's me," Thomas sheepishly conceded.

The caseworker shot him a look of rebuke. Others giggled as a chagrined Thomas shuffled off behind the woman into the bowels of the building. Don't get the caseworkers angry, LaJoe thought. If they aren't your allies, at the very least you want to make sure you don't antagonize them.

It was clear that no one wanted to be here. Of the dozen or so people waiting, none looked up from their laps—except to catch a glimpse of Thomas. They all kept on their heavy coats, as if they were on their way out rather on their way in. LaJoe kept her denim jacket on, even during the hearing.

"LaJoe Rivers," a caseworker finally called. LaJoe, clearly thinking of Jesse Thomas, punched her hand into the air, and then got up to follow the caseworker through a tangled maze of desks and dividers to the interrogation room. It was not one office but rather a bank of windowless rooms that lined the far wall. It was where recipients were questioned about their eligibility.

A few months earlier, LaJoe had received notice from the Department of Public Aid that it had launched an investigation into her eligibility. She knew nothing more than that. The $931 she received each month, a combination of both welfare and food stamps, was her only income. She spent most of the money within three days of receiving it: nearly $400 for groceries, which she bought in one shopping trip; $80 for burial insurance; $122 for rent, and $8.00 to cash the check at the currency exchange. She used the remaining $300 or so to purchase clothes for the children, most of which had been placed on layaway. She planned it so that she finished the payments on the clothes three times a year: Easter, the beginning of school in September, and Christmas. She also used the remaining cash to buy small items that she couldn't purchase with her food stamps, such as school supplies for the children, laundry detergent, hair grease, soap, and other cosmetics. The money also went to buy food as needed during the month. What remained had to last the family until the next check, four weeks later.

A handwritten sign adorned the door where LaJoe was led:

HEARING ROOM ONLY
OTHERS KEEP OUT

The room itself was small, perhaps eight feet by eight feet. The combination of its fluorescent lights, four strategically placed metal chairs—one facing the other three—and a large metal desk, devoid of papers, pencils, or books, gave the room the appearance of a place meant for interrogation. There was nothing to distract the inquisitor or accused, no windows or clocks to give any sense of location or time, no pictures or posters to give the room any personality.

LaJoe sat in the chair clearly meant for her, the one standing apart from the others. She folded her hands and waited: Someone brought in one more chair and lined it up with the other three. "All of them on one little old me?" she whispered to herself. Ten minutes later, three women and a man filed in. They did not introduce themselves.

The oldest of the three women, Edith Rogers, whose job it was to investigate welfare fraud, explained to LaJoe that she was here for a "pre-appeal hearing" in which she would get a chance to hear the charges being brought against her and, if she desired, to respond to them. Another of the women then took over.

"We're doing everything by policy," she explained, citing Chapter 320 of the Public Aid statutes, which outlines how the department may verify proof of residence. "We have found a substantial amount of information that your husband has claimed your residence as his home. Do you have anything to dispute that?"

LaJoe nervously fingered her gold-colored loop earrings. She spoke for the first time since she had been led into the room. "He's at his mother's and sister's. Here, there." She spoke so softly that the four inquisitors had to lean forward to hear her. LaJoe went on to explain that she gave Paul his mail when he came around.

"Was there a place you could always find him?" the woman asked.

"He was always on the corner of Lake and Woods," said LaJoe, referring to a local liquor store where men of Paul's age hung out.

The woman continued to rattle off the proof that the department had compiled, placing Paul at LaJoe's. It was damning. She cited joint income tax returns for the years 1982, 1983, 1984, and 1985.

"Did you report those to the agency?"

LaJoe shook her head. "No."

The woman noted that Paul had received unemployment benefits for thirty-eight weeks between July 1984 and March 1985 at LaJoe's apartment; that Paul's driver's license, issued in July 1986, indicated his address as 1920 West Washington; and that Paul had been personally served with a court summons at that address on October 25, 1981. A four-page, single-spaced summary of the investigation outlined the charges. A fifth page listed the benefits LaJoe had received since 1974; they totaled $109,373 in financial assistance and food stamps, the bulk of it after 1980. There was also $97,903 in medical benefits, most of which had gone to care for the triplets, who were born prematurely and had had to spend much of their first year in the hospital.

The woman concluded the fifteen-minute hearing by explaining to LaJoe that "you have to prove to us that our findings are false. We have a substantial amount of evidence placing him in your home."

"Is that it?" LaJoe asked, referring not to the evidence but to the meeting itself.

"Yes," the woman replied.

Confused and upset, LaJoe walked silently out of the room, slamming the door behind her. She would later apologize to her inquisitors for her impoliteness, but she wouldn't offer much defense against the department's charges. She didn't deny that Paul occasionally stayed over. She didn't ask whether she was entitled to legal counsel. She didn't ask where she would get money to feed her children. She didn't ask for a caseworker to come out and look at her home. Now, as she made her way through the labyrinth of desks, she wondered how to break the news to the kids.

Lafeyette knew his mother had gone for a hearing and that the department was considering cutting her benefits, so when she came home that afternoon he was by the door to greet her. As she walked into the apartment, his eyes locked with hers. His long fingers cupped her face.

"What'd they say?" he asked.

"Off," LaJoe replied in a voice that barely approached a whisper. Lafeyette's shoulders sank. LaJoe hugged him.

She chose not to tell Pharoah, at least not yet; she was protective of him. Because he had lately responded to nearly every instance of violence and family trouble with the same refrain— "I'm too little to understand"—she feared that the problems, when he was at last ready to confront them, would be too deeply buried for him to resolve. Now, though, she was convinced that Pharoah's attitude gave him some peace of mind and the strength to push on, so she avoided burdening him with stories of hardship.

"The reason I don't go to Pharoah is because I like Pharoah just being a kid," she explained. "I better enjoy it now, because I don't know how long it's going to last."

She wished, in fact, that she hadn't told Lafeyette, but he was the only person she felt she could talk to about it. It was as if he were as much a husband as he was a son. He was her confidant.

Lafeyette believed that the only person he could depend on was his mother, and he would do anything to protect her. A year ago, when two teenagers robbed her and Rochelle, one of the assailants severed the nerves in the middle and ring fingers of LaJoe's right hand with a butcher knife. The fingers now often swelled and were painful. The assailants stabbed Rochelle seven times. Lafeyette told his mother, "If I was around and I had a gun or something, I'd of shot him in the head or the chest or something. I don't play that about my mother."

Later, he said, "Sometimes I be in my bed crying so God can hear me so my mama's fingers get well. She can't hardly do nothing with them. If she has to open up a can I'll help her open it." He would also help scrub the family's dirty clothes because he knew the work hurt his mother's hand.

The night of the hearing, after the other children had gone to sleep, Lafeyette got out of bed and joined his mother on the living room couch. Shirtless—he wore only his dark blue jogging pants—he propped his bare feet on the scratched and sticky coffee table. A late night movie on the television went unwatched. The steadily running bathtub water could be heard even through the closed bathroom door.

"What you worrying about?" Lafeyette asked.

"I ain't worried," LaJoe lied.

"Yes, you is. Don't worry 'bout nothing. I be worrying for you. I'm gonna help you." Lafeyette drew closer to his mother, placing his arm awkwardly around her shoulders.

"Lafie, I'm not worried about nothing. We're gonna be all right." LaJoe then explained to Lafeyette that the reason she had gotten into trouble with the Public Aid Department was that she had let Paul use their address.

"Why don't you just say that he didn't?" Lafeyette demanded.

"If I told them that I didn't know he was using the address, it would be a lie in my face. I knew he was using the address."

"You ought to put them out, all of them," Lafeyette said of his father and his older sister.

"If I put them in the street—they live their lives in the street —they'll look like the street. I can't put them out."

"If they ain't helping me the way you helped us, I wouldn't help them. I wouldn't care 'bout them."

"It ain't them. They not even theyself," she said referring to their drug problems.

"You should stop being so weak-hearted." Lafeyette could see his mother's pained expression. That remark hurt LaJoe because she knew there to be some truth in it. She *was* "weak-hearted." She *didn't* have the resolve to kick her older children out of the apartment or, for that matter, to put her foot down and not allow Paul to stay over on occasion. She sometimes seemed passive, unable to act on what she knew was right. But her strength was also her weakness. She gave and gave and gave —and then didn't get it back. The problem was that she didn't know when to stop giving.

"No, I don't mean weak-hearted," Lafeyette corrected himself. "You strong-hearted too, but you should stop being weak-hearted too. You don't like it here. You don't like nothing that be going on at this time. I would leave. If we weren't here, Terence wouldn't of gone to jail. They wouldn't of handcuffed him, took him out like a dog. One day I might just walk up and find a whole bag of money and bring it home, Mama, and then we can move out of the projects. When I grow up, I don't know where I be headed, but I'm gonna have a white house. It'd be made of wood, and Pharoah and all them, they're gonna be my kids. I won't need to have kids."

Lafeyette talked frequently of getting out of Horner, and sometimes would feel such urgency about it that he would get angry at his mother for not trying harder. He once demanded that she wait on line to apply for one of 285 rehabilitated apartments that were federally subsidized. She did, but there were over a thousand people on line ahead of her, some of whom had been camped out since the previous morning. Another time, Lafeyette insisted that she inquire about some new rental units in one of the few restored brownstones in the neighborhood. She did that too, but they cost far too much. It turned out later that they were owned by a couple who were allegedly among the west side's biggest drug suppliers, so the property was confiscated by the federal government.

Lafeyette suggested that he quit school and find work to help feed and clothe the family. LaJoe told him that was nonsense; they would manage, and he should stay in school. The two talked until about two in the morning. Now and then they fell silent, and Lafeyette rested his head on his mother's shoulder. During their talk, he confessed, "Mama, one time I had said to myself I wasn't gonna talk no more. I got tired of peoples talking to me and I wasn't answering them. What I try to say ain't worth saying to nobody anyways. Nothing happens."

Lafeyette had become more and more reticent, keeping to himself. He relied on as few people as possible: his mother, maybe his brother Pharoah, and himself. These were the only ones he knew for certain wouldn't cross him, who wouldn't desert him.

James Howard, one of Lafeyette's closest "associates," had moved out of Horner in April. For ten years, his mother had been on a waiting list for Section 8 Housing, a program in which the government subsidizes rents in private housing. Their name had finally reached the top of the list and they found a two-bedroom apartment about a mile south of Horner. Their apartment complex had a twenty-four-hour-a-day security guard, a swimming pool, and a basketball court. At first, James visited Horner on weekends, but then he spent more of his time with his new friends at the apartment complex. In those first few months, he knelt at his bedside before he went to sleep and prayed that God would not make him move back to Horner.

So many friends and acquaintances passed through Lafeyette's life that he didn't seem to give James's absence much thought. He would occasionally spend a night over at the Howards', but as the months passed the two boys were together less and less.

Lafeyette was used to being disappointed. No one else, it seemed, ever held up his end of a bargain. Lafeyette was certain that a neighbor or friend had called the Public Aid Department and told of Paul's occasional presence in the apartment.*

"The things I should of been talking to Paul about I was talking to Lafie," LaJoe said. "I put him in a bad place. But I

---

* A spokesman for the Illinois Department of Public Aid later conceded that it had launched the investigation as a result of an article I had written for *The Wall Street Journal.* The story chronicled a summer in Lafeyette's life, detailing the almost daily violence he had to contend with. One line in particular caught the attention of the department. It read, "Lafeyette's father, a bus driver for the city, stays with the family sporadically." According to the spokesman, the department regularly combs newspapers for possible hints of welfare recipients who may be ineligible for benefits.

didn't have anyone to talk to. Lafie," she said, regretfully, "became a twelve-year-old man that day."

LaJoe had to figure out what to do, how to put food on the table and pay the rent. She had five children to worry about. Terence was now in jail, and Weasel had moved in with friends for a few months.

The next day after school, Lafeyette brought home seven loaves of bread he received as giveaways at a local church. LaJoe thanked him, though she had to throw them out because all seven were moldy. Pharoah didn't find out about Public Aid's decision until a couple of weeks later, when LaJoe didn't go to do her usual monthly shopping. Pharoah loved to help his mother carry in the groceries and then organize them in the cabinets and refrigerator, but when it became apparent that his mother wouldn't be shopping on the usual day of the month, Pharoah asked what had happened. His mother explained their situation.

"Old girl, we're really poor now," Pharoah said.

LaJoe laughed and thought to herself, As if we weren't poor already.

Pharoah surprised her. He seemed to take it all in stride. One afternoon, he asked her for a quarter but, before she could refuse him, covered his mouth in embarrassment. "Oops, I forgot," he apologized, and went on about his business. Timothy, one of the triplets, had watched Lafeyette comfort LaJoe. He told his mother, "Your head be hurting all the time. Lemme worry for you."

LaJoe leaned on friends and family. One of her sisters gave her $65 worth of food stamps. Rochelle supplied her with some food. But her family and neighbors, who for the most part were not much better off than she, were limited in what they could give her. So LaJoe played cards for money.

Both of LaJoe's parents had loved to gamble. Her father played poker and blackjack and occasionally shot dice. Her mother would drink Pepsi and take aspirins to stay up all night, playing cards with lady friends. LaJoe, in fact, was named after an uncle who was a riverboat gambler. It seemed to be in the family's blood.

Like housecleaning, it got her mind off her problems. A

friend's mother ran an all-night card game for women, and LaJoe had occasionally joined in. The game was pitty-pat; players won by accumulating pairs. Now, she played almost nightly, winning $35 one night, $20 another. She rarely played in the same game as Rochelle; the two didn't want to win money from each other. Many weekends and some weekdays, LaJoe spent her nights away from home playing cards. She'd leave after putting the children to sleep and not come home until morning, usually early enough to help prepare the kids for school. On occasion, though, the children had to ready themselves. Lafeyette would take charge. If Timothy needed a new hole to tighten his belt, he'd punch it through with a nail. If Tiffany or Tammie needed a blouse pressed, he'd iron it. Though there was always an adult in the house with the children, either Paul or Weasel or, in later months, Weasel's girlfriend, who was in her late twenties and seemed wise beyond her years, the children worried about their mother. It was while she'd been away one night that she'd been mugged and her fingers sliced.

In addition to relying on the generosity of friends and her luck at pitty-pat, LaJoe looked for work. She applied for jobs at three local hospitals but couldn't get interviewed at any of them. They had no openings for someone with her limited clerking experience. She spent a day in the Loop, checking with stores for a job as a clerk, but could find nothing. Part of LaJoe's difficulty in finding a job was her timidity. It sometimes made her seem unusually tense or, worse yet, aloof. Also, she had not held a job in seven years, and even then it had been at only one place, the Miles Square Health Center. She lacked the ability to combine her self-assuredness and humility—two powerful traits that alternately dominated her personality—in her job interviews. After staying home with her children for the past seven years, she was unprepared to re-enter the job market. She had no skills to offer. And there were few jobs to be had.

Frustrated and bitter, and worried about each coming day, LaJoe slept little except for occasional catnaps in the afternoons while the children were still at school. She drank tea and Pepsi to keep going, but the chronic fatigue worked on her. She unleashed her temper on her children, shouting at them to sweep the floor or take out the garbage. But usually, after one of these outbursts, LaJoe sought out Lafeyette or Pharoah or one of the triplets to hug and make up to. In apology, she braided Tammie's and Tiffany's hair or, if she had the money, gave Pharoah a couple of quarters to play the video games at the corner store. During this period, LaJoe found solace in the realization that there were those yet worse off. On a frigid spring night, two homeless people, an unshaven man in an oversize trench coat and a young woman dressed in a white T-shirt and ragged denim jacket, wandered into her building. They were hoping to find a vacant apartment. Instead, LaJoe insisted they use her couch; fully clothed, the man and woman stretched out feet to feet like bookends. LaJoe couldn't sleep anyway. "I'm just tired from worrying; you're just tired from being out," she told the woman.

LaJoe still had an appeal hearing in which an administrative law judge would hear first Public Aid's case against LaJoe and then her response. It didn't go well.

LaJoe had become resigned to losing her benefits. She knew that technically, on paper, Public Aid had a strong argument. Yes, Paul used her address. Yes, she conceded later, they had filed joint income tax returns—though she never saw any of the money. And, yes, Paul lived at her home off and on, depending on whether he could find shelter with other friends or family. But despite all that, Paul spent much of his paycheck for drugs. He felt guilty and responsible for the family's predicament, so he visited a caseworker before the appeal to tell of his history with drugs and his separation from his wife. He asked that the conversation be kept confidential from his employer. The caseworker, Ms. Rogers, understood that to mean confidential from everyone. She didn't mention his visit at the appeal hearing.

But what upset LaJoe was knowing that any caseworker who visited her apartment would have realized that she could not be double-dipping. Lafeyette and Pharoah slept on lumpy and torn mattresses older than either of the two boys. The triplets and LaShawn's daughter Tyisha were so crowded in their one bed that they often woke up tangled with one another, their arms and legs aching from a night fighting for a comfortable position. Many of the children's clothes were secondhand. The parishes from suburban churches donated used clothing, so the area's children wore T-shirts promoting suburban sports teams from such foreign places as Berwyn and Oak Park. Also, LaJoe and other residents relied on two volunteers from a northern suburb, a housewife and an airline pilot, who drove a van through Horner twice a week, distributing free clothing and food. One company had donated five thousand pounds of meat, another contributed two hundred pairs of gloves, all to be distributed in the Horner neighborhood.

LaJoe's living room couch had cost $45 at the local Goodwill; the matching black-cushioned chairs, $20. The olive-green curtains still showed the two bullet holes from the gang battle outside the apartment. The family had no kitchen table; the children ate their meals seated in the living room. Besides, LaJoe thought, if she had had the benefit of Paul's full income, they would have long ago moved from Henry Horner.

Also, and this LaJoe failed to make clear to Public Aid, Paul had been suspended from his job in January, four months earlier, for drinking. The transit authority sent him to a rehabilitation center, but Paul had started drinking and taking drugs again. In effect, he had been permanently suspended. He now had no income.

LaJoe felt so defeated that she barely put up a fight with Public Aid. At the appeal hearing, she mentioned only in passing that Paul had been suspended from his job. She didn't refer to his drug problem, perhaps to protect him. And she hadn't known he'd been interviewed by the caseworker. Not surprisingly, the administrative law judge, Edward A. Disch, who LaJoe felt had been courteous and understanding, nonetheless ruled against her. Public Aid would strip her and the children of their benefits. If she wanted, however, she could reapply.

Little else changed. As the summer of 1988 approached, the shooting picked up. Twice in May, LaJoe herded the children into the hallway, where they crouched against the walls to avoid stray bullets. Pharoah's stutter worsened, so that he barely talked and stayed mostly by himself. He continued to shake whenever he heard a loud noise. Lafeyette told his mother, "Mama, if we don't get away someone's gonna end up dead. I feel it."

On Sunday, May 22, a nine-year-old friend of the boys was shot in the back of the head. Alonzo Campbell had been walking into his building, just across the street, when he was hit by a bullet meant for someone else. The shooting might have gone unnoticed outside Horner had it not offered such a stark contrast to what had taken place two days earlier in Winnetka, an affluent northern suburb.

Laurie Dann, a thirty-year-old emotionally disturbed woman, had walked into the washroom of Winnetka's Hubbard Woods Elementary School and shot a six-year-old boy. She then entered a second-grade classroom and shot six children, killing eight-year-old Nicholas Corwin and wounding the others. Later that same day, Dann killed herself.

The murder-suicide made national news. The local papers ran banner headlines. In Winnetka, the citizens mobilized to deal with the tragedy. They brought in a crisis team of psychologists and social workers to help them and their children deal with the trauma. Teachers received instructions on how to comfort the kids. Governor Jim Thompson called for increased school security. Others demanded tighter gun control laws and a tougher examination for mental illness.

To many at Horner, the two shootings served to highlight everything they didn't have. Alonzo's shooting received extensive coverage in one of the local newspapers, but only because its aftermath so sharply contrasted with the response to the Winnetka shooting. No one counseled Alonzo, who survived, or his friends. Lafeyette and Pharoah talked to no one about the incident, though they prayed for their schoolmate. One neighborhood, rich in community and professional talent, mobilized to comfort its wounded; another neighborhood, poor in spirit and resources, did nothing. In Winnetka, the shooting was an aberration; in Horner, it was part of normal life.

"I've got to keep smiling to keep from crying," LaJoe counseled herself. "If I ever slow down, I'll lose it."

Eleven

LAJOE, LAFEYETTE, PHAROAH, and the
triplets walked through the guarded fence, past
the man-made pond, through the revolving
doors, and into the visitors' waiting room of Division Four of
the Cook County Jail. The fifty-four-acre complex sits on the
city's south side, conveniently set behind the Criminal Courts
building. Built in 1929 to house twelve hundred prisoners, it
now holds seven thousand, a thousand of whom sleep on mattresses on the floor. Nearly all the people here are awaiting
trial. They stay an average of 138 days, though the jail authori-

ties, to relieve the overcrowding, under a controversial program first introduced in 1982 may release any inmate who has committed a crime against property. In 1988 alone, the jail set free twenty-five thousand accused criminals because it didn't have room for them.

The jail has eight divisions. The oldest building, which is fortified with two-foot-thick concrete walls, houses those accused of such violent acts as murder and rape. Most inmates there have bonds of over $500,000. Division Four, where Terence now resided, houses those who have been assigned low- to medium-priced bonds, usually not more than $40,000. Terence's bond was set at $20,000, which meant that to be released he'd have to post 10 percent of that, or $2000.

Built in 1975, the Division Four unit is, like Henry Horner, made of cinder block, which jail authorities quickly learned did not provide the best of security. Because prisoners scraped through the mortar with metal spoons, the jail switched to plastic utensils in 1979. And after several inmates used the top of their dressers to beat through the walls, some in as little time as a minute and a half, the dressers were finally removed in 1981. To outsiders, though, the place looked impenetrable.

After a twenty-minute wait, a guard pointed LaJoe and the children to a room on the right. They could meet Terence there, he told them. The children eagerly followed LaJoe. They hadn't seen their brother since he'd been arrested two months earlier.

"Where's my Terence? Where's my Terence?" Tammie asked her mother in hushed tones.

"In there," replied LaJoe.

The rectangular visiting room has a countertop running its full length. It could pass for a small diner, if it weren't for the pane of inch-thick, bulletproof glass, which extends up to the ceiling, cutting the room in two. Six stools face each side of the glass.

Set into the glass is a circular metal grate about ten inches in diameter through which the inmates and the visitors communicate. To hear a person on the other side, you must place your ear flat against the cold metal while the other talks in a loud voice to compete with the other visitors and inmates in the room. There used to be telephones, but they were removed after many were ripped out by temperamental inmates. There was also a handwritten sign that read BEWARE OF PICKPOCKETS AND THIEVES.

As LaJoe and the children crowded around the one free stool, Terence walked into the room on his side of the glass. He spotted his family, and broke into a huge grin. So did Lafeyette, Pharoah, and the triplets. Terence, who wore his long hair plaited tightly against his skull, stood still for a moment, reared his head back, and then pointed at each of his brothers and sisters as if to acknowledge their presence. They all pointed back. Then Terence sat down. Beaming.

Tiffany pulled herself onto the countertop and pressed her lips against the metal grate. "I love you," she told her brother. "I love you, too," he replied. Then they all, in turn, told Terence they loved him. Lafeyette shared the stool with LaJoe, trying to catch Terence's every word. He was nursing a mild case of flu, so he sat quietly and uncomfortably through much of the visit. Pharoah stood on the other side of his mother. He fought to restrain Timothy, Tammie, and Tiffany, who, in their excitement, clamored for space on the countertop. Once Pharoah calmed them down, though, he found himself distracted by all the commotion in the room. He heard little of what Terence had to tell him and his siblings that morning.

Most distracting to Pharoah was a young girl, perhaps seventeen, who sat perched on the stool next to theirs. She was dressed in a denim miniskirt, which exposed a pair of shapely legs and which, one suspects, had the intended effect of teasing her incarcerated boyfriend, with whom she obviously was not at all pleased. She held a letter up to the glass. "This is bullshit," she said, loud enough so that Pharoah turned his head to see what was going on. "I ain't taking this crap no more." She went on to dispute the missive, which apparently her lover had sent her from prison, calling her a "no good bitch" and other assorted names for not having visited him. "I got a job and more important things to do," she lectured him. "I'm gonna get the last laugh." Pharoah covered his mouth, embarrassed by the fighting and foul language. This lovers' quarrel continued throughout the visit and made it necessary for LaJoe and the others to press their ears even closer to the metal grate to hear Terence.

As the joy of seeing his family wore off, Terence grew tense.

His smile disappeared. "I'm hurting," he told LaJoe, his clenched left fist slowly and rhythmically drumming the countertop. LaJoe worried that Terence, whose pounding became harder and harder, was going to explode. "I wanna be outta here. I wanna be outta here," he said, his pleading sometimes lost in the din. He rocked back and forth on his stool in rhythm with his drumming fist. "It's bogus," he asserted. He insisted repeatedly that he hadn't robbed the Longhorn Saloon. LaJoe, who had seen Terence arrested many times before, believed him. So did Terence's public defender, whom LaJoe would meet in coming weeks. Only once before, in his over three dozen arrests, had Terence professed his innocence. And that one time he had, indeed, been wrongly accused. "Don't give up hope. Be a man," LaJoe told him. She repeated it. She couldn't think of anything else encouraging to say.

Lafeyette pushed his way through the triplets and leaned the full weight of his body on the countertop; he pressed his lips against the dirty cold metal. "Hi, Terence," he said meekly. Terence smiled, shaking his head and pointing. "Hey, homey, you look good," Terence told him as he launched into a ten-minute lecture, urging Lafeyette to stay in school and to keep to himself. Lafeyette listened raptly, his head pressed firmly against the grating, so hard that the angled metal strips left marks on his cheeks and forehead.

"Lafie, you know, don't never come to jail 'cause this ain't no place to be," Terence told his younger brother. "It's hard. You go to school. Get your education. Do what Mama tell you to do. And stay away from crooked people. If they come at you to do something with them, tell them no. That ain't the way to go. I'm telling you, Lafie, stay in school and do something positive. Get you a successful job. I don't want you to follow my footprints. The things that I did. I want you to be better. You won't be like me. You'll be better than me."

Lafeyette nodded. Terence, who seemed eager to impart these guidelines to his brother, rambled on. By the time he finished, Pharoah had taken a seat on the floor in the corner, away from the hubbub, tending a headache. Tiffany and Tammie had gone to the bathroom down the hall. And Timothy, with his thumb in his mouth, sat perched next to Lafeyette, trying to eavesdrop on the conversation between his older brothers.

"Time to go," a guard called to Terence. Nearly an hour had passed. "Keep the house clean. Do your homework. When you're through, read a book," Terence urged Lafeyette in a rush. "And watch out for Mama."

"I will," replied Lafeyette.

"Mama, come here." Terence gestured to LaJoe. He gave her lengthy instructions to say hello to his three children and their mothers.

"Man, it's good seeing you," he said, shaking his head from side to side.

"Time to go," the guard said again.

"Okay, man!" Terence yelled.

He stood up from his stool and blew kisses to Lafeyette, Pharoah, and the triplets. "Send me some pictures!" he hollered. They could understand him only by reading his lips. He turned and walked back toward the cells.

As LaJoe and the children walked out the revolving doors and across the front lawn, Tiffany tugged at her mother's coat. "Mama," she asked, "how does Terence get out from behind that glass?" Before LaJoe could think of how to answer her, Lafeyette cuffed the back of her head. "Shut up," he ordered.

A couple of weeks later, Lafeyette and Pharoah curled up on the sofa, watching Saturday morning cartoons. The beige couch collected dirt and odors quicker than any other piece of furniture in the house. The pillows were so dirty, it was hard to make out their original color. LaJoe had placed an old lavender sheet over the seat cushions in an effort to hide the smells, particularly the scent of urine. A relative of LaJoe's had passed out here from drinking and, in his drunken stupor, peed in his pants. Some of it had leaked onto the couch.

LaJoe sat on a nearby chair talking with Rochelle. "When's Terence getting out of jail?" Lafeyette interrupted his mother.

"I don't know," she replied.

"Guess," he demanded. "By the summer?" His already high-pitched pubescent voice rose even higher.

"Lafie, I don't know," she said.

"When's he coming home? Could he come home tomorrow?" he persisted.

"I don't think so, Lafie," she repeated. "I just don't know. Stop asking."

Lafeyette let out a low grunt of dissatisfaction, and went back to watching cartoons. Since Terence had been arrested, Lafeyette asked about him regularly. This conversation, in one form or another, had been repeated often. He had even been having dreams about Terence, dreams that woke him in the middle of the night, dreams he refused to share with anyone.

Pharoah, too, thought a lot about Terence. It especially upset him that he might be serving time for something he didn't do. Pharoah's sense of justice, of right and wrong, was so powerful that it sometimes took the form of righteousness. No one could get away with doing anything, including himself. This past Christmas, he had awakened early, before the other children, and stolen a look at the presents piled in the back room. Among the wrapped games and toys, he couldn't find one with his name on it. He burst into tears and ran to his mother, complaining that she had forgotten him. Of course she hadn't, LaJoe assured him. His gifts had been squirreled away in the front closet. For weeks afterward, Pharoah apologized to his mother for questioning her love for him. "It bothered my conscience," he explained.

At school, he sometimes raised his hand to tell on himself. If he'd been chattering and Ms. Barone asked who'd been talking, he'd confess quickly. LaJoe would say of Pharoah, "That's a doll. He got a heart. He couldn't do nothing and get away with it. He'll tell on himself."

Pharoah knew that Terence had once before been locked up for something he hadn't done. Two years ago, nineteen-year-old Maggie Atlas told the police that Terence had shot her in the stomach. He spent five months in the county jail awaiting trial on charges of attempted murder. In January of 1987, shortly before Terence was to go to trial, Atlas called the Public Defender's Office and said that she had lied: Terence had not shot her. A friend who was a Vice Lord had tried to kill her and then had told her to finger Terence, a rival gang member. But the friend had since been killed, so she had decided to come forward. It was a harrowing experience for the family. They knew Terence wouldn't have shot a girl. He didn't have it in him.

"What would you do if someone said you did something and

FALL 1987—SPRING 1988

you didn't do it?" Pharoah asked a friend. "What would you do if they still said you did it?" He paused. "If the judge said you did it?" He paused again. "If they didn't believe you?" The incident so unsettled Pharoah that he cried whenever he re-counted it.

Terence's arrest had shaken both boys. In a neighborhood of losses, it was yet another family member or friend gone: an aunt murdered, their brother Paul jailed, their neighbor William shot accidentally, their friend Bird Leg killed, and now Ter-ence. LaJoe tried to reassure both boys about him. Maybe, she told them, he was better off in jail. He's off the streets and can't get in more trouble, she told them. But they wanted him home.

Pharoah sent Terence a black-and-white photo of himself. He was wearing a button-down shirt, standing in front of the build-ing, smiling, his head cocked to one side like a puppy's, similar to the pose he had assumed in the Boys Club brochure. On the back, he wrote in clear, crisp block letters: "TERENCE I'M TO LIT-TLE TO UNDERSTAND WHAT IS HAPPING. BUT I WANT TO TELL YOU I MISS AND LOVE YOU. PHAROAH."

Twelve

PHAROAH would have liked Rickey to root him on at the school spelling bee, but his friend spent the period in the principal's office, where he sat out most assemblies. Ms. Barone had sent him there as a precaution, because, if he felt moved to, he could have disrupted the entire proceedings. Lafeyette couldn't make it either, since the contest was only for the middle grades.

Pharoah prepared diligently for the annual spring event, which pitted the school's top third-, fourth-, and fifth-graders against one another. A dozen students competed, two from each classroom. Ms. Barone had conducted her own class bee to choose two representatives. Pharoah was one; the other was a boy named Jimmy. Clarise, the class's star pupil, was absent the day Ms. Barone chose the contestants.

Pharoah wanted badly to do well, but he knew that to do so he'd have to control his stammer, which had worsened with his family's troubles. He wanted to succeed at everything he took on. He liked to stand out. He relished the attention. And, he figured, if he tried hard enough, everything would work out okay. (He was just as hard on others as he was on himself. A loyal Chicago Cubs fan, Pharoah would berate players if they didn't get a hit in a critical situation. "Man," he'd say, "Andre Dawson didn't try hard enough.") He felt confident that he would at least place second or third in the spelling bee.

He established a routine for himself in which he'd first sound the word out in his head, pause a moment to remind himself to take his time, and then spell it, drawing out each letter slowly and deliberately so as not to stutter. For over three weeks, he had studied fourteen mimeographed sheets of words.

On the day of the competition, Ms. Barone asked the two young contestants to come to the head of the classroom. "We wish you lots of luck," she said to the two nervous boys. "I know you can do it. I know you can win. Remember the rules. You have to say the word. Spell it. And then say it again. Good luck." Their classmates applauded and on the way to the auditorium tugged at their arms and told them to do well.

Pharoah and the other eleven contestants lined up on the small wooden stage in the school's gymnasium, which doubled as an auditorium. They faced the judges, who sat to the side, so that their right shoulders were turned to the audience. Pharoah was bright, Ms. Barone thought. He'll do okay. He looked handsome in his freshly pressed turquoise cotton shirt, buttoned at the collar. The name tag she'd printed for him stood out as she hoped it would. Made of bright yellow construction paper, it read PHAROAH RIVERS in huge block letters. It looked weighty on his tiny frame; he was considerably shorter than the other contestants.

Pharoah was much more nervous than anyone knew. He was praying that he wouldn't stutter. If he did, people would laugh and make jokes. It would be humiliating. Not in front of all these people. Please. He started wringing his hands in apprehension.

The head judge took the lecturn and explained the rules, repeating Ms. Barone's instructions. Pharoah, though fidgety, listened attentively. There was a stool for those, like Pharoah, who couldn't reach the microphone. If a word sounded unfamiliar, the students could ask to hear it used in a sentence. Few, though, ever made that request. If a student misspelled a word, a buzzer would sound and he or she had to leave the stage.

Pharoah was so focused on controlling his speech and spelling the words right that he paid little attention to the other contestants. The first few rounds were a blur. All he remembers were words like *Catholic* and *abandonment, adjust,* and *Appalachian.* He knew how to spell them all. As student after student walked off the stage in defeat, Pharoah realized he was getting closer and closer to winning. He spelled *kangaroo,* a word he knew but had never seen in print before. His classmates, who were asked to hold their applause, clapped their hands silently.

But as the contestants were whittled down to five, Pharoah's nerves began catching up with him. He could feel himself losing the self-control he'd fought so hard to retain. He had unconsciously untucked his shirt. His hands balled up beneath it, playing with the fabric. His next turn came around quickly.

"*Endurance,*" the teacher announced. "*Endurance.*"

Pharoah felt his heart pumping fast and loud. He knew how to spell the word. He knew, in fact, what it meant. He couldn't restrain his joy, and, abandoning his usual routine, he spoke in a rush, quicker than he should have. His eyes darted around excitedly.

He repeated the word. "*Endurance,*" he said, spitting out the three syllables as if they were one. He then started to spell it: "E-N-D-U . . ." He couldn't hear a thing. Nothing came out of his mouth. Nothing. He tried again. Nothing. His stutter, which had gotten worse in recent months, devoured him. The letters knotted up in his throat; the veins in his neck strained as he tried to get them out. The buzzer sounded. Pharoah's lips quivered in disappointment. He did all he could to keep from crying in front of his friends.

When he went to sit down with his class to watch the rest of the bee, Ms. Barone put her arm around him and pulled him to her. "You did a good job, Pharoah," she told him. "We're proud of you."

When Pharoah got home from school that day, he walked straight back to his room. LaJoe, who was at the sink washing dishes, knew something must be wrong; he always greeted her. She went back to see him. He was lying on his bed.

"How'd you do today, Pharoah?" she asked. He told her. LaJoe assured him there was nothing to be ashamed of. "It's going to be all right. You okay in my book." She tried to soothe him, stroking his head. "I love you. You can spell for me whenever you get ready to." He had tried his hardest.

"Pharoah is Pharoah. He's going to be something," she would tell friends. "When he was a baby, I held him up and asked him if he'd be the one. I've always wanted to see one of my kids graduate from high school. I asked him if he'd be the one to get me a diploma."

But for Pharoah that wasn't good enough. He knew how to spell better than most kids his age. He should have won, or at least placed second. He was just going to have to work harder. Pharoah promised his mother he'd do better next year. Pharoah was not one to break his word.

_____ Summer 1988 _____

Thirteen

IN HINDSIGHT, it was a summer of disappointment and, ultimately, of tragedy. At the time, though, LaJoe thought it a season of hope, an unusually calm, even radiant few months, certainly a respite from the family's recent troubles. It was a dramatic change from what she now referred to as "the war-zone summer" of last year.

On this blistering, humid May afternoon—the thermometer would top 100 degrees seven times this summer—the plaintive falsetto of pop singer Keith Sweat floated from a record player placed outside Lafeyette and Pharoah's building.

> Let me hear ya tell me you want me
> Let me hear you say you'll never leave me baby
> Until the morning light
> Just make it last forever and ever.

Please, LaJoe thought to herself, make this moment last forever. Over fifty adults and children had gathered by the front entrance of 1920 West Washington, their bodies jiggling and pulsating to Sweat's hit tune. It was an unusual sight at Henry Horner—a large crowd of people mingling and laughing together, as if they hadn't a worry in the world. Even Lafeyette, who stood to the side, his back and shoulders rattling rhythmically, smiled at the scene. His mother noted that she had never seen him so at ease.

The young man responsible for this musical gathering was Craig Davis, a good-natured eighteen-year-old who didn't even live at Horner, but at another public housing complex, the ABLA Homes. (ABLA, a mile and a half southeast of Horner, is a complex of four developments: the Jane Addams Homes, the Robert Brooks Homes, Loomis Courts, and the Abbott Homes.) Craig's girlfriend lived with her mother on the second floor of Lafeyette's building, and Craig visited her regularly after school. He spent a great deal of time in the building, and though it took a few weeks before the Vice Lords and Stones were assured that Craig didn't belong to a rival gang, he quickly won the hearts of the younger children. When he walked the distance from Horner to ABLA, he usually stopped to shoot baskets on the jungle gym with Lafeyette and others.

His ambitions in life were to be a good father—he had two daughters by another girl—and to be a disc jockey. He told Lafeyette he planned to get a job once he graduated from high school so that he could buy a house in a quiet neighborhood where he could raise his kids.

Craig was currently enrolled at Cregier High School. Though slowed down by a slight learning disability, which his school's psychological report identified as "a problem with audio-visual coordination and poor memory," Craig had managed to make it to his senior year, something three fourths of his freshman class had failed to do. He particularly impressed his teachers with his creative writing.

But Craig lived for his music. Whenever he had a spare moment, he wrote raps, which he sent to local radio stations in the hope that they would be read on the air. He shared some of them with Lafeyette and would often ask for his opinion. He had told Lafeyette he was planning to apply to a broadcasting school, where he could learn to be a radio dee-jay.

Craig was different from all the other teenage boys Lafeyette knew. Here was an older boy who not only paid attention to him, but took him seriously. What's more, Craig had thought about the future, something most young men in this neighborhood rejected—often for good reason—as a waste of time. He had the grandest of dreams: a home out in a safe and neat neighborhood and a family. He warned Lafeyette to stay away from the gangs.

"I liked how he thought," Lafeyette later said. "He used to talk about a lot of good things."

Lafeyette often admired Craig from a distance, watching him walk through the projects, headphones hugging his head, his hands knocking out a beat, his long legs striding smoothly and quickly, always as if he had a destination and purpose in mind.

On this particular afternoon, as Craig would do numerous times through the summer, he set up two turntables and a speaker in front of Lafeyette's building, on what tenants there generously referred to as "the porch." In reality, it was a slab of concrete about ten feet deep and twenty feet across that led into the building's dark breezeway. The corners where the slab met the building bore the unmistakable smell of urine; it was a nook where drunks could relieve themselves without being seen. Since an overhang covered the entrance, tenants from the upper floors couldn't watch the activities on the porch, where gang members dealt drugs. The overhang, like the porch, was made of concrete. It served as a landing place for junk thrown from the upper floors—a black vinyl car seat, a baby bottle, Coca-Cola bottles, a suitcase, shoes of various sizes—that might otherwise have struck the children below.

The overhang had the acoustical effect of directing the music outward, into the playground, so that people in the three sur-

rounding buildings could hear of Craig's arrival. Like the Pied
Piper's followers, they drifted to the front of 1920 West Washington, lured by the blasting beat of pop stars, rap groups, and soul
singers. Paul Rivers could hear the music even a block away,
where he was hanging out with friends on the street corner.

As the evening wore on and the crowd swelled, Craig per-
suaded even the shyest of friends to start dancing. "Mama,"
Pharoah yelled over the rowdy raps of the group El Jabbar,
"W-w-watch . . . w-w-watch me. It's the w-w-wop." Pharoah's
shoulders and arms began to move in military syncopation as
his legs, which he jerkily bent at the knees, propelled his upper
body up and down. Adding to the frenzy of the new dance, he
thrust his small chest forward and back, like the proudest of
peacocks. LaJoe poked Rochelle. "Will you look at the old boy,"
she said, laughing with a freedom she hadn't felt in a long
while.

Next to LaJoe and Rochelle stood Rickey, Lafeyette, and
James. James, who on occasional weekends still came back to
visit Horner with his mother, didn't like to dance with adults
around. He mischievously circled the crowd, tapping friends on
the shoulder or back. Then, before they could turn to see who
had beckoned them, he ran to another part of the crowd to
blend in among his friends. James, too, adored Craig. "Look at
how he makes all these people laugh," he said to Lafeyette.
"Man, people enjoy him."

Rickey seemed to revel in the joy and energy of the dancers.
A self-conscious child, he buried his hands deep in his pockets
and smiled nervously. "Hey, Lafie, man, look at Pharoah," he
said, pointing to the writhing youngster. Lafeyette looked and
laughed. "Man, he don't know what he doing," Lafeyette said,
launching into an exaggerated imitation of his brother's rendition of the wop.

As Rickey came to spend more time with Pharoah, Lafeyette
began to accept him. The three boys played tag or basketball,
and Lafeyette enjoyed having Rickey around. He could be generous if he had any money and would occasionally buy a hot
dog or a soda pop for Lafeyette or Pharoah. If Pharoah trusted
Rickey, Lafeyette now figured, so could he.

"C'mon out here. Let's dance," Rochelle urged Lafeyette.

"C'mon, Chicken Legs." Rochelle had nicknamed him that because he was so skinny.

Lafeyette shook his head. "Go ahead," said Rickey, who himself was not about to leave the sidelines.

"C'mon. You don't never dance," Rochelle insisted. She grabbed one of Lafeyette's hands and began to drag him into the group of dancers.

"I don't wanna. I just wanna look," he protested. But children and adults alike began a quiet chant: "Dance, Lafie, dance. Dance, Lafie, dance." He did. Reluctantly. His long arms moved tentatively and awkwardly as his upper body moved back and forth in time with the music. Rochelle edged him slower and slower into the middle of the dance floor, where, for just a moment, he let loose, his legs and torso moving with surprising grace to El Jabbar's raps.

For those few minutes, he was at peace with himself, his facial muscles relaxed into a full, unencumbered smile. His eyes focused on Craig, whom he considered a friend, not an "associate." He idolized the teenager. Craig's energy and joy had made even Lafeyette momentarily forget about his troubles.

From the porch, Craig smiled and waved at Lafeyette, which made him feel self-conscious about dancing. "That's all," he told Rochelle. She reached out to grab him, but he snaked through the crowd to watch from the sidelines with Rickey and James. The dancers continued to gyrate and whirl through the hot, humid night. LaJoe, Lafeyette, and Pharoah would remember this night and the others that Craig dee-jayed as some of the most spontaneous and spirited fun they had ever had at Horner.

When Audrey Natcone, a public defender, first met Terence she was struck by how young he seemed. A skinny, painfully shy boy among strangers, Terence, seemed much younger than eighteen, Audrey thought, not much older than her own son, who had just turned fourteen. She felt sorry for him, as she did for many of her clients. He was nervous, his right leg often bouncing nervously. He was so reserved that he never corrected her when she called him by his alias, Bobby. She discovered his real name from reading court papers. Going to prison, she thought, would quickly change this adolescent.

Audrey, thirty-six, had been a public defender for three years.

Her political roots were in the 1960s, when she had been active in the antiwar movement and had picketed in support of the United Farm Workers. She had run a crisis-intervention hotline and worked at a battered women's shelter before going to law school, where she decided to do criminal work. She was now thinking of teaching. "I don't really enjoy the combat," she said. "It's too destructive—for the client usually." She had for months been battling on behalf of another young man who was from Henry Horner and was accused of murder. She felt he was being framed.

With more cases than she could properly handle, she couldn't spend enough time on Terence's. Moreover, unlike some of her other clients, Terence rarely questioned or challenged her about his case, and he didn't have a phone, which made it impossible for her to get quick answers to questions that came up. She had to reach him through a neighbor's phone. The only time they could meet was at each court date before his case was called.

In May a friend had helped bail Terence out of jail. He spent most of the summer inside the apartment, sequestered in one of the back rooms. On occasion, though, he and a friend took the El to O'Hare Airport, where they shined shoes at a dollar a polish. On a good day, Terence earned as much as $100. Frequently, though, the airport police booted them out for not having a vendor's license.

What most impressed Audrey about Terence was his close family ties. Usually, parents and siblings didn't visit her clients or show up on court dates. With Terence, it was different. His case had been assigned to the county's criminal court branch in Skokie, a northern suburb. Because of the huge burden at the main Criminal Courts building on the city's south side—the number of cases jumped from thirteen thousand in 1982 to eighteen thousand in 1987—four judges in the suburban courts now handled Chicago cases. In order to get to the Skokie branch, Terence had to find a friend to drive him or take three trains and a bus. Each time he had a court date, LaJoe was sure to join him—and the three, Terence, LaJoe, and Audrey, could discuss the case together before or after the court session.

Because of LaJoe's unbending loyalty to her son, Audrey paid closer attention to the case. LaJoe strongly believed that Terence hadn't robbed Ann's Longhorn Saloon. And as Audrey spoke to Terence about it, she too began to believe that he may have been wrongly accused. It wasn't that Terence wasn't capable of participating in the caper at the bar. After all, he'd been arrested numerous times as a juvenile for similar crimes. It was just that the evidence didn't point unwaveringly to his presence there. Moreover, Audrey was struck by Terence's earnest and seemingly genuine assertions of his innocence.

For months, the police delayed providing photographs of the lineup from which the victim had identified Terence. Audrey had requested them so many times without success that the judge had threatened to issue a contempt order if they weren't produced. It raised the defender's suspicions that all was not right. Was there something about the lineup that would have made it particularly easy for a witness to pick out Terence? she wondered. She had already suspected that the police had shown Ann Mitchell, the owner of the saloon, snapshots of Terence before she picked him out of the lineup. If that was the case, she planned to argue that that had prejudiced Ann. Audrey would move to suppress the prosecution's main evidence.

What Audrey didn't know was that Johnny Adams, the young man who orchestrated the robbery, could have testified that Terence was not with him the night he robbed Ann's Longhorn Saloon. But Johnny didn't come forward because in doing so he would have incriminated himself; he would have had to put himself at the scene of the crime. It is the law of the streets. You watch out for yourself first, then family, and then friends. It wasn't until an interview a year later, after he'd been convicted for his part in the robbery, that Johnny Adams talked openly about the crime and said that Terence had not been with him.

Even without such testimony, though, Audrey felt confident that she could win the case.

It was a Friday afternoon in late June, and a swirl of adults and children filled LaJoe's apartment. The kitchen table, a recent hand-me-down from a friend, was loaded with platters of food; the guests could barely see the tabletop. Baked ham. Spaghetti with meat sauce. Macaroni and cheese. Collard greens. Corn bread. Sweet potato pies. "It was," LaJoe later said, "the happiest moment in my house."

There was much to celebrate.

Terence, it appeared, would beat his case. That particularly relieved Lafeyette and Pharoah, who knew, as did most of the children, that prison consumed and mangled its inhabitants quicker than the neighborhood. They were also glad to have him home, out on bond, out of the overcrowded Cook County Jail. Their family was whole again.

Also, LaJoe had reapplied for welfare, which is an option for those who feel they have unjustly been denied benefits. The caseworker had accepted her application and told her she would soon have her benefits restored. Public Aid could no longer claim that Paul supported the family. He was still out of work, and as the months passed his chances of returning seemed slimmer and slimmer. He continued to drink and take drugs, though with some moderation since his release from the rehabilitation center. Knowing she would start receiving benefits next month, LaJoe felt a huge burden lifted from her shoulders. Public Aid, however, didn't reinstate her medical benefits; she would have to use the Cook County Hospital as her family doctor. With the family's income restored, LaJoe promised her five youngest children new bunk beds. I'll get them on layaway, she assured them. You'll have them by Christmas.

And there was Craig Davis. His very presence seemed to calm Lafeyette. Lafeyette had found an older boy who could serve as his model, who articulated much that he felt. LaJoe was sure that Craig could be nothing but a good influence on her son.

But the reason for the feast had nothing to do with Terence or Public Aid's decision to restore her benefits or Craig's friendship with Lafeyette. Dawn Anderson, LaJoe's niece and Porkchop's older sister, was to graduate from the Richard T. Crane High School. She was to be only the second of Lafeyette and Pharoah's generation in the Anderson family to graduate from high school. Nine children had already dropped out.

LaJoe was very close to Dawn. The girl, whose name everyone pronounced "D'won," leaned on her aunt for advice and support. She could open up to her and know that LaJoe wouldn't reveal her troubles to her mother, LaJoe's younger sister.

Dawn was a feisty, scrappy girl, who was quite pretty. Broad-shouldered and strong, she backed down from no one—and had had her share of fights in the neighborhood. But it was that determination and fearlessness which had got her this far and, everyone hoped, would carry her even farther.

Dawn's accomplishment was made even more notable by the fact that she had, at the age of eighteen, four children, aged four, two, one, and three months. She raised the kids with the help of her boyfriend, the children's father, Demetrius Nance. Earlier this year, deciding she wanted to be on her own, she had moved out of her mother's home to a third-floor apartment in LaJoe's building. She, Demetrius, and the children lived there illegally, since the rightful tenant had moved out and had let Dawn take over the unit and pay the rent. (Such illicit arrangements are frequently made in Chicago public housing because the waiting list for units is so long. In addition, because the CHA is so strapped for funds, once an apartment becomes vacant chances are the authority won't have the money to fix it up for a new tenant. The vacancy rate at Horner alone had ballooned to 40 percent.) LaJoe helped Dawn get through her senior year by baby-sitting for the children on occasion.

Lafeyette and Pharoah revered Dawn. Lafeyette told her he would do twice as many years of college as she. "I have to do a lot of studying to bring up my grades," he said. "I wanna be like my cousin D'won." Pharoah told her he'd beat her reading scores. But however proud they were of their older cousin, both boys were emphatic about one thing: they didn't want to attend Crane.

Crane is one of the city's worst high schools. It stretches for an entire city block just a quarter of a mile south of Horner, a grim, squat stone structure with pillars marking its entrance. Since the early 1960s, when the school changed from 85 percent white to 93 percent black, it has been a troubled institution. As far back as 1965, a newspaper series on the school showed that because of de facto segregation in the school system, Crane had been forced to enroll fifteen hundred more students than its capacity. Nearly 60 percent of the freshman class never made it to their senior year. The series described the fear felt at Crane by both faculty and students. In one three-month period, six teachers had been attacked by students, and after a small riot broke out in the lunchroom, the school ordered plastic utensils in place of the metal ones.

It hadn't necessarily gotten worse at Crane, but it certainly hadn't gotten much better. Today, about half the entering freshmen never makes it through the senior year. In 1985, the seniors' reading tests were in the eighteenth percentile nationwide. One semester, the school decided to raffle off a bicycle among those who passed all their classes. That involved only 287 of its 1220 students.

Security was still a problem. In Dawn's yearbook, two full pages were devoted to photos of the school's eleven security guards, some of whom were moonlighting Chicago police officers. Students were prohibited from wearing jackets in the lunchroom because they might use them to conceal weapons. James, Lafeyette's friend, so feared going to Crane that he tried to get held back at Suder. " 'Cause I was real short and I know a lot of tall people be there so I thought they'll probably try to beat me up, take my jacket and stuff, and make me pay peon fees," he said. So, James figured, if he messed up his standardized reading test, maybe Suder wouldn't graduate him from the eighth grade. James filled in test answers randomly, and received scores that showed him over a year below grade level, despite his having a perfect attendance record. But that was hardly bad enough to keep him from graduating. Suder gave James his diploma. James, however, chose to attend Westinghouse, another local high school whose reputation was not quite as bad as Crane's. Some children went to live with relatives in other neighborhoods and even other states to avoid attending Crane and the area's other high schools.

Dawn was in a special honors program at Crane in which she took courses with other good students. They were given special attention and, as a result, were resented by some of the other students. Dawn had thought of dropping out numerous times. But LaJoe pushed her. "You can't stop, girl. You got too far," LaJoe would tell her. "Continue to go, just go. Whenever you don't want to go to school, D'won, just go 'cause it's going to pay off. You're going to live like the people on the south side, like in Beverly [a south suburb]." Dawn's persistence culminated in her graduation—and the party thrown by LaJoe.

Cousins, aunts, and friends piled into the apartment, where

they drank beer and wine coolers and filled their stomachs with LaJoe's homemade dishes. Pharoah told his mother that when he graduated he planned to rent four white horses and a carriage to take him to his prom. Even five-year-old Timothy told his mother he intended to get his diploma. Everyone seemed almost giddy at Dawn's accomplishment. Toasts were made to Dawn's future and her health.

"She got to make it," LaJoe said. "She got to. She got to get a job. If they don't see her life take her nowhere after finishing school, it will be the truth. Only thing out here left is to sell drugs. D'won got to be the one to prove it's not true."

LaJoe, who is not a very religious woman (a minister once made a sexual advance to her, which turned her away from the church), nonetheless offered a prayer: "God gave D'won a gift and she carried it on. And that gift, I hope she shares it so it'll go on within the family. Thank God for making it possible." Glasses and bottles clinked in celebration.

A month later, *The Chicago Sun-Times*, as part of a series on education, published a short article about Dawn and Demetrius under the headline HOW YOUNG PAIR BEAT ODDS IN PUBLIC HOUSING.

> She was 13. He was 16. They were at an arcade.
>
> "Can I have a quarter?" she asked him. He forked it over. Love blossomed.
>
> Now she's 18 and he's 21. Their kids are 4, 2, 1, and 3 months.
>
> They are still in love. And together, they wrote one of the rare success stories of Henry Horner Homes.
>
> Dawn Anderson, 18, mother of four, graduated from Crane Vocational High School. She is planning to start college in the fall.
>
> "Everybody says I made history. I never stopped going to school. He took care of the kids while I was at school," she said.
>
> Says the children's father, Demetrius Nance, "I've taken care of them all—from the first little girl up to her"—the baby, 3-month-old Demeca.
>
> Dawn was seven months pregnant when she graduated from eighth grade. A mother

at 14, she lived with her own mother in the
Henry Horner Homes.

Demetrius would pick up the children—
Demetra, now 4, and later sons Demetrius
Jr., 2, and Demond, 1—at Horner in the
morning and take them to his mother's
Northwest Side home to watch them while
Dawn was in school.

"I'd have one in the front of the buggy,
one in the back of the buggy, and I'd hold
one in my arms," he said. "The only thing
I'd hate was when it was cold. But it was
important. I didn't get to finish high school
like I wanted to. (He earned a GED.) I
wanted Dawn to finish."

"All I ever wanted was to get my diploma," said Dawn. "I had to prove to them
that I could do it. I am not a loser."

And now that she has her diploma, the
two are looking at new horizons. Besides
college plans, they are thinking about join-
ing the Army. They are looking for jobs.
And they are eager to leave public housing
far behind.

"I've been around this all my life. It's time
to get out," Dawn said.

"I hate this, I hate the hell out of this. I'll
come home from the park with the kids and
see this and I get so angry. I want better for
them, for us."

How has this young pair survived so far?

"We've struggled. We've had good times
and bad times," Dawn said. "I take half and
he takes half. We never let anyone break that
bond between us. I respect and trust him.
He respects and trusts me. That was all we
needed. We've always communicated. We've
always been understanding."

The wedding is set for Oct. 15.

An accompanying photograph showed the happy couple
walking their children in Horner's playground. Dawn was
wearing a pantsuit; Demetrius a tank top and jeans. The photograph, were it not adjacent to the story, might be mistaken for
that of a suburban family out for a morning stroll. One line in
the story stood out: "And together, they wrote one of the rare
success stories of Henry Horner Homes." Lafeyette and
Pharoah each held on to a Xeroxed copy of the article and
showed it off to friends.

Fourteen

THE 1988 INVENTORY for the Cook County
Criminal Courts included 14 perjuries; 103 briber-
ies, 23 impersonations of physicians, judges, and
government officials; 260 indictments for official misconduct; 20
charges of obstruction of justice; 3647 aggravated and heinous
batteries; 8 charged with possession of explosive devices; 993
caught with burglary tools; 162 home repair frauds; 380 home
invasions; 1312 charges of unlawful restraint; 830 kidnapings; 84
jail escapes; 8419 rapes; 1584 armed robberies; 1351 accused of unlawful use of a weapon; 10 police officers disarmed; 73 gambling

charges; 5 food stamp frauds; 3101 thefts; 232 attempted burglaries; 6160 burglaries; 81 charged with intimidation; 1 unlawful discharge of hazardous waste; 1219 bail bond violations; 867 forgeries; 388 arsons; 156 charged with deceptive practice; 429 retail thefts; 2568 auto thefts; 2569 incidents of armed violence; 104 reckless homicides; 3 solicitations for murder; 953 attempted murders; 1905 murders; 6 charges of endangering the life of a child; 4 child abandonments; 36 charges of cruelty to children; 1 reckless homicide of an unborn baby; 2 involuntary manslaughters of unborn children; 7 intentional homicides of unborn children; 53 child abductions; 7 solicitations of juveniles; 1 juvenile pimping charge; 174 child pornography charges; 27 charged with taking indecent liberties with children; 14 incest charges; 10,518 drug charges—24,390 cases and 56,204 charges heard by thirty-two judges.

Of those, two held special significance for the residents of Henry Horner. One case had to do with an eight-year-old girl, Urica Winder; the other, Jimmie Lee. Both cases involved drugs, and both cases, unlike most incidents at Horner, made the newspapers. And yet, despite the publicity, the people of Horner refused to talk about them.

Eight-year-old Urica Winder leaned over the witness stand, her braided head poking above the top. The jurors and others in the packed courtroom, which included reporters, Urica's family, and lawyers intrigued by the case, could just make out her face, which, given the gravity of the event, seemed unusually calm. The prosecutor had rehearsed the testimony with the girl many times, so she was perhaps the only one in the courtroom who didn't show much emotion.

"Did you notice anything unusual about Lawrence Jackson, the man you have identified here in court today?" Paula Daleo, the prosecutor asked her.

"Yes," replied Urica confidently.

"What was that?"

"He had a knife in his hand."

"And can you show the ladies and gentlemen of the jury how big that knife was?"

Urica held her hands about a foot apart.

"And who was Lawrence Jackson facing at that time?"

"Shirley."

"What did you see Lawrence Jackson do?"

"Stab her in the heart."

"And what did— Did Shirley say anything to Lawrence before that?"

"Yes."

"What did Shirley say?"

"I love you."

"And did Lawrence Jackson reply to that?"

"Yes."

"What was— What did he say?"

"I don't love you."

"And then what did he do?"

"Stabbed her in the heart."

"Did you see what happened to Shirley after she got stabbed in the heart?"

"Yes."

"What happened?"

"She started sliding down the wall . . ."

Urica also testified that she had watched Lawrence Jackson and his partner, Bobbie Driskel, kill her mother, her mother's boyfriend, and her four-year-old sister. Shirley had been a friend of the family's. The quadruple murder happened on September 24, 1986, in a second-floor apartment across the street from the Riverses'.

At one point in the trial, the prosecution asked Urica to show her scars to the jurors. She unself-consciously opened her black-and-white dress with ruffles, uncovering an ugly wound that ran from just below her left armpit to her navel. She had been stabbed forty-eight times and left for dead. Two things saved her. So much blood had collected in her body cavity that it virtually stopped the bleeding from her punctured aorta and heart. Also, from the time of the murders, around midnight, until the next morning, when she was discovered, she remained amazingly calm. A cousin found her the next morning, still conscious.

The prosecutor, Daleo, asked Urica about Bobbie Driskel. She had already established that he, like Jackson, had a knife in his hand.

"What did he do?"

"Stabbed me."

"Where did he stab you, Urica?"

"In my stomach."

"Do you know how many times?"

"No."

"Did he have anything else in his hands?"

"Yes."

"What?"

"A pen."

"And what did he do with that pen?"

"Digged my guts out."

Urica's grandmother left the courtroom, shaken. A juror wept. A newspaper reporter turned to a colleague and whispered incredulously, "Did she really say that?"

It took the jury one hour to find Jackson guilty on four counts of murder; he was sentenced to death. In a second trial, Driskel was sentenced to life in prison. Urica had been the only witness to the crimes. Were it not for her testimony, the police might never have found the killers. The prosecution argued that Jackson and Driskel, looking for money to buy cocaine, robbed the family of a television set and a videocassette recorder. They pawned the two items for $120. Driskel was a cousin of Urica's mother's boyfriend.

Mothers at Horner called Urica "the miracle child." Not only had she survived the attack, but she had had the courage to testify, something many people at Horner wouldn't or couldn't do.

Many children had seen the bodies carried out of the building. Lafeyette and Pharoah heard the tale at school and later learned the details on the evening news. LaJoe told them to put it out of their minds. She couldn't tell them it wouldn't happen again. It could. Besides, she warned them, what happened that night was between family. They shouldn't talk about it. The wrong person might overhear. Other mothers did the same.

After the trial, there was no community celebration. People just whispered among themselves about an eight-year-old girl having such strength, perhaps more than they might have under similar circumstances. And they marveled at—and were at the same time saddened by—Urica's continuing to live at Horner with her grandmother, just two floors above the apartment where the attack occurred. The family had been offered a new apartment house in Cabrini-Green, but they turned it down. At least at Horner, they knew people.

Even in victory, the silence was deafening.

A few weeks earlier, in a courtroom two floors above where Urica's testimony was heard, Jimmie Lee stood and faced Judge Robert Boharic. To the judge's left hung a hand-drawn smiley face.

Unlike the attendance at Urica's case, only a few spectators sat in the hard-back wooden seats. Sophisticated gang leaders like Lee knew better than to have their members attend trials; the judge might take it as an attempt to intimidate the court. Lee looked impassive, as he had throughout the two-day trial. Nothing seemed to unsettle him. Boharic, a former prosecutor who was known for his toughness as a judge, had decided early on, when he learned that Lee was a known gang leader, that if he found him guilty he would give him a long sentence. He would set an example with Lee.

Lee, Lee's wife Geraldean, and another woman, Donna Scoyners, had been charged with possession of sixty-nine grams of heroin. It had an estimated street value of $7500, not an unusually large amount, but enough to incur up to a thirty-year sentence under Illinois law. Lee had also been charged with unlawfully possessing an automatic weapon.

The police officers in the city's gang crimes unit are some of the most streetwise and savviest among the city's cops. Their job is to keep track and detail the workings of the city's street gangs. On the west side, Michael Cronin, a seventeen-year police veteran who had lost his left foot in Vietnam, was one of the best. He followed the Vice Lords. He probably knew the organization as well as its members, if not better. He knew, in great detail, of Lee's operations—and he knew Lee. But even Cronin hadn't been able to catch him with any weapons or drugs. Lee never carried a gun or, for that matter, drugs. He always had intermediaries do the dirty work.

Lee so frustrated the police that Charlie Toussas, the plainclothes cop who had stopped Lee from retaliating after Bird Leg's death, reached a kind of agreement with Lee's gang after one of his squad car's windows had been busted while parked in front of a Vice Lords' building. He told Lee's second-in-command that if it happened again, he would sit in the building's breezeway through his entire shift and disrupt the drug trafficking. From then on, whenever Toussas parked his car on Wolcott, the gang had two or three young Vice Lords watch the sedan. Toussas liked to say that he could leave his wallet on the car seat with the doors unlocked and it would be there when he returned.

Cronin and others in the gang crimes unit were somewhat constrained. Because of the police department's own internal workings, the gang crimes cops couldn't launch extensive narcotics investigations, even though selling drugs was the major activity of the gangs. Such efforts were reserved for the department's narcotics unit. But Cronin had obtained a warrant to search Lee's apartment on the tip that he kept an automatic weapon there.

On November 1, 1986, Cronin and five other officers raided Lee's second-floor west side apartment. After forcing open the door with a sledgehammer, they found Lee standing in the hallway, shirtless and barefoot. Cronin discovered more than he had bargained for. On the bedroom and kitchen floors and in the toilet were hundreds of packets of heroin plus various items of drug-packaging equipment, including two triple-beam scales, blenders, strainers, two beepers, two walkie-talkies, and three Daisy sealers. From an open window, Cronin spotted at the bottom of the air shaft a nine-millimeter assault rifle with a banana clip. It held twenty-eight live rounds.

Cronin also found Lee's clothes in a closet, which would help prove in court that this was, indeed, his residence. In one suit pocket were the obituaries of two gang members, one of whom, Neal Wallace, Cronin remembered. A leader of the Traveling Vice Lords, Wallace had only recently been killed. When Cronin had searched Wallace's apartment after his death, he found an essay the gang leader had written to himself. The handwritten composition explained that he sold drugs to make it easier for the next generation of black children to become lawyers and doctors. Like many of the others, Wallace, who used to give out Easter baskets every year filled with food and candy, clearly saw himself as a hero.

Despite the arrest and his previous record, Lee was released.

He raised the $5000 in bail money. For a year, including the warring summer of 1987, he continued about his business. But, again in 1987, he was arrested for the alleged attempted murder of a policeman, a charge of which he was eventually acquitted. He again got the necessary bond money and was released.

At the trial, Lee's attorneys raised doubts that the semi-automatic rifle belonged to him. His wife and the other woman were acquitted of all charges. Judge Boharic, however, found Lee guilty of possession of a controlled substance with intent to deliver.

In a presentencing report, Lee stated that he had supported himself by working as a manager of a car wash and that his wife received assistance from Public Aid. He also said his plans included the possibility of opening his own car wash.

But in the presentencing hearing in front of Judge Boharic, the prosecution attempted to establish Lee's high ranking in the Vice Lords. Charlie Toussas told about the time Bird Leg had been shot and Lee led a band of his soldiers over to the Disciples' turf. Cronin testified that the Vice Lords had expanded their operations to Iowa, Minnesota, and Mississippi. Another police officer estimated that the Conservative Vice Lords, the faction controlled by Lee, sold "thousands of dollars a day in both heroin and cocaine."

The prosecutor, William O'Brien, in his closing statement asked that Lee be sent to prison for a long time. "The people would stress that we wish that this court would listen to the people at Henry Horner Homes, listen to the people of Chicago, and remove Jimmie Lee . . . to weaken the grip of gangs upon the public housing projects as well as the neighborhoods in Chicago." O'Brien went on to suggest that a long sentence would send a message "that this court and the people of Cook County will not tolerate the type of behavior."

Lee's attorney, Maurice Scott, was the last person to address the judge that day. "I think that this man is on trial as an individual, not as a symbol of all that is wrong with out society," he told the court. "To treat this case as a cause célèbre, to give this man some long, long term in prison, is not going to change the narcotics problem. I wish I knew the answer—maybe some form of legalization, something to take the profit out of it. I don't know. But I know it doesn't stop it by giving people long terms in prison." Scott also argued that the heroin that had been found was far from pure and therefore was nowhere near as much as it seemed.

The judge then asked Lee whether there was anything he wanted to say before he was sentenced. "No, sir," he replied.

"Organized evildoers cannot expect mercy from this court," Judge Boharic told Lee and the assembled attorneys. "I feel that under the circumstances here there is a need to deter others from committing the same type of crime and from entering into the same path of life that the defendant apparently has chosen. It is all too often pointed out that persons who grow up in the area where the defendant lives are given tough choices in life and one of the very attractive aspects of being a gang member and being involved in the dope selling is the money and prestige that that brings. But I'm here to enforce the law and I'm here to show that there is a downside and a big cost involved sometimes when a person is caught with those very serious crimes that this defendant was involved in. We must teach people in the community here that society will deal harshly with those who prey upon the weaknesses of those people in the community. In the long run we must teach the youth of this community the old aphorism that crime does not pay."

Judge Boharic then announced Lee's sentence: the maximum term possible, thirty years. "If I could give him more years in the penitentiary under the law, I would," the judge told the attorneys.

Word of Lee's extraordinarily long sentence traveled fast. Gang members stationed at the courthouse inquired about the outcome of various trials and then, like eager stockbrokers, got on the telephone to deliver the news. By the time Cronin drove the four miles to Horner, people there had already heard of Lee's sentence.

A neighbor delivered the news to LaJoe. "What?" Lafeyette asked, overhearing the hushed conversation.

"Shut up," LaJoe told him. "I don't want to hear it. You don't talk about them peoples. They still got peoples out here."

"Why?" asked Pharoah.

"He might be gone but there's always someone out here. They could get the family hurt."

A few days later, *The Chicago Tribune* ran a story on the front page of its Metro section about Lee's sentence. In the accompanying picture, a teenage boy, maybe thirteen or fourteen, had his arms raised. He didn't want to answer a question posed by the reporter, so he shrugged his shoulders and thrust his arms into the air. The Vice Lords thought he was celebrating Lee's sentencing. The next day, they beat him up, badly enough that the boy's father went to the police. Even without their leader, there was discipline among the ranks—and some ready to fill in for Lee. Jimmie Lee, it was clear, wouldn't be missed long.

Fifteen

THE WHITE GYPSY CAB pulled up to the back of 1920 West Washington, its back seat and trunk loaded down with bags of groceries. LaJoe and Rochelle sat squeezed in the front seat. Once a month, when LaJoe received her public aid check, she hired a cab to take her shopping; it was nearly impossible to persuade a licensed taxi to come into the neighborhood. Rochelle often joined LaJoe so that she had some help. LaJoe would have the cab take them to three different stores—Jewel, Aldi, and a discount butcher store—all of which charged less than the hiked-up prices of the closer markets. Some local markets charged 30 percent more for food than other stores did. It was July and she had just received her restored benefits, and she resumed her routine as if it had never been disrupted.

LaJoe bought enough to feed herself, Lafeyette, Pharoah, the triplets, and LaShawn, LaShawn's boyfriend and his brother, LaShawn's two children, Terence, and Weasel, who had moved back home. LaShawn contributed her food stamps to this monthly venture. LaJoe never needed a shopping list and always came within dollars of the $542 she had in the combined sets of food stamps. The food was almost always the same—and because there was so much, LaJoe stored some of the meat in the freezers of two neighbors.

15 packs of bacon
8 packs of sausages
12 dozen eggs
6 loaves of bread
8 packages of hot dog buns
10 packages of hamburger buns
3 gallons of milk
6 gallons of orange juice
2 gallons of apple juice
4 six-packs of fruit juice cartons
6 packages of sliced American cheese
12 boxes of cereal, including oatmeal and grits
24 cans each of ravioli, Campbell's soup, peas, carrots, mixed vegetables, applesauce, creamed corn, whole corn, baked beans, spaghetti, peaches, fruit cocktail, tomato paste, and tomato sauce
24 boxes of corn bread mix
4 packs of hamburger patties
14 round steaks
2 canned hams
7 packages of chicken
4 packages of pork chops
8 pounds of ground beef
20 packages of hot dogs
4 pot roasts
2 pounds of veal

4 packages of beef liver
10 packages each of salami and bologna
4 packages of ham
8 packages of frozen perch
2 boxes of frozen fish sticks
4 packages of cookies
4 packages each of doughnuts and Danishes
6 boxes of spaghetti
12 boxes of macaroni and cheese
6 cans of Spam
14 cans of sardines

and assorted fresh vegetables, including cabbage, onions, carrots, lettuce, collard greens, tomatoes, and potatoes, as well as sugar and seasonings.

As a special favor for Lafeyette, she had bought some cans of oysters, which he loved to eat with just a touch of hot sauce. For Pharoah, she bought ripe pears. For all the children, to celebrate the restoration of her benefits, she bought apples, grapes, plums, peaches, and Popsicles. The treats would all be gone within a few days.

Lafeyette and the triplets raced out of the building to help their mother carry in the bags of food. Timothy grabbed two containers of milk. Tiffany and Tammie rummaged through the bags for the sweets. Lafeyette, who was growing taller and stronger, picked up two heavy sacks, teetered for a moment, and then walked back toward the building. Where was Pharoah? LaJoe wondered. He always showed up to help. She had told him she was going shopping. Maybe he forgot. That was just like Pharoah to forget, she thought. Daydreaming again. Oh, that Pharoah. Still, she wondered where he could be.

Three blocks south of Horner sits a condominium complex called Damen Courts. Its manicured lawns and graffiti-free walls seem immaculate next to the rubble of Horner. The three-story red brick buildings look elegant and proper beside Horner's grim and worn high-rises.

Pharoah can't recall when he first discovered this small paradise, but when he did, he retreated regularly to the comfort of the lush lawns that circled the buildings. He was there when his mother returned from shopping.

The grass carpet offered a quiet resting place; it was like going to the beach. Pharoah found a shady place on the lawn and shot marbles or read a *Captain America* or *Superman* comic. Or, if the mood fit him, he just sat and daydreamed. He thought about school and next year's spelling bee. He urged on the Chicago Cubs and imagined himself a professional wrestler. It was at Damen Courts that he came up with the name for a scraggly gray cat that was now staying with the family: Useless. "He hardly don't catch no mice. He just want to freeload off our heat," he explained.

Pharoah had long sought such a refuge. For a few months last spring, he'd attended Bible classes at the First Congregational Baptist Church. Washington Boulevard was lined with churches, but most of them now served people who had since moved from the neighborhood. Churches had lost their authority in areas like Horner. Pharoah grew bored with the classes and began to question whether there was indeed a God. He often prayed to him, asking that he let them move from the projects. But, Pharoah would say, "I be praying but he don't do nothing. Maybe there ain't no God." It was as much a question as it was a statement.

At Damen Courts, Pharoah found some respite. No one knew of his discovery, not his mother, his cousin Porkchop, his friend Rickey, or Lafeyette. He wanted it that way. He wanted a place that he could escape to by himself, where nothing would interrupt his daydreaming, where no one would try to fight him, where he didn't have to worry about gunshots or firebombings. When his mother asked where he was going, he said to the corner store to play video games. He didn't want anybody to know about his hideaway.

In the weeks immediately following Jimmie Lee's conviction, an unusual calm descended over Horner. Several other gang leaders had been jailed. The drug dealing and beatings didn't stop, but they certainly slowed down in comparison with the relentless battles of the previous summer.

With fewer shootings and a reprieve from some of the family's troubles, Pharoah's stutter became less noticeable. In later months, it would recur, but never would it get so bad that it would immobilize or silence him as it had during the past year. LaJoe had taken Pharoah to the Miles Square Health Center, where a counselor urged Pharoah to slow down when he spoke. Think about what you want to say before speaking, he told Pharoah. The stuttering is partly due to nerves, he explained. Pharoah was bewildered. "What's it got to do with nerves?" he later asked his mother, who did her best to explain that when people started fighting and shooting, he got nervous and scared and would begin to stutter. It acted as a kind of warning mechanism to himself to be vigilant and cautious. Pharoah understood. He always seemed to understand—when he wanted to.

With the uneasy calm, Pharoah found other distractions in addition to Damen Courts. He and Lafeyette frequented the outdoor swimming pool in Union Park, four blocks to the east, and in this large pool filled with flailing bodies, both boys learned to swim. They also regularly visited the Boys Club to play basketball or shoot pool or to get free sandwiches, which had become endearingly known among the children as a "chokes." Or they might just hang about their building, playing basketball on the jungle gym or wading in the permanent pool created by the fire hydrant. Sometimes Red, a small man in his fifties who lived in their building, would ride around the high-rise on his adult-size tricycle with presents for the neighborhood children stuffed in his basket. He found the used gifts in trash bins or behind stores. He'd give the little girls plastic necklaces and metal pendants; the little boys got tennis balls. To LaJoe and the other mothers, he presented gladioli and daisies which, in their late bloom, florists had thrown away. Over the years, Red had become like a year-round Santa to the building's kids. The triplets in particular adored him, and on his arrival on his tricycle could be heard screaming, "Red, oh, Red! What it is, Red?" as they ran up and surrounded him and gave him hugs in exchange for the presents.

Pharoah continued to badger Lafeyette and Rickey and any other older friend he could corner to take him back to the railroad tracks, which he remembered for the quiet and solace he'd found there. But no one would take him. The stories from last year of lost legs were still fresh in their minds. And now there were exaggerated children's tales of "raper mans" and other loonies hiding in the buildings by the viaduct. So, with the older boys' refusal and his own fear of what he might meet at the tracks, Pharoah spent more time at his private sanctuary.

He stayed on the lawn at Damen Courts until a security guard or janitor shooed him away, but he always left happy and satisfied. Being there for even an hour gave him a chance to catch his breath, to find the tranquillity he treasured.

On this particular afternoon, after his mother had finished putting away the groceries, Pharoah wandered through the front door, his head cocked slightly to one side. "Where you been, Pharoah?" his mother asked.

"Nowheres," he said, turning away. It was hard for him to lie, especially to his mother.

"Pharoah?"

Pharoah thought about telling her but didn't. "I been playing video games with Porkchop," he said and walked back to his room.

In later weeks, he finally confided in his mother about his discovery. "My mind be cleared of everything there," he told her.

_____ Fall 1988–Winter 1989 __

Sixteen

IN THE INTERVENING MONTHS, Lafeyette and Rickey had become friends or, in Lafeyette's word, associates. Closer in age, they seemed a more likely pair than Pharoah and Rickey. LaJoe speculated that Lafeyette first started hanging out with Rickey because he wanted to keep a close eye on Pharoah. But Rickey and Lafeyette took a liking to each other.

Rickey introduced Lafeyette to some of his friends, many of whom had been in trouble with the law. A group of them, including Rickey, had been arrested regularly for what was known as "smash and grabs." They smashed the windows of cars stopped at the traffic light on the corner of Damen Avenue and Lake Street and then grabbed jewelry from the motorist or snatched a purse or valise from the passenger seat. It had become such a troublesome problem at Horner that the police had assigned two young plainclothes officers to watch for the thefts. Rickey had also been picked up for stealing a car. The police caught him and a friend driving it around Horner's parking lots; Rickey could barely see over the Cadillac's steering wheel.

Rickey had been arrested at least half a dozen times and was known by all thirty officers in the Thirteenth District's tactical unit. "By the time he's eighteen, he'll be dead or in the penitentiary," one cop prophesied. They had once found two bullets in his bedroom—which they searched after Rickey's mother gave them permission. And Rickey's close friend Terrell had been picked up for possession of a zip gun that was constructed from a toy plastic pistol.

Because of Rickey's troubles at Suder, he had been sent to the Moses Montefiore School, a school for troubled boys. It enrolled 152 children from throughout the city and provided them with individual counseling and special instruction. No class ever had more than eight students, compared with as many as thirty at Suder. Most of the students had behavioral problems and tested at two to six years below grade level.

Pharoah remained friends with Rickey, though now that Rickey was at Montefiore the two saw less of each other. Rickey still gave Pharoah money or candy, and he still watched after the younger boy. But he moved with a crowd that was too old and brazen for Pharoah. Lafeyette was torn. He liked Rickey and, unlike Pharoah, could hold his own among Rickey's friends.

On a Saturday two weeks before Christmas, Pharoah, Rickey, Lafeyette, and several other friends went window shopping. They walked the six blocks to Chicago Avenue, which in this part of the city was a distinctly unfashionable strip of discount stores. The children didn't have much money between them, perhaps enough to buy some french fries and soda pop, so they wandered in and out of stores, admiring the large boom boxes at JB Electronics, the shoes at Chicago Avenue Discount, and the clothes at Goldblatt's. Ordinarily, Lafeyette didn't like coming here with other kids from Horner. "It make me feel embarrassed 'cause I'm walking with a whole lot of dirty kids," he would say. "They know we come from the projects and they think we wanna start something."

So he suggested they walk another half mile north to a videocassette store on Milwaukee Avenue, an even larger and more bustling boulevard of small shops and fast-food restaurants. Lafeyette desperately wanted a VCR for his birthday, but he knew his mother couldn't afford one. Still, he thought, nothing wrong with make-believe.

"Let's go see what we could be buying when we get some money," Lafeyette said to his friends. The six of them straggled into Erol's Video Club, a spacious, well-lit store with row upon row of videotapes. Pharoah wandered through the stacks until he found the Wrestle Mania movies, where he surveyed the pictures of the massive-chested men. An avid sports fan, Pharoah was particularly captivated by professional wrestling; he regularly watched the matches on television. He, Porkchop, and a couple of other young friends tag-team wrestled in the hallway of their building's second floor. The loud, savage theater of professional wrestling, seemed an odd love for Pharoah, but he delighted in it, closely following the dubious careers of such characters as the Iron Sheik, Hulk Hogan, and Jake (the Snake) Roberts. On the surface, it didn't make sense, but wrestling offered the gentle Pharoah an innocent entrance into the brutal world about him. It was one way he could, albeit vicariously, fight.

As Pharoah admired the wrestling movies, Lafeyette and Rickey looked at the new releases, which included various Ninja and horror films. "Hey, Lafie," Rickey whispered, "let's take us some." Pharoah, who was standing nearby, overheard him. Before Lafeyette had a chance to respond, Pharoah sidled up to his brother.

"Lafie, let's go leave them," he pleaded. Lafeyette hesitated. "Let's go home, Lafie."

"I'm still looking 'round, man. If you wanna go, go!" Lafeyette said in a loud whisper.

Pharoah and the others left. Pharoah was disappointed in Rickey, but even more so in Lafeyette, who seemed to bow to the pressure of his friend. Maybe they wouldn't get caught, he hoped. "I'm never going to jail," he had said more than once.

Rickey grabbed a Ninja movie and slid it under his coat. He nudged Lafeyette, who pushed a tape under his loose-fitting Chicago Blackhawks warm-up jacket. The two boys walked quickly toward the exit.

Mario Vera, the assistant manager, had been watching them on a videocamera from the back of the store. When he saw the children bunching up together and whispering, he knew from past experience that they were thinking of shoplifting, so before they could leave, he grabbed them. He had seen young kids do this before; they always wore an air of innocence.

"What you doing?" Rickey boldly asked.

Vera smiled. "Now, come on, just give us the tape."

"What tape?" Rickey said. Lafeyette remained silent.

"The tape you have there." Mario pointed to the bulge in his coat.

"Man, you don't leave me alone, my big brother, he be burning this place down." Rickey didn't have a big brother.

Another store employee, who held Rickey from behind, began to pat him down. The Ninja tape slipped out from under his jacket. Lafeyette then produced his.

"Rickey—" Lafeyette started to say.

"Shut up, dummy," Rickey snapped, worried that Vera now knew his name.

"They don't know what we be talking about," Lafeyette assured him.

"What's your name?" Vera asked Rickey.

"Joe Styro." Rickey evidently had gotten the idea from a nearby Styrofoam cup stand.

While Rickey stood there, unflustered if not somewhat cocky, Lafeyette looked worried. "Since you got the tape, mister, why don't you lemme go?" Lafeyette asked Vera. "I'm sorry. I won't come back again."

"Sorry?" Vera replied. "It doesn't work that way." Vera, though, felt bad for Lafeyette, who seemed genuinely apologetic. Privately, he wanted to let the two boys go. But he couldn't. Store policy demanded that he report to the police any incidents recorded on the hidden camera.

While they waited for the police, Vera took the two boys to

the back of the store, where he seated them in folding metal chairs. "Is this the first time you've done this?" Vera asked Lafeyette.

"Unh-unh," Lafeyette mumbled.

"Like what?"

"Twinkies, cupcakes, potato chips."

Both boys were nervous. Lafeyette sat with his arms tightly crossed against his chest, his face revealing little. Rickey leaned back in his chair, his arms slung over the back as if he had nothing better to do that afternoon than to pass the time with Vera. Vera sensed that beneath Rickey's tough demeanor he was scared.

"You guys want something to drink?" Vera asked.

Lafeyette nodded. Rickey looked at Vera defiantly. Vera brought Lafeyette a root beer. "Thanks," he said. Lafeyette was surprised at the friendliness of their captor. In later weeks, he expressed a desire to meet with Vera to apologize for his actions.

Vera beckoned the two boys to a one-way window to show them how he could see the entire store from this back room. "Why don't you lemme go?" Lafeyette asked again.

"All they have to do is turn their back and we be gone—" Rickey said to Lafeyette.

"We'll give you a head start, and if you make it to the door you're gone," interrupted Vera.

"Really?" Rickey asked. Mario laughed at the boy's innocently earnest response.

When the police finally arrived, Vera didn't press charges. Instead, the cop gave the two boys a short lecture about shoplifting and dropped them off at Chicago Avenue. They walked the rest of the way home.

LaJoe might not have found out about the shoplifting had a neighbor's daughter not told her. She began to think of Terence and how quickly she had lost him to the neighborhood. She worried that she might be losing Lafeyette, but hoped the incident might serve some good. It was, after all, a relatively minor violation, considering the crimes of the neighborhood. And it showed Lafeyette that he could get caught. She also knew that Lafeyette, who would turn fourteen next June, would have to make some choices in the coming months and years. It would be easy for him to get caught up with boys who were more daring. She made Lafeyette stay in the house for a week and a half. Lafeyette didn't seem to mind the punishment. He knew that what he had done was wrong.

LaJoe had begun to place more responsibility on Lafeyette, partly in the hope that her son would rise to the new duties and partly because there was no one else she could turn to. She made him the beneficiary of her $4000 life insurance policy. She told him she wanted him to take care of Pharoah and the triplets should anything happen to her. She also asked that she be cremated so as to save him the cost of a funeral. Lafeyette protested. He didn't want his mother burned up. LaJoe promised to take him to a funeral home to see the cremation boxes. She didn't, however, want the ashes scattered in a lake, she told him. She didn't like water. She told Lafeyette that he or one of his sisters or brothers could keep the ashes.

Talk of death upset Pharoah. He worried that Lafeyette wouldn't provide for him if his mother died. "Yes, I will," Lafeyette reassured him. "I'll always take care of you, but I don't want my money like that." Me neither, thought Pharoah, who had begun to resign himself to the possibility that he might die young. "I don't be scared only 'cause when it's time to let you go, God will let you go," he told his mother. Pharoah told friends that Lafeyette had become his mother's "obituary." He meant beneficiary.

The shoplifting incident also unsettled Pharoah. He began to distance himself from Rickey, not because he didn't like him anymore—in fact, he was still fond of his older friend—but because he worried that Rickey might get him into trouble. As for his older brother, "he was dumb for listening to other people."

Pharoah became more alert and prudent. He had never stolen anything. Nor had he ever gotten into any trouble other than talking in class. He wanted it to stay that way. The best way was to hang out more by himself. Pharoah decided he no longer had any friends. Like his brother, he just had associates.

"You don't have no friends in the projects," he said. "They'll turn you down for anything."

"I was figuring to go back and help," explained Pharoah.

"How could you help?" chided Lafeyette.

"Shut up."

"You couldn't fight him," said Lafeyette.

Seventeen

WHAT HAPPENED THAT NIGHT wasn't clear—and probably never will be. But by the time it was over, Lafeyette was wet and hurting and unusually angry at the police. And Pharoah was confused and disappointed with himself for not doing more to help his brother.

The late afternoon rain had warmed the December air ever so slightly, enough for Lafeyette and Pharoah to decide to work the Chicago Blackhawks game that night. Lafeyette wore his nylon Blackhawks warm-up jacket. Pharoah refused to wear what the kids called "starter jackets," the nylon jackets with the logos of various sports teams. They had become so popular that teens were stealing them off others' backs. During the next year, at least two boys in the city would be killed when others tried to steal their jackets.

Pharoah, instead, had a black polyester coat, which at first glance looked like leather. The white cotton stuffing poked out through three rips in the sleeves. Pharoah refused to wear the hood for fear it would mess up his new curls. The fancy hairdo made him look older. He had gotten many compliments on it. One woman wanted to know who had done his hair.

For decades, children of the west side viewed "stadium nights" as a way to make a few dollars' spending money. When the Chicago Bulls or Blackhawks played, thousands of well-dressed, mostly white sports fans poured into the neighborhood. The children would offer to watch people's cars if they parked on the side streets instead of in one of the numerous parking lots. If the driver refused to pay a couple of dollars to have his car watched, the children might smash a window with a handful of ball bearings and steal the radio or a jacket or anything else left behind. But mostly the children had no intention of breaking into the cars; they just wanted to earn some spending money.

Pharoah took the job seriously. He and Porkchop were partners. If someone paid them to watch a car, they would stay by it at least fifteen minutes past game time and then retreat to Pharoah's apartment, where they would watch the game on television. They checked on the car three or four times during the evening. Once, they went back outside at the end of a game only to find the driver's window shattered on a car they had been paid to watch. Pharoah apologized profusely to the driver, and was upset the whole day after. He said, as he had before, that "my conscience bothered me." He didn't like to let down others or himself.

When asked his name by stadium patrons, Pharoah always told them "Jimmy." Porkchop told them "Michael." Lafeyette once used the name Todd, which was the brand of his jogging suit. Everybody had an alias, even the young children. Rarely did they give their real names to the authorities or to strangers;

the belief that they could hide behind false identities gave them a sense of anonymity and, perhaps, invulnerability.

Pharoah, because he was so small and nonthreatening, was successful at picking up extra tickets from stadium patrons. "Any extra tickets?" he'd ask, looking longingly at a passerby. How could you turn down that face? It was so sweet and open. Sometimes, Pharoah would hand the tickets over to LaShawn's boyfriend, Brian, who would then scalp them and give Pharoah a few dollars for his help. Mostly, though, Pharoah and the others would use the tickets to attend a game. They loved to watch Michael Jordan and the Bulls. But there were times when the stadium's attendants wouldn't let the children in, even if they had tickets. The children would curse the stadium and the ticket takers. Who were the attendants not to let them in? After all, they lived right next door. Besides, if they wanted, they could make life hell for the stadium's patrons. Some of the patrons—the stupid ones, they'd say—even parked their cars in Horner. It was almost inviting trouble. Once, a stadium attendant humiliated James by tearing up his ticket as other patrons waited to get in. Another time, when Pharoah handed his standing-room ticket to the attendant, the man firmly told him, "No neighborhood kids allowed." Pharoah got in through another entrance.

The relationship between the stadium and the neighborhood had long been tense. Built in 1929, the immense concrete monolith has, in addition to serving various sports teams, been host to four Democratic National Conventions, all of them during the Roosevelt and Truman eras. Although they were built nearly thirty years apart, the stadium and Horner mirror each other's architecture: drab and just plain big.

Over the past twenty years, the Wirtz family, the stadium's owners, have helped change the character of the neighborhood. The name of Arthur Wirtz, the family's patriarch, who has since died, is anathema to some residents of this area who believe him to have been a private demolition crew; he bulldozed blocks of homes to make way for his paved parking lots, forty-eight acres in all. But Mr. Wirtz alone did not alter the landscape. The riots following the death of Martin Luther King, Jr., in 1968 turned to rubble the bustling, brightly lit two-mile commercial strip along Madison Street, which runs just two blocks south of Horner, right past the stadium. Fires set by the rioters destroyed an estimated $10 million worth of property; dozens of other stores shut down, their owners fearing for their safety. It was not a proud moment for the west side—nor for Mayor Richard J. Daley, who ordered the police to shoot to kill. Eleven people died in the rioting, two of them killed by police officers; five hundred were wounded or injured; and three thousand were arrested. Madison Street and the surrounding neighborhood never fully recovered from those two days of rioting. Today, it is lined with liquor stores, currency exchanges, and storefronts overflowing with used refrigerators, stoves, sofas, and other household items.

In the mid-1980s, angry residents feared that the only improvements planned for the area were the construction of two new stadiums, one for the city's basketball and hockey teams, the other for its football team. When talk of such plans first surfaced, real estate speculators began buying up property in anticipation of rising land values. Some walked the length of Lake Street, under the El tracks, offering to purchase storefronts.

Since the city's downtown—the Loop—can't expand to the east because of Lake Michigan, it has crept westward, past the Chicago River and through the city's once notorious skid row, certain to bump eventually right up against Henry Horner. There are many who believe that with a new stadium the area will become gentrified. The absentee owner of one gutted gray stone building just across the street from Henry Horner was asking $150,000 for the property. And artists and professionals have begun to move into the area just north of Horner, converting aged factories to loft spaces. Some smaller companies have also opened up shop there. The city, for its part, has repaved parts of Lake Street and built a ramp onto the expressway to handle the expected influx of fans. These were, residents point out, the first infrastructure improvements in the area in years.

As this period of real estate speculation began, Henry Horner went into a tailspin, leaving residents, local businessmen, and politicians to whisper of a conspiracy. The thinking went as follows: the housing authority, through neglect and attrition, would empty Horner so that it could be torn down to make way for yet more parking lots or upscale housing. The housing authority's lack of money to fix up vacant apartments for new tenants fed the conspiracy theory, particularly as the complex's number of vacancies soared from 501 to 699 in only a year's time.

Even passersby who knew of the stadium plans couldn't help wondering what the city fathers had in store for Horner, which suddenly sat on thirty-four acres of very valuable real estate. Many of the buildings boast more empty units than occupied ones, thin plywood replacing the windows. In some, the black scorching of fires, recent and old, surrounds empty and boarded-up window frames, which look like the blackened eyes of a defeated boxer.

Authorities assured residents that they had no plans to demolish Horner. They cited a 1987 law passed by Congress prohibiting the razing of public housing unless replacement housing is provided. Moreover, the city's football team, the Bears, chose to continue to play in its stadium by the lake, so only one new arena was planned. Nonetheless, skeptics abounded.

The stadium has caused bad feelings among residents for other reasons as well. On stadium nights, the neighborhood overflows with police. There are so many that two years ago Jimmie Lee, according to the police, had to shut down his drug operations during ball games. Why can't we get more protection for ourselves? the residents asked. Why does it take all these white people, all these outsiders, to flood the area with police? Why is it that only on stadium nights the area is well lit? The questions, rarely posed directly at the stadium or the city, come up in conversations at Horner. The Interfaith Organizing Project, an organization of local churches, challenged the construction of the two stadiums, but its complaint was merely a whisper compared with loud and well-orchestrated voices heard two decades ago. In the late 1960s and early 1970s, numerous community organizations, most notably the Miles Square Federation, vigorously fought for and won neighborhood improvements, including better schools and health care. Demonstrations were frequent. Today, the tensions simmer below the surface.

Lafeyette, Pharoah, and Porkchop joined some friends as they got to Washington Boulevard, which runs along the southern edge of the complex. "The police told us to get away, not to watch no cars," one boy told the others. A disjointed conversation ensued. Should they turn back? There had been nights when the police seemed more intent than at others to keep the boys away from the stadium. Sometimes, the children would heed the cops' warnings. Other times, they would continue their efforts to watch cars, careful to avoid the police. This night, Pharoah and Porkchop turned back, choosing instead to play basketball on the jungle gym. Porkchop, always filled with mischief, hollered at a teenage sentry for one of the gangs, "Police!" The young gang member jerked his head around. "Where? Where?" Porkchop and Pharoah burst into laughter at their joke. Lafeyette went on to the stadium with his friends.

Lafeyette helped a parking lot attendant wave in cars. The boys could make $5.00 to $10.00 flagging cars into the lots. A policeman approached and told Lafeyette and a few of his friends, who were waiting for cars to pull into the side streets, to go home. Lafeyette may have talked back to him or he may have been slow in moving, but two other boys have separately recounted what happened next. The policeman grabbed Lafeyette by the collar of his jacket and heaved him into a puddle of water. He then kicked Lafeyette in the rear. "What you doing here?" the officer demanded of the boy. "Little punk, you ain't supposed to be working here. These white people don't have no money to give no niggers."

One of Lafeyette's friends ran to the safety of Horner, where he breathlessly told Pharoah what had happened. Pharoah panicked. He stood by himself in the middle of the playground, shivering more from fear than from the cold. He didn't want to go to Lafeyette because he was afraid the policeman might kick him, too. He didn't want to summon their mother because he worried that "she probably would of gotten involved and they would of taken her to jail for keeping her kids out too late." He was paralyzed with fear.

Meanwhile, two boys had sprinted to get LaJoe, who bolted from her apartment without her coat. By the time she reached Washington Boulevard, Lafeyette was in the back seat of the squad car. She started arguing with the policeman who had thrown Lafeyette to the ground. Two other officers then showed up. They released Lafeyette. He wasn't arrested; no charges were filed.

Lafeyette later recalled that one of the policemen had warned him he could get hurt out there at night. "I've been living around here all my life and I ain't got hurt so far," he told the officer. "Only the police have hurt me."

No one got the name of the patrolman or his badge number, so there was no way to pursue the case with the police department. Besides, it would be the boys' word against his. That night ushered in a period of confusion for Lafeyette as he began to question his relationship with the police.

For several weeks, neither Lafeyette nor Pharoah worked the stadium. LaJoe told the two never to go back, but eventually they went. Sometimes LaJoe knew about their forays; sometimes she didn't. She had trouble saying no to them, as she had had with the older children. Besides, working the stadium was the only way the children could earn spending money.

Pharoah returned to the stadium first. It would be spring before Lafeyette tentatively made his way over there. Pharoah had found a new way to make money. He and his friends performed what was called "the chicken wing" for one of the stadium goers. The man, who was white, would chuckle at the frenzied dance, in which the children mimicked a squawking chicken; he'd give them a few dollars. Pharoah must have realized there was something demeaning about his performance, because when he told the story to others, he would feel embarrassed and would turn his head away, giggling nervously.

For the first time, Pharoah, now ten, began to wonder aloud about being black. "Do all black people live in projects?" he asked his mother. "Do all black people be poor?" He was upset that Michael Dukakis hadn't chosen Jesse Jackson as his running mate. "He might of won then," he thought out loud. "Why don't people elect black people?" The incident at the stadium had unnerved him. He felt that "the police probably don't like black children or something. The white polices don't like the black children. That's what I believe." It was the first time Pharoah had acknowledged any bitterness toward anybody.

The incident involving Lafeyette and the policeman brought back unsettling memories for LaJoe. Like other long-time

Henry Horner residents, she had mixed feelings about the police—and her ambivalence was passed on to her children.

On the one hand, LaJoe and others had sympathy for the
police. What young cop, after all, would want to be stuck alone
in a neighborhood like Horner after dark? The residents knew
this and understood. It wasn't safe for them. Why would it be
safe for anyone else? In one nearby neighborhood, not too long
ago, a youth got down on one knee, put a rifle up to his shoulder, yelled out the name of his gang, and then opened fire on a
squad car. Most officers wouldn't venture into Horner by themselves even during the day. Who could blame them?

But the residents didn't fully trust the cops. For one thing,
residents felt stuck in the middle between the drug gangs and
the police. The cops came and went, but the gang members
were there twenty-four hours a day, every day. It wasn't a question of allegiance; it was common sense. Few residents, after all,
would call 911 for fear that the gangs would discover that they
had snitched.

But much of their wariness was rooted in the past. Memories
died slowly. And Horner, like so many other inner-city black
communities, had been a victim of the police's overzealousness
or brutality, depending on the way you looked at it. As early as
1968, the Kerner Commission, appointed by President Johnson
to explore the problems facing the nation's inner cities, charac-
terized the relationship between the armed authorities and the
black community nationwide as "explosive." The antipathy of
Henry Horner residents toward the police crystallized a year
later, in 1969, when four young men were killed by the authorities. Their deaths forever changed the way people at Henry
Horner viewed the police.

In the late 1960s, the nation's black ghettoes were filled with
rage and fury, a stark contrast to the resignation and personal
excesses of the late 1980s. It was a period when people felt that
they could do something, that they could find allies in the "system" to help make it work for them. And when that began to
fail them, so did their hope and sense of justice.

First the War on Poverty, despite its grandiose intentions,
flickered in its failures, and then the leaders, Malcolm X and
Martin Luther King, Jr., were gunned down. White America
seemed intent on ignoring pleas for equality in the schools, in

housing, and in health care. The Kerner Commission, which issued its report only months before Dr. King's death, presciently warned: "Our nation is moving toward two societies, one black, one white—separate and unequal."

During those years, the residents of Henry Horner, like many others, organized. They were galvanized by what they considered the neglect and outright exploitation of their community. Pressuring the federal government, they were able to get funds for the founding of a neighborhood health clinic, the Miles Square Health Center. They put pressure on schools, like Crane, to bring in more sympathetic principals. They helped get a swimming pool built at the Boys Club in 1967. And then, in the fall of 1969, residents demanded a traffic light.

Given all the turmoil of those years, it didn't, at the time, seem an extravagant request. Washington Boulevard had become a virtual expressway for commuters driving from the Loop to the western suburbs, and because there was no traffic light for the one-mile length of Horner, motorists passed it at high speeds. Since the opening of school, two children had been hit by motorists. So it seemed reasonable to the parents in the neighborhood that the city install a traffic light; the city needed to do something to slow down the traffic. But the city refused. It would impede the flow of commuter traffic, officials said.

Parents and children, reinforced by the Vice Lords, who wore red tams and who at the time were making an effort to become a constructive part of their community, turned out in protest. They considered stringing a human chain across Washington Boulevard, but they could have been arrested for impeding traffic. Instead, they formed a never-ending picket line that moved back and forth across the boulevard. They were pedestrians, they argued, simply trying to cross the street. They couldn't help it if it just happened to be rush hour. They called their picket "the funky four corners."

Tensions heightened with the arrival of busloads of police, in full riot gear, who stood menacingly across the street, ready to make mass arrests. The confrontation never materialized, though the police did arrest a few protesters. During one confrontation, twenty-one-year-old Michael Soto, who was home on a thirty-day leave after a year of service in Vietnam, got into a shoving match with a policeman and was arrested for obstructing traffic and resisting arrest, charges that were eventually dropped.

On October 5, nineteen days later, Michael's younger brother, sixteen-year-old John, berated two white policemen who were arresting two of his friends. One of the officers shot and killed John Soto. The police said it happened when the boy started to scuffle with the officer; witnesses said the policeman shot John Soto without provocation.

On October 10, five days later, only hours after burying his younger brother, Michael Soto, while standing on a concrete landing between the first and second floors of the Horner highrise where his family lived, was also killed. Also by a policeman. The police said he had just robbed someone. Within minutes, the residents of Horner, on hearing the news of yet another dead Soto brother, rose in indignation and for an hour waged furious combat with the police. Snipers shot from the high-rise windows. Residents ran out of nearby stores, brandishing revolvers and shotguns. The police took cover behind their squad cars and under the El tracks. A helicopter hovered overhead. When the shooting subsided twenty minutes later, ten policeman and a twelve-year-old girl had been wounded by gunfire.

The city installed a traffic light. But there was trouble only two months later. Two more blacks were killed by the police.

On December 4, only a few blocks from Horner, thirteen policemen stormed the home of several Black Panthers, killing twenty-one-year-old Fred Hampton, head of the Illinois chapter, and twenty-two-year-old Mark Clark. The police at first contended that the Panthers had opened fire on them as they tried to serve a search warrant. A later FBI investigation, though, found that the Panthers fired one shot to between eighty-three and ninety-nine shots by the police. The Panthers lived only a few blocks from Horner; they were viewed with a mixture of awe and respect. They had started a breakfast program for the children. They held inspiring rallies at their headquarters on the corner of Western and Madison. And they had helped with such seemingly minor things as the traffic light protest.

Their death became a cause célèbre not only in Chicago but across the nation. Five thousand mourners attended a memorial for Hampton. Books were written about the incident and the subsequent trial of the state's attorney, who ordered the raid, and the police officers. They were all acquitted.

The four killings—the Soto brothers and the two Panthers—left an indelible scar on the people of Henry Horner. Twenty years later, those deaths at the hands of the police lingered in the memories of Horner's adults. "What you thought would protect you, you found out that you couldn't trust," said LaJoe, who was seventeen at the time. "How can people kill a person like that? And lie? And cover it up? When all they had to do was simply say it was a mistake and everything wouldn't have got like it had got."

LaJoe knew that most police weren't bad people. One of the boys she grew up with had become a detective who worked at Cabrini-Green. He frequently came back to visit. Another policeman had personally warned a gang leader to stay away from the Riverses after he had threatened LaShawn. LaJoe knew how scared some of them must be when patrolling her neighborhood. In 1975, Officer Joseph Cali had been killed by a sniper while writing a parking ticket at Horner. When police left their patrol cars unattended, residents would sometimes toss heavy objects from upper floors. Someone once threw a bowling ball onto a squad car. Another time, someone threw a refrigerator out of an upper floor, barely missing a policewoman. It got so bad that the police had trouble finding volunteers to patrol certain neighborhoods, including Horner.

What's more, many of the individual policemen LaJoe knew genuinely cared about the children. One, Bill Spencer, who worked at Horner every day, was a favorite among the kids. He understood them, and would give them second and third chances. He was so well liked that when he was transferred residents demanded—and won—his return. Another officer, William Guswiler, a lieutenant in the district's plainclothes unit, had recently given Lafeyette a ride to a restaurant, and, in a friendly manner, warned him about hanging out with the wrong people.

The police weren't all bad. It was just that when something tragic happened, like the Soto brothers' killing, LaJoe couldn't understand why the police didn't apologize, just admit they had made a mistake. And now, Lafeyette had been roughed up by a policeman. The incident itself wasn't that big a deal, she thought. Lafeyette's back hurt for a couple of days and he had to stay home from school, but there were no serious injuries. What worried LaJoe, though, was that Lafeyette's cynicism had begun to define his person. When the Public Aid Department had cut off his family's income, he immediately suspected a neighbor of telling on them. He had been disappointed so many times that when people let him down, his response was simple and direct: they had lied to him. Why else would they not hold up their end of the bargain? And now he was losing faith in the police. That wariness would only grow in coming months.

The apartment bulged with people that winter. Weasel's girl-friend moved in, as did LaJoe's mother, Lelia Mae, who had been depressed from a stroke that paralyzed one side. She had been shifted from one child's or grandchild's house to another.

Lelia Mae was initially invigorated by her move to LaJoe's. She slept on the couch and would tell the children stories of the old Horner, though they had to listen closely, because her speech has become slurred. The old days she spoke of seemed bright and cheery. She told the children, to their disbelief, that families used to keep their doors unlocked at night. During the summers, she told them, they might even spend the nights outside, sleeping on the lawn.

Lafeyette was particularly glad to have her there. He liked to take care of old people. It made him feel needed. At McDonald's, he would help older people with their trays. He ran errands for his grandmother. They'd always been close. When Lafeyette was younger and Lelia Mae healthier, Lafeyette would ride his bike over to her house. Now, he helped his mother bathe her and would rub her feet with alcohol. And he frequently ran to the local restaurant to buy his grandmother her favorite food: a hot dog with raw onions.

Moreover, Lelia Mae brought her small black-and-white television with her. Lafeyette and Pharoah kept it in their room, where they could watch in private and not put up with the commotion of the young kids.

The apartment seemed to collapse under the weight of all these people. The oven stopped working, and for most of eight months LaJoe couldn't bake. The wooden door to Lafeyette and Pharoah's room could be opened and shut only with great care;

otherwise, the top came unhinged and the door leaned precariously into the room as if it had been battered down. A cheap, unadorned light fixture, which the housing authority had only partly installed, hung loosely from the wall, unfinished. A friend of Lafeyette's stuck a screwdriver in its opening—and recoiled from the electric shock.

And the pipes leading to the kitchen sink sprang a leak. LaJoe tied rags around them to keep the water from dripping onto the floor, and for two weeks, while she waited for them to be repaired, she washed the dishes in the bathtub, which still ran day and night.

In all this activity, both Lafeyette and Pharoah were most troubled by their father's depression. It didn't look as if Paul would get his job back. He still drank and occasionally took heroin. He knew he would have trouble passing another urine test. He had become so desperate for money that he stole the television LaJoe's mother had given the boys and pawned it for $15. Lafeyette and Pharoah figured that one of their siblings' friends had walked off with it. They got a lock for their room. Paul felt so guilty that he pulled the money together and got the television out of hock, and returned it without their knowing who had taken it.

Lafeyette deeply resented his father. He didn't feel he had lived up to his promises to the family. When he was younger, Paul had told Lafeyette he would move the family out of Horner to a quieter neighborhood. "One of these days, son," he had promised, "you'll have your own big back yard to play in, have some room for a dog." The house, he went on, would be big enough so that he and Pharoah could have their own bedrooms. And there'd be a playroom where they could entertain friends. As LaJoe once had done, Paul dreamed out loud about the future. Nothing had seemed impossible. Both he and LaJoe were working at the time, and though the two had their problems, money wasn't one of them. Until Paul's habit overtook him.

"To look back at it, drugs really tore my life down, got my family in the shape it's in now," Paul reflected. "I'm sure the kids know. They don't say anything to me about it, either 'cause they respect me as their father or they don't feel big enough to get angry at me about it. It's deprived my family of a lot of things. I chose a way of drugs instead of necessities for my family."

Paul, who despite his problems had retained his fighter's physique, had not only welshed on his promises, but he was too dejected to be of much support for the kids. "I remember times when I would come to the house drunk or high, and the kids would seem to detect it," he said. "Everybody would be sitting in the living room, sitting up, and when I came in, I'd sit down and one by one they would leave and head to the back. As if to say, Hey, y'all, watch it, Daddy drunk. At times they just totally disregard me. I'm not allowed in my sons' room. I'm not allowed in my daughter's room. And if I want to go in any part of the house I have to knock on the doors. That's rough."

LaJoe didn't talk much to Paul either. She had never forgiven him for taking drugs. She was restrained, though, in the way she spoke of him: "He could do what he wants to do. I can't be angry with him, 'cause he doesn't even understand himself. I can't be angry with someone who's not in control of his self. If he can't help himself, how's he going to help me?"

Paul respectfully called LaJoe a "conscientious objector," since she didn't drink or get high. Her only habit, he would joke, was cigarettes. Even though LaJoe virtually ignored Paul, he still had strong feelings toward her. "I love that woman," he would say. "I'm the one that care but I can't show how much I care."

Paul continued to come around because he wanted his children to know their father. He felt bitter about his own childhood. His father had left when he was two. "It bothered me for a long time," he said. "When I questioned my mother about it, she'd get mad, and that would make me more bitter. She won't talk about it. That's what pisses me off. That's one of the reasons I visit with my kids despite my domestic problems with LaJoe. If I left now, they'd never forgive me. At least they have a daddy."

And at least Paul had Pharoah. Pharoah felt sorry for his father and often tried to cheer him up. If there was a basketball game on, Pharoah would try to get his father involved. He'd make a gentleman's bet on one team; his father would take the other. Anything to keep his father from becoming too pensive. Then, Pharoah knew, his father would only get depressed.

One balmy December afternoon, Paul sat at the edge of the double bed in the front bedroom, his eyes staring at the brown floor. Pharoah lay on his belly, his chin in his hand.

"Let's go outside," Pharoah urged.

Paul shook his head. "I'm all right here. Why don't you go on out?"

"Is you going back to work?" Pharoah asked.

"I'm off temporarily. It's a suspension," explained a sullen Paul.

"What the difference be between that and being fired?"

"It's only temporary."

"If you ain't working, how you gonna keep some of your promises to us?" Paul had promised to buy bicycles and snow-suits for the children. "Daddy, you can't buy it if you ain't working, can you?"

"Don't worry about it. Sooner or later I'm going to get back to work and I'm going to try and hold them promises. Try to stay to them." The two sat in silence for a few minutes. Pharoah looked at his dad, who stared at the floor.

"Why you drink? What you get out of it?"

The question stunned Paul. Pharoah would rarely have the courage to ask his father about his drinking, even though it upset him when his father came to the house reeking of alcohol and talking excitedly. Pharoah would always say that what his father did was his father's business. But it bothered everyone: him, Lafeyette, and, in particular, LaJoe, who would get angry with Paul and demand that he leave the apartment.

"Why you don't want me to drink? When I play with you and what-not, you smell it on my breath?"

"It stinks and you don't look right. You act funny," Pharoah said.

Paul sat motionless. He said nothing. He knew Pharoah was right. He should stop drinking. He had slowed down in taking drugs, but he should stop. He desperately wanted to return to work, but hadn't had any success in getting rehired at the transit authority. More than anything, he felt that he had let his children down.

Pharoah got up and sat behind his father, tenderly placing a hand on his shoulder. He made a point of looking cheerful.

"You gonna get your job back, Daddy. If not that one, then

another one. Remember you used to pick up them big old garbage cans? You want that job back?"

Porkchop's grinning face poked through the door. Pharoah looked at his father and stood up to leave. "Daddy, 'bye, I'm going." Pharoah hopped out of the room. Paul couldn't help cracking a smile.

Eighteen

AS IT DID EVERY WINTER, the temperature in the apartment approached a dry, crackling 85 degrees. Stripping down to their underwear was of no relief to Lafeyette and Pharoah; it was like being inside an oven. Their only remedy was to open a window, even in the dead of winter, but then they had to put up with a frigid draft. Pharoah had developed a blistering cough; his throat was parched and sore. The scorching heat tired the boys and put everyone on edge.

LaJoe wanted to find some excuse to get them out of the

apartment. Weekends were the worst. Besides the Boys Club, the kids had nowhere to go, so they would sit around all day. As Christmas approached, LaJoe wanted to do something special, for herself and the children. She had already promised them they would be getting bunk beds for the holidays, but that was beginning to seemed unlikely. After buying the children their Christmas presents, she didn't have the money for the beds. They'd have to wait until spring.

LaJoe decided to take the younger ones to see the Christmas windows downtown, something she had done with her mother as a child. The triplets had never before been in the Loop; Pharoah, only a couple of times. LaJoe didn't think to ask Lafeyette. She figured he'd feel too grown for such a tour.

So on a Thursday after school, two weeks before Christmas and a few days after she'd won $38 playing cards, LaJoe gathered the children. In addition to Pharoah and the triplets, she invited three of her grandchildren, Tyisha, Baldheaded, and Snuggles, and a friend of the triplets whom everyone called Esther B.

She walked the young battalion to Madison Street, where they hopped the bus and where all the kids, including ten-year-old Pharoah, got on for free. As LaJoe and the eight youngsters filed on, the driver joked, "Next time you get on the bus, you pay nine dollars." LaJoe, already tired, managed a half smile. The trip, she hoped, would lift her spirits.

"Why's that window so clean?"

"Where them lights come from?"

"Ooooh, look at them tall buildings."

"Them's glass."

"No, they ain't."

"Is too."

"If a hurricane hit them buildings, everybody gonna die. The glass will get them."

"Ain't no hurricane gonna hit it."

"Stop lying."

And so the banter went as the bus was swallowed by the city's downtown; the skyscrapers seemed to rise forever into the darkening sky. The children tried to look straight up, to spot the buildings' tops, but, with their necks craning back as far as they would go and their faces pressed against the bus windows, their warm breath clouded the glass. Frantically, they rubbed off the mist as they caught a few more glimpses of the high-rises that dared to tower over their own.

LaJoe began to share their excitement. "When we're through," she promised the distracted crew, "I'll buy you some popcorn like you never tasted before." She remembered the popcorn her mother treated her to when as a young girl she had visited her at her job in the downtown county building. LaJoe was beginning to feel a part of an ordinary family, a family without problems.

"Here you go, ma'am," the bus driver told LaJoe as he pulled up to State Street, home of the downtown's major department stores and their elaborate Christmas windows. The children pushed and tumbled off the bus.

"Ain't no one going anywhere," LaJoe shouted. All except Pharoah, who felt he was big enough to go it on his own, clamored to hold LaJoe's hands. "I can't hold you all. Pharoah! Pharoah!" she called. But Pharoah was mesmerized by the afternoon rush. Men in suits and ties walked past him, their eyes focused straight ahead, their faces fixed with determination. And the women. They looked so pretty in their long wool coats, brightly colored scarves draped around their rosy faces. He twirled 180 degrees as his gaze followed one passerby after another.

"Pharoah!" LaJoe shouted again. "PHAROAH!" He drew upright at the sound of his name, which for the past minute had fluttered by him like the rush-hour shoppers. "Pharoah, take Tammie's and Tiffany's hands." He gripped the bare hands of the two five-year-olds. Tyisha grabbed Timothy and Snuggles. LaJoe picked up Baldheaded in one arm and held Esther B. with the other. Like paper chains, the eight of them floated down State Street, in and around the hurried businessmen and women, toward the crowds surrounding the windows.

The children screamed in delight at the sight of the two-foot-high mechanical children in the windows, some singing carols, two celebrating Christmas in a spaceship. "Are they real little kids?" Timothy asked.

"No," LaJoe told him. "Them's dolls and they make them move by battery."

"I wish I could go in there and live with them," Timothy said.

The kids argued. Was it real or fake snow? How about all the Santas ringing bells on the street corners? How could there be so many? "Them Santa Clauses just want money to buy people gifts," Pharoah explained to the younger ones. Pharoah himself had begun to doubt Santa's existence. "I don't think there's a Santa Claus," he whispered to his mother. "I don't think he could make it in every state in one day. He couldn't go to Detroit in one whole day."

Pharoah guided LaJoe and the others from window to window, block to block. He'd fly ahead of the pack, with Tammie and Tiffany as his wings. "Mama, come see this! Mama, come see this!" he'd scream. At one window, Pharoah read for the little ones: "Singing carols on the steps of the Art Institute has a way of making even Scrooge look cute . . . There's Tiny Tim and Bob Cratchit from Dickens' past. But who's teasing the dogs?"

"Perfect," said a young couple who had stopped to listen. Pharoah smiled proudly.

LaJoe led the children to McDonald's, where they ate and talked feverishly. "Where we going next?" they asked. "Mama, where?"

"One more stop. The big Christmas tree," she told them.

They hiked one more block, where they oohed and aahed at the huge city tree, which was actually tens of smaller trees neatly sculptured to look like one. "Is that God's tree?" Tiffany asked. "It's almost in the sky."

"No, that's everybody's tree. But God probably be around here somewhere," LaJoe told them, as their small bodies moved in rhythm to the Christmas carols emanating mysteriously from the tree's center. Finally, LaJoe brought them to Garrett's, a downtown popcorn emporium, where, despite Pharoah's protestations that she keep the rest of the money for herself, she bought them two huge bags, one of cheese-flavored and the other of caramel popcorn. She popped a kernel of each in each of their mouths as they giggled and chewed and asked for more. It was, they told LaJoe, the best popcorn they'd ever had.

On the bus ride home, Tiffany and Tammie walked up and down the aisle and in clear and precise tones, meant to imitate adults', said to each other and the other children: "Oh, we had a lovely day. Didn't you have a lovely day?" Before long, all eight had joined in the game. "Oh, we had a lovely time, Mama," one would say to the giggles of the others. LaJoe sat back in the seat, her head against the cold window. She was physically exhausted, but, in an odd sort of way, had more energy than she had had in a long time. It felt good to see the children giddy with excitement. They seemed so unencumbered. She promised herself she'd take the children on more trips. It gave them—and her—such satisfaction. "Oh, what a lovely day," she repeated to herself, imitating her daughters. She laughed softly.

Pharoah, too, sat in the bus exhausted. It had been an extraordinary day for him. He got to help his mother take care of the kids and to read to them from one of the windows. But more than that, he liked just spending time with his mother. He wished she'd take him on more trips. "I'd like to go again, Mama," he told LaJoe.

"Me too." LaJoe smiled and patted Pharoah's head.

LaJoe's only regret was that she hadn't asked Lafeyette. She didn't think he would have wanted to go; he would have thought himself too old for such a tour. But when they got home, Lafeyette was seated on the couch.

"Why didn't you take me, too?" he demanded.

"I didn't think you'd want to see a Santa Claus and a Christmas tree and the windows with all those dolls in it," she said.

"I wanted to go."

Next time, LaJoe promised herself. She had to remind herself that Lafeyette, despite his adult worries, was still a thirteen-year-old boy.

Lafeyette got angry when he heard the news. There was no way their brother could go to prison for ten years. No way. He wasn't *that* bad. When LaJoe had told Lafeyette, all he could muster was "I hope Terence get less time than ten years." He then disappeared into the bathroom, where he remained for nearly half an hour. Like his father, he felt his stomach tie up into knots when he got anxious. He had terrible bouts of diarrhea.

When Pharoah heard that his brother might be sent away for ten years, his face dropped. "I be thinking," he told his mother, "why they be locking people up and taking them away from their parents?" LaJoe tried to explain why it happened; it was a form of punishment for Terence's doing something wrong.

"If he get the ten years, then he'll be home when he's twenty-eight. I'll be twenty," Pharoah said, calculating the years with his fingers.

"Y'all just will have to catch up a little," LaJoe told him. "That'll be all right." LaJoe was concerned about Pharoah because his teacher had called her one afternoon after school and said that Pharoah had been daydreaming a lot in his class. Was there something wrong? the teacher had asked LaJoe. She suspected Pharoah was troubled about Terence. Neither Pharoah nor Lafeyette liked to let his mother in on his worries, because he thought it would just burden her more. As a result, a lot went unspoken.

"Terence is gonna be a man about what they give him," LaJoe assured Pharoah. "And you have to be a man for him also, no matter what they do. You have to be Pharoah and you can't worry about Terence if it make you to the point you have to daydream, thinking on him. Your brother's gonna be all right, so don't worry about him."

"Mama," Pharoah interrupted, "I'm just too young to understand how life really is."

The prosecution had offered Terence ten years if he would agree to plead guilty. That may have seemed an outrageous offer, particularly since he adamantly proclaimed his innocence. But Terence had been arrested again. Another armed robbery. Only this time, the police had substantial incriminating evidence.

Over the summer, Terence, while out on bond, had been determined to stay out of trouble. He spent some afternoons and evenings shining shoes at the airport, but mostly he lounged in the bedroom he shared with Weasel. Friends would visit him there. He didn't leave the apartment much. He felt good about his public defender, Audrey Natcone. She cared and she believed him. Nonetheless, Terence didn't share her optimism about his getting off. Hadn't he once spent five months in detention for a crime he hadn't done? No one came to his rescue then, he thought. Luck saved him. Had the girl he'd allegedly shot not come forward and changed her testimony, he might have been sent to prison. Because of the severity of the alleged crime, aggravated battery with a gun, he would have been tried as an adult. The judge could have sent him away for ten years. He just didn't trust the system. *They* didn't listen. *They* didn't understand. So if *they* thought he was a bad guy, if they wanted him to be a bad guy, then he'd be a bad guy. If *they* wanted to put him away for something he didn't do, then he'd give them something to put him away with. It was a tangled and tragic form of reasoning, but then it was a tangled and tragic life that had got him into trouble. It was his own confused method of seeking justice. And so he told a friend over the summer, perhaps somewhat presciently, "Man, they ain't gonna convict me with something I ain't do like that. I'm gonna give them something to convict me for."

On September 5, Terence and an acquaintance held up Mazury Tavern, a working-class bar on the city's north side. The stories vary. Terence says he went for a car ride with a few friends, only to learn that they'd planned a robbery. They paid Terence a few hundred dollars to stand as the lookout.

The police reported it differently. Two men, Terence and his friend, entered Mazury Tavern, where the friend held the bartender at bay with a pistol while Terence jimmied open a video game and the cash register and withdrew an estimated $1000 in cash. The police said they found indisputable evidence: Terence's fingerprints. Moreover, the police said Terence gave them an oral confession, though he refused to sign it. In the statement, he said he agreed to accompany his acquaintance to a north side tavern and that for his role in the robbery he received two bags of heroin.

Whatever the true version, Terence knew the prosecution had a good case. The police had reason to prosecute him. Now if he served time, at least it would be for something he'd done, not for some "bogus case." After they arrested him, he didn't confess to Audrey. But she could tell. She just knew.

His arrest upset Audrey, but it didn't come as a surprise. Many of her clients committed crimes while they were out on bond. She had hoped it would be different with Terence. She also felt they had had a strong case. She believed Terence hadn't committed the first armed robbery. The police still hadn't produced the line-up photos, which made her think something was amiss. But now it didn't matter. The prosecutors could try the second case first—and Terence didn't seem to have a chance.

The prosecution, though, was already overburdened with cases. It didn't want to go to trial. The three prosecutors in the courtroom where Terence's case was to be heard handled about 450 cases at a time, up from 250 cases the year before. They suspected part of the reason for the increase was political. Their boss, Richard M. Daley, was running for mayor, so the more cases they prosecuted, particularly those related to drugs, the more convinced the electorate would be that he was a strong law-and-order man. In fact, of the twenty-five thousand drug defendants in the county the previous year, over half had had their cases dismissed or their charges dropped, according to one study. As a result, the prosecutors—or state's attorneys, as they are called in Chicago—plea-bargained nearly 90 percent of their cases. They just didn't have the time to go to trial.

They had told Audrey they would offer Terence ten years in exchange for a guilty plea. She thought that was too much for him, especially since she believed he didn't commit the first robbery. It was also his first offense as an adult. She wanted to get him six. She had yet to talk to Terence about it other than to inform him of what had been offered. She believed she could negotiate a shorter term with the prosecution.

Nineteen

THE HOLIDAYS came and went without incident, though on December 30 Pharoah insisted on staying up all night so that he would be exhausted the next night. He wanted to sleep through the ritual celebratory shooting on New Year's Eve. Both boys had had a good Christmas. LaJoe had begun buying the children gifts on layaway back in September. It was her way of putting away savings; she didn't have a bank account. Lafeyette received a radio; Pharoah an Atari video game. Both boys also got $10 watches as well as clothes, mostly slacks and shirts for school.

The family had a small tree, which LaJoe decorated with candy canes and tinsel. She hung lights in her windows. Christmas, LaJoe would joke, was the only time of the year the neighborhood was well lit.

In early February, Pharoah returned from watching cars at a Blackhawks game. Lafeyette met him at the door.

"What you make?" Lafeyette asked.

"Two dollars," Pharoah replied.

"That's stupid. Working all night for two dollars. I make seven dollars when I work."

Pharoah didn't put up a fight. He just shrugged and shuffled to his room, where he folded the two dollar bills and stuffed them into a jacket pocket. He always saved his money. LaJoe joshed him about it. "What you gonna to do with all that money?" she'd ask. Pharoah just giggled. Usually he ended up spending it on video games or candy. This time he had a purpose. He was saving it for the Boys Club annual talent show. He and Lafeyette never missed going.

The Boys Club's one-story building was as old as Henry Horner. In the club's game room, Pharoah shot pool and became proficient at eight ball—though none of the pool cues had tips. Lafeyette played basketball in the gym. The club's indoor swimming pool, which had been closed for nine years, was scheduled to open in a few weeks. The club was an oasis for the neighborhood's children, though it served mainly those who lived east of Damen Avenue. Those children on the other side, who couldn't cross the boundary for fear of being attacked by rival gangs, frequented Chicago Commons, which boasted a gym and a new literacy center. There, they could find a quiet spot to do their homework or read. Commons also had a daycare center and Head Start program. For the talent show, however, the gangs' geographic boundaries temporarily disappeared. There, adversaries mingled. The police turned out in large numbers, too. It was one of the few community gatherings.

The show was as old as the Boys Club. Local children and young men and women put together singing, dancing, and comedy acts. In the 1960s and 1970s, local radio stations sent talent scouts. The members of the rock group Earth, Wind, and Fire, all of whom grew up in Horner, got their start here. Lafeyette and Pharoah looked forward to the show every year; they wouldn't have missed it for the world.

On this Friday evening, the club's gym filled up quickly. Pharoah and Lafeyette found a place on the top row of the bleachers, where they could stand and have a clear view of the stage. Children, teenagers, and young mothers filled the folding chairs. The Vice Lords cocked their hats to the left; the Disciples to the right.

Lafeyette, in his Chicago Blackhawks starter jacket, looked around the gym for his "associates." Pharoah, dressed in a gray sweatshirt with a drawing of San Francisco's skyline on the front, stood with Porkchop, who restlessly bounced from foot to foot, grinning with excitement. He said little to Pharoah except to nudge him now and then to point out something funny or odd. A teenage boy hawked rainbow-colored fans, though it wasn't very hot in the gym; another sold headbands with SU-BARU printed on front. "Ain't nobody gonna want to buy those," Pharoah told Porkchop, who nodded in agreement.

"How you doing out there?" the show's master of ceremonies, a club staff member, shouted into the microphone. The antiquated sound system made it sound as if he were hollering through a tin can. "Fine!" Pharoah and Lafeyette yelled back in unison with the crowd.

In preparation for the singing of the national anthem, the emcee yelled, "Don't you love this country?"

"Nooooooo," the crowd roared, drowning out Pharoah's meekly spoken "yes." Only a few in the crowd, including Pharoah, placed their hands on their hearts during the anthem's singing.

The first act was one of the crowd's favorites. Five teenage boys from Rockwell Gardens put together a highly choreographed routine. They called themselves the Awesome Force, and introduced themselves by telling the audience their astrological signs. "Hi, I'm Donnell and I'm Pisces, the sign of the fish." The girls in the gym yelled and screamed and nearly fainted at the sight of these young stars. Pharoah bounced to the music as he tried to keep from getting pushed off the bleachers. The gym was getting more and more crowded.

Lafeyette wandered away with a companion. They swiped some straws from the concession stand and snaked through the crowd, blowing spitballs at young girls. *Swwwooosh.* One smacked a girl in the back of her neck. She turned around. "Get your hormones together!" she screamed at her assailants. Lafeyette and the other boy guffawed, repeating the retort to one another with obvious adolescent satisfaction. "Get your hormones together. Maaan, get your hormones together."

Everyone was in good spirits. Even a young overweight girl who sang Keith Sweat's "Make It Last Forever" off key and who was booed off the stage managed a smile at the crowd's reaction. It upset Pharoah, though, who commented to Porkchop, "They booing her. They shouldn't be doing that."

Pharoah and Porkchop giggled at the next performance. A boy about twelve did convincing imitations of Pee-wee Herman and Popeye. Next, a teenage girl in a snug-fitting dress sang "Superwoman," a song made popular by the pop star Karyn White. It had become something of a theme song for the women in the neighborhood, so all the girls in the audience, most of whom were young mothers, sang along, belting out the lyrics. As they harmonized, some turned to their boyfriends with obvious glee.

I'm not your superwoman
I'm not the kind of girl that you can let down
And think that everything's okay
Boy, I am only human
This girl needs more than occasional hugs as a token of love
    from you to me

"Hey, Pharoah." Rickey had spotted his young friend in the bleachers. "Hey, Pharoah." Pharoah clambered down to greet him.

"Wanna hot dog?" Rickey asked.

"Sure," Pharoah replied. He followed Rickey, who bought him a hot dog and pop and also gave Pharoah $2.00.

"Thanks, Rickey."

"You straight, Pharoah." Pharoah rejoined Porkchop and shared the food with him. Rickey returned to his friends.

Late in the evening, a young man got on stage to rap. He looked around the audience. "All the Travelers in here holler travelers." The crowd roared back, "TRAVELERS."

"All the Fours say solid." "SOLID."

"All the Stones says Stone Love." "STONE LOVE."

"All the C's in the house say Conservatives." "CONSERVATIVES."

The gangs had called a truce to attend the talent show.

As the show wound down toward midnight, a rumor floated through the crowd that would prey on both Lafeyette's and Pharoah's minds in the weeks to come. A teenage girl named Alice had been shot in the head four times somewhere farther west. Some had her already dead; others had her holding on for her life. Lafeyette and Pharoah just listened to the talk. They both knew her, though not well. They both prayed for her and asked about her well-being for weeks after.

Lafeyette had looked for Craig Davis at the talent show but couldn't find him. Craig, who had brightened everyone's summer with the dance parties on the front porch, had turned Lafeyette on to music. Lafeyette now listened to cassettes regularly and would often bring the older boy new rap tapes for him to hear.

A few evenings after the show, Lafeyette heard that Craig was in the building, visiting his girlfriend, so he went upstairs to see him. Craig was sitting on the couch, writing a poem. A music tape he'd put together was blaring in the background.

"What it is, Laf," Craig said.

"Hey, Craig." Lafeyette sat down next to the older boy and watched him scribble on a sheet of looseleaf notebook paper. Lafeyette needled him a bit about his girlfriend.

"She gonna be my girlfriend," he told Craig.

"You can have her."

"Okay, I can have her?" Lafeyette said, chuckling to himself. Craig continued to write.

"What you think?" Craig asked, showing Lafeyette the poem. It was entitled "Children of the Future," and though its grammar and spelling were rough, Lafeyette understood it fully. It was an ode to learning. Craig was always telling Lafeyette how important school was.

> I can't blame the teacher for teachen
> I shoulden criticize the speaken
> Because the less I knew the more I weaken

The teacher gave a lesson.
If I was there I learned.
What's the use of letting it go to waste
    win I can show what I earned.
I took advanedge of the education
Not advanedge of it being free
If I took advanedge of both
It wouldn't mean much to me.

"Straight out," said Lafeyette, who was tickled that someone older than he would ask for his opinion. Lafeyette so admired Craig. Despite his kinetic energy, there was something soothing about just being around him. Craig told Lafeyette he was going to dee-jay a party at the Boys Club in a couple of weeks on March 3. He told Lafeyette to stop by.

It was a Thursday in late February, and in the cold and dreariness of a Chicago winter afternoon, Pharoah could be found locked in his bedroom. It was what he had begun to call his "brain day."

Flopped face down on his bed, he had spread about him mimeographed sheets of words, hundreds of words. He was studying for the upcoming spelling bee.

"*Dodgery,*" he asked himself out loud. Looking away from the paper, he spelled the word. Slowly. "D-O-D-G-E-R-Y." If he started to stammer, he'd stop and take a breath. Slow down, he'd tell himself. Slow down. He was in training. Both to learn the words and to conquer his stutter.

One of the triplets, Timothy, banged on the door. "Who's there?" Pharoah asked.

"Me," Timothy said. Curious, like Pharoah himself, he wanted to know what those sounds were coming from the other side of the door. Why was his brother talking to himself?

"What you want?" Pharoah hollered.

"Let me in," Timothy pleaded.

Pharoah opened the door slightly. "I'm studying, Timothy. Now get on outta here." When Timothy took a step into the room, Pharoah swatted his younger brother on the back of his head, hard enough so that Timothy started to cry. It was out of character for Pharoah, but he wasn't messing around. He was going to do okay in this spelling bee. Nothing was going to distract him. Almost every day after school, Pharoah headed directly for his bedroom and went through his practice routine. Sometimes he'd have his mother bring him his dinner so that he didn't have to interrupt his studying. On occasion, Lafeyette joined Pharoah on the bed and, as if he were a Marine drill sergeant, flung words at his brother, hoping to find particularly difficult ones to stump him with. *Obedient. Soybean. Hazardous.* He never asked Pharoah the same word more than twice. If he couldn't get it on the first go-round, he thought, then he never would.

Pharoah also studied hard at school. This year Clarise, one of the school's brightest, was chosen as the other class representative for the bee. An unusually mature fifth-grader, Clarise Gates had been the youngest Suder student selected to travel to Africa. When Pharoah had lost last year, she had pulled him aside and to try to cheer him up, whispering, "That's all right, Pharoah. You know you're gonna win next year."

She and Pharoah liked each other. Both were curious and studious and forever cheerful. They both had wonderfully open smiles. Clarise, though, towered over Pharoah, who was almost six inches shorter than his friend. On Tuesday and Thursday mornings, the two got to school half an hour early so that they could test each other. There were some words Pharoah had trouble pronouncing because of his stutter. "I can't say this right," he'd cry out in frustration. "No such thing as can't," Clarise would remind him, like a mother encouraging her son. And the two would work at sounding out the word, syllable by syllable.

One morning Clarise, with a slight frown on her face, told Pharoah, "I ain't even gonna be in it. I'm gonna let you win it yourself."

"What?" Pharoah cried. He too began to frown. How could his friend desert him?

"Naw, Pharoah, I'm gonna be in it. I was only joking," she assured him. The two giggled and kept at their studying. Over the weeks, as they prepared for the contest, Pharoah and Clarise came to call each other "partner."

• • • •

The week before the spelling bee was a disturbing time for the family. On Friday, February 24, two men, neither of whom lived there, had a fight in the house. A neighbor from upstairs whom everyone knew as Tough Luck had accused a man named Willie, who sold fake jewelry with LaShawn's boyfriend, of stealing a tire from his car. LaJoe had seen the dispute simmering for days—the men had exchanged heated words in the parking lot—so she warned LaShawn about letting Willie and his problems into the apartment.

On this afternoon, Paul and LaJoe's mother were sitting on the sofa when Tough Luck stuck his head through the unlocked door. "Mister Paul," he said, "I just wanna talk to the man who's got my tire." Tough Luck was from the Deep South and still addressed people as "mister" and referred to his car as a "skillet." Willie, who was standing at the end of the hallway, shouted, "Man, I don't have your tire. Just take a tire."

"Mister, I don't want no problem, but I be damned if I'll let anyone take anything from me," Tough Luck said diffidently.

"Willie," Paul urged, "get on out of here with this thing. You too, Tough Luck."

Willie ignored Paul. He got louder. "If you want it, take it. I ain't got nothing. If you can see it, take it. If you insist I took it, I took it!"

Tough Luck's calmness worried Paul. It was, he thought, like the lull before a storm. "Man, give me my tire. My skillet's missing a tire. I ain't gonna let no one take nothing from me," Tough Luck said. He then reached into his back pocket, pulled out a pistol, and shot, almost randomly, at Willie. Paul dove over the couch. Lelia Mae, whose movement was constrained because of her recent stroke, rolled off the sofa onto the floor. "The kids!" she hollered. "The kids!" Pharoah and Lafeyette weren't in the house at the time, but the triplets, who had been watching the argument, ran for the front bedroom, where they took refuge in the doorless closet. They pulled clothes over them as if the fabric offered some protection.

The bullet, which missed Paul by inches, embedded itself in the wall. Tough Luck, who either wasn't a good shot or, as was more likely the case, didn't really want to wound anyone, started moving in on Willie, who jumped into the room with the triplets and pulled a dresser in front of the door. Tough

Luck, in his quiet determination, pushed open the door a few inches and stuck the gun through. Willie slammed the door on his hand. Tough Luck dropped the gun—and then, as calmly as he had entered, left.

When LaJoe arrived, shortly after the shoot-out and just when the police got there, she went into a spiraling rage. She took the elevator to Tough Luck's apartment and banged on his door. "Open this door!" she screamed hysterically. "You came into my house and almost shot my kids. Open the door!" Her friend Rochelle and her neighbor Red had to restrain her. The two brought her back home.

A few days later, Lelia Mae moved out. The ceaseless activity in the apartment had become too much for her. She wished LaJoe wouldn't leave to play cards or to visit Rochelle some nights. And the violence, both inside and outside, brought back memories of her daughter's murder nearly ten years earlier. She made arrangements to live with another one of her daughters, who had her own house. "I already miss my grandma. I hope she come back," Pharoah told his mother. "I don't," said Lafeyette. "There be too much danger over here." LaJoe later covered the bullet hole with a small wicker wallhanging. It was, like much else, a bad memory to be papered over.

Five days later, LaShawn went into labor with her third child. In her seventh month of pregnancy, she had stopped smoking Karachi. She went cold turkey when she was arrested on an old warrant for stealing a car. During those days, she could feel the fetus in her curl up into a tight ball. It went through the withdrawal with her. She wanted a healthy baby.

On March 1, LaShawn went to Rush–Presbyterian–St. Luke's Medical Center, a private hospital where she had given birth to her first two children. She went in around midnight, and the next morning, when the new shift of doctors came on, they determined that she was not yet in labor and sent her to Mount Sinai Hospital, because, they said, that was where she had had her prenatal classes. It was not the first time Rush-Presbyterian had sent a patient elsewhere. Critics called it dumping. A doctor at Cook County Hospital, which sits just across the street from Rush and is the hospital of last resort for Chicago's poor, told the story of a pregnant woman who, kicked out of Rush, presumably because she was on public aid, gave birth to her child as she tried to walk across the street to the neighboring hospital.

A few days later, at Mount Sinai, LaShawn gave birth to a five-pound-fourteen-ounce boy, whom she named DeShaun. He was tested and found to have opiates and cocaine in his system and so had to stay six days at the hospital while the Department of Child and Family Services paid LaShawn a home visit. DCFS eventually permitted the child to go home. LaJoe and the boys helped care for him.

Despite this flurry of activity in the family, Pharoah remained remarkably focused on the spelling bee. He and Lafeyette talked about the Tough Luck shooting as if it were the most natural of occurrences. Pharoah didn't tell Clarise about it. Even the triplets, one of whom later found the bullet for the police, enjoyed recounting the events of that morning. As for DeShaun, both Lafeyette and Pharoah viewed the new addition to the family with a combination of worry and pleasure. They were concerned that yet another baby would stretch the family's resources; it meant more money for things like diapers and clothes. It also worried LaJoe that the drugs might have had an effect on him. But LaJoe and both boys, Lafeyette in particular, adored small children, and the idea of another baby to cuddle excited them.

Pharoah, perhaps in anticipation of the spelling bee, began having pleasant dreams, one of which he particularly liked to recall. In it, he was a grown man looking for employment, and people down the street were calling him because they thought they might have a job for him. Pharoah was so touched by the fantasy that he remembered the smallest of details, like the blossoming white roses he could see from his office window and his new clothes: a starched white shirt and blue tie with matching vest and pants, and spanking new black shoes. He had indeed gotten the job, and at work people started calling him "the brain." He can't recall what kind of work the job entailed, though he had "a big metal desk, a pencil sharpener, a paperweight, and papers spread all over." He does, however, remember how good the dream made him feel: "I started thinking about if I do be a lawyer or something, then I'd make a better living and my mama be outta the projects."

He had also recently finished reading *Old Yeller*, a book about a boy and his dog. It was, he told his mother, one of his favorites because "Old Yeller used to fight other animals for [the boy]. I believe the others would be dead" had it not been for Old Yeller. Pharoah was also taken by "the way the boy talked so country," and, trying not to giggle, he launched into a perfect imitation of a Southern accent: "Ain't nawbody gonna take ma dawg." LaJoe thought Pharoah was managing to control his stutter. Maybe he'd do better in the spelling bee this year. She knew how much it meant to him.

Spring 1989

Twenty

ON THURSDAY, March 2, winter seemed intent on unleashing some of its final fury. The day began with a soft, comforting snowfall, but by midafternoon, when the temperature rose to the 20s, the swirling snowflakes turned to hard-driving droplets of frozen rain. Coupled with the thin layer of snow already covering the ground, it made for an icy and slippery turf. Had Craig Davis been able to foresee the ugly intersecting of forces that night—the wretched weather, official duty, and lonely fear—he might have stayed inside. But Craig wasn't one to sit still.

Craig left work that afternoon and headed directly to Henry Horner to visit his girlfriend. He had graduated from Cregier High School two months earlier and quickly landed a job as a stockboy at Order from Horder, a stationery store chain. He worked at one of the downtown stores, where he earned $4.50 an hour. Craig so impressed the manager there, Percy Anderson, that he was thinking of training Craig in sales. "He caught on fast," said Anderson.

That evening, Craig briefly visited with his girlfriend and then took the bus home. Craig lived with his uncle and his uncle's girlfriend in a two-story row house in the ABLA Homes. ABLA differed from the other projects in that it included both high-rises and row houses. The latter, many felt, were preferable to the sixteen-story fortresses, but, like the tall buildings, they were in terrible physical condition. What's more, they were laid out in such a confusing way that strangers walking through the maze often got hopelessly lost.

With his customary high spirits, Craig greeted his uncle and his uncle's girlfriend, and placed on a set of speakers two albums he had just purchased, Frankie Knuckles's *You Can't Hide* and Dada Nada's *Haunted House*. He grabbed a turntable needle and two cassette tapes of rap and pop music he had assembled. He stuffed the tapes and needle in his pockets. Craig always had music with him. During lunch at his job, he would sit in back of the store listening to tapes on his headphones. Tomorrow night was his debut as a dee-jay at the Henry Horner Boys Club.

"I'm going right out. To a friend's. Be back real soon," Craig yelled to his uncle.

"Are you coming right back?" the uncle asked.

"Yeah," Craig replied as he trotted out the door.

Craig was on his way to pick up two turntables and speakers from a friend's for tomorrow night's dance. His uncle, who knew Craig went to bed by eleven every night, left the door unlocked.

Francis Higgins and Richard Marianos cruised the streets of ABLA in their unmarked sedan. Higgins, thirty-four, was a Chicago police officer assigned to a new gun task force devoted solely to investigating the illegal shipment of arms. In its first four and a half months, the unit, whose members called themselves the Gunbusters, had seized 334 guns. Marianos, twenty-three, was an agent for the Bureau of Alcohol, Tobacco, and Firearms, a division of the U.S. Treasury Department. The Bureau of Alcohol, Tobacco, and Firearms, or ATF, originated in the 1920s to battle Prohibition; the famed Eliot Ness was an ATF agent. But the last illegal still in Chicago was discovered in 1980. Tobacco no longer occupied much of the bureau's time either. Occasionally, the agents captured illegal interstate shipments of cigarettes.

So, over the last ten years most of ATF's work had been focused on firearms. With the rise in drugs, the weaponry had become sophisticated. The ATF had seen more and more automatic weapons, including Uzi machine guns, Mac 10s, and Intertec 9s. Only three weeks earlier, the ATF and the Gunbusters, working in tandem, had raided two suburban homes, where they confiscated twenty-three live grenades, ten fully automatic machine guns, thirty-one handguns, seven sawed-off shotguns, a semi-automatic weapon, a cluster bomb, and thousands of rounds of ammunition. The police believed these guns belonged to a west side gang that used the suburban homes as safe houses. This night, though, Marianos and Higgins were looking for someone they knew only as "Craig" and who they'd heard had purchased a sawed-off shotgun in recent days.

While driving through the labyrinth of ABLA's streets, the two officers came on three teenage boys, including Craig, on the 1300 block of Thirteenth Street. The boys were on their way to pick up the stereo equipment. It wasn't clear why the police thought they looked suspicious or had any cause to stop them. It was only eight at night and, though dark, certainly early enough for teenagers to be walking about. One of the boys, Craig Davis, on seeing the two white officers, turned to one of his friends. "I ain't going to no jail again," he said.

Five months earlier, Craig had been arrested with four others for allegedly stealing cookies from a delivery truck. It had been his first arrest and was such an upsetting experience, he had cried. He had been recording music tapes at a friend's when the police came in on another matter and saw boxes of chocolate chip cookies in the living room. The police arrested all five boys in the apartment. When Craig was released the next morning, he told his uncle's girlfriend he hadn't had anything to do with taking the cookies. He had just been at his friend's mixing tapes. Now, Craig feared the police, so on this cold night he ran. Craig, everyone said, was always moving. He took off, and took off fast.

Marianos, only a few years older than Craig, gave chase. Higgins meanwhile questioned the remaining two youths. In a later police report, Higgins said they told him the boy who had run was named Craig. They say, however, that they refused to give the police Craig's name. Higgins let the two boys go and caught up with his winded partner a couple of blocks away. Craig had eluded Marianos.

The boys saw Craig one more time. Having outmaneuvered Marianos, Craig was intent on picking up the stereo equipment for his big debut the next night. From about a half block away, Craig spotted his friends and hollered at them, "Let's get them turntables!" At that point, the squad car turned the corner. Marianos got out of the car and resumed the chase.

They ran down one street and up another, then through a darkened breezeway. Marianos lost sight of Craig for "a split second," according to a later police investigation, and so unholstered his service revolver, a .357 Smith and Wesson. Craig turned to his left to get back to the safety of his uncle's house. Marianos caught up with him there, grabbed him from behind, and shoved him up against the wall.

Marianos had his revolver near Craig's head. He later told homicide detectives that Craig struggled, that he "began to twist and turn his body and then reached over his shoulder and made contact" with Marianos's right hand. But the medical examiner's report later cited evidence of "soot staining within the wound," which indicated that the barrel of the gun may have been pressed up against Craig's skull when it discharged. Whatever the case, it appeared that Marianos slipped and fell backward onto the fresh sheet of ice, and when he did, the Smith and Wesson accidentally discharged.

The pop of the pistol echoed off the brick row houses. But few paid much attention to it. There had, after all, been gunshots just about every night in recent weeks.

Craig's mother, Christine Davis, who lived on the fourteenth floor of a high-rise just a block away, heard the shot as she returned from buying cigarettes and a six-pack of beer at a local store. People started running around her. "They shot some nigger," she heard someone say. She hurried to her apartment to avoid the scene that was sure to follow.

Even Daniel Davis, Craig's uncle, thought nothing of the noise outside his door. "When we heard the shot, we just figured it was more shooting," he later said. "They got a lot of shooting around here." Ten minutes later, when it was clear from the commotion that someone had indeed been wounded outside his apartment, he opened the door.

There lay Craig face down in a pool of blood, which seemed startlingly red and thick against the thin layer of white snow and ice.

The police had strung yellow tape from tree to tree to keep the angry spectators at a distance.

"You shouldn't done that!" someone yelled.

"We see you 'round here, man, we're gonna kill you!" The anonymous threats rose from the growing crowd.

"Them sons of bitches shot him in cold blood," one resident said to another. "They ain't got no reason to have done that."

"Man, who care? They don't. It's just another nigger to them."

An acquaintance of Craig's banged on his mother's front door. At the same time, she received a phone call from a friend. They both told her, almost simultaneously, that her son had been shot. Christine raced downstairs to the low-rises, where she learned that Craig was being taken to Mount Sinai Hospital, the very place where she had given birth to him. Some friends offered to drive her there.

The medical technicians in the ambulance had hooked Craig up to an IV and administered oxygen. They attached him to a cardiac monitor, which showed no activity. By the time they got him to the hospital, Craig had no blood pressure, pulse, or respiration. Four doctors administered cardiac massage. They injected him with adrenaline and atropine in the hope that they could stimulate the heart into pumping again. They then tried shocking the heart. No response. In the meantime, X-rays showed that the bullet, which had entered through the back of the head, had fragmented through both hemispheres of the brain. Craig Davis was pronounced dead at 8:48 P.M.

• • • •

A spokesman for the ATF told reporters that Craig was a Black Gangster Disciple and suspected gun runner. Two days later, a one-paragraph account of the shooting appeared in *The Chicago Sun-Times:*

> A reputed street gang member was fatally shot Thursday night when a federal agent's revolver discharged during a scuffle, investigators said. Craig Davis, 19, of 1262 S. Throop, who was shot once in the head, was pronounced dead at Michael Reese Hospital [sic]. A spokesman for the federal Alcohol, Tobacco and Firearms Bureau said the agent and a Chicago police gang crimes officer approached Davis to interview him about illegal firearms trafficking and Davis grabbed the agent, touching off the scuffle.

Twenty-one

ON FRIDAY, March 3, the day of the spelling
bee, Pharoah looked his best. The night before he
had washed his good clothes in the bathtub and
then dried them with a fan. This morning, he ironed his ever-
green-colored sweater and a pair of new blue jeans on the
family's makeshift ironing board, a broken microwave oven.
And he shined his Fila high-tops with white shoe polish. After
he was dressed, he sneaked into his brother Weasel's room to use
some of his cologne; he patted the strong fragrance on his neck
and cheeks. If he was going to be in front of a big crowd, he

wasn't going to let people talk nasty about him. He appraised himself in the mirror and turned to the side, fidgeting with his sweater. He looked okay.

When Pharoah got to school, Clarise couldn't believe her eyes. She'd never seen Pharoah looking so natty. And that smell! What was he doing, wearing cologne? Clarise giggled to herself. "I couldn't believe that was Pharoah that day," she said later. Clarise had dressed up, too, though she didn't look quite as spiffy as her friend. She wore yellow jogging pants and a clean white shirt with an emblem of a small mouse. She had curled her hair for the occasion.

The two contestants, Clarise and Pharoah, led their fifth-grade class into the gymnasium, and as they entered Clarise leaned over to whisper, "Pharoah, if I miss, you keep on going for our class."

"You do the same," he replied.

Pharoah seemed surprisingly calm. He wasn't wringing his hands or balling them up under his sweater as he'd done last time. Nor was he bouncing from foot to foot as he was apt to do when he got antsy. Yet, though nobody could tell, he was nervous. He didn't want to stutter and mess up again. He felt confident he could spell well enough to win, but he reminded himself all morning to take his time and to speak slowly.

Their teacher, Mr. Rogers, who was at Suder only temporarily, promised them a party if either of them won. "Good luck," he said, patting the two children on their backs. Pharoah and Clarise marched onto the wooden stage.

The judge ran through the rules, though Pharoah and Clarise hardly listened. Pharoah was too busy thinking about not stuttering. When his turn came, he stood poised and ready.

"*Acceptable*," the judge said. "*Acceptable.*" Pharoah drew a deep breath and took his time.

"*Acceptable*," Pharoah repeated. "A-C-C-E-P"—he pulled the microphone down toward him so that his voice would be amplified—"T-A-B-L-E. *Acceptable.*" He went to the back of the line.

Clarise, shaking slightly from nerves, was given the word *abdicate*.

"*Abdicate*," she repeated, in a forceful voice that carried through the gymnasium. She almost shouted the individual letters into the microphone. "*Abdicate.*"

By the third round, four students had missed words. It was Pharoah's turn again. As the contest progressed, he felt more self-assured. Nary a stutter, and the competition was nearly half over.

"*Aerial,*" the judge said. "*Aerial.*" Pharoah wasn't sure how to spell it. He'd never seen the word in print. He wasn't even quite sure what it meant. He paused and then guessed.

"A," he said tentatively, almost asking. No buzzer. Fifteen seconds elapsed. E-R-I-A-L." He thought he'd gotten it wrong and, his head bowed, started to head for the steps off the stage.

"Come back. That was right," the judge yelled out to him.

"It was?" Pharoah said in disbelief. Mr. Rogers gave him an okay sign with his hand. Students giggled. Pharoah put his hands over his eyes in embarrassment.

The words kept coming, round after round, until there were only three contestants left: Pharoah, Clarise, and a boy named William. William went first.

"*Amendment,*" the judge said. "*Amendment.*"

"*Amendment,*" William repeated. "A-M-E-N-D-M-A-N-T. *Amendment.*" The buzzer sounded, and William walked off the stage. Pharoah broke into a big grin and, as if he'd just scored the final point of a basketball game, threw a fist into the air. He quickly caught himself and pulled his hand down. But he didn't stop smiling. He was guaranteed at least second place. Now it was between him and Clarise. Both wished they could have stopped right there and shared first place, neither wanted the other to lose.

Clarise got the word *catbird.*

"*Catbird.*" She enunciated each letter with precision and punctuation. She liked compound words; they were easier to sound out in your head. "*Catbird.*"

The judge gave Pharoah *cellblock.*

"*Cellblock.* S-A-L-E-B-L-O-C-K. *Cellblock.*" The buzzer sounded. Clarise now had to spell it right to win. She stepped up to the microphone and twisted it so that she didn't have to bend over.

"*Cellblock.* S-A-I-L-B-L-O-C-K. *Cellblock.*" The buzzer sounded again. They would get one more word, the judge told them. Otherwise, he'd declare it a tie.

"*Darken,*" the judge said. "*Darken.*" Clarise looked at her partner. She knew how to spell it. Pharoah wasn't so sure. But he proceeded as if he knew. He couldn't or wouldn't lose it now.

"*Darken,*" he repeated. "D-A-R-K"—he hesitated for a moment—"I-N. *Darken.*" The buzzer sounded. He'd gotten it wrong. Now, Clarise had to spell it correctly. She stepped confidently to the microphone.

"*Darken,*" she repeated. "D-A-R-K-E-N. *Darken.*" Her classmates erupted in wild applause. Pharoah might have been upset, except that he was happy for his friend and satisfied with second place. The two children embraced each other, their faces radiant in victory.

"Congratulations," they muttered to each other. Pharoah felt good. He'd accomplished what he'd set out to do. He hadn't stuttered. Not once. Not even close. From her seat in the audience, their fourth-grade teacher, Ms. Barone, thought her two former students looked proud and charming in their celebration. She had never doubted they would win. Huge grins covered both their faces. Pharoah thrust his fist into the air, waving it back and forth. This time, he didn't bring it back down.

In his joy, Pharoah alternately skipped and ran home from school, a pad of paper and a textbook clutched tightly in one hand, his red ribbon flapping in the other. He couldn't wait to tell his mother of his triumph and show her his award. He had kept his promise. Though not the champion, he had done better than last year.

Pharoah pushed open the door to the apartment, which his mother left unlocked when school let out. Everyone and everything was eerily quiet. The television was turned down. The triplets were in their room. Pharoah could even hear the running bathtub through the closed bathroom door. Lafeyette sat perched by the window on the microwave-turned-ironing board, his arms around his bent knees. He strained to hear the conversation at the kitchen table between LaJoe, Rochelle, and a neighbor, Clementine, whom everyone called Dutt; it was conducted in hollow whispers.

Pharoah first stood at the entranceway—"That little round pie of a face," his mother later recalled, "it looked like the pie had just got cut all up and ate up; he was so happy"—and then went to his mother's side, thrusting the ribbon in her lap. "I-I-I c-c-came in second place." In his excitement and in the spooky stillness, his stutter had returned.

LaJoe returned Pharoah's smile. "Second place; that's still good."

"Mama, if-if-if I hadn't m-m-missed a word . . ." He stumbled over his words and for a moment, flustered by the silence, lost his train of thought. "You know what they do?"

"What?"

"If-if you m-m-miss a word, Mama, they make you just get off the stage. That was so embarrassing to peoples. And, and w-w-when I saw that I couldn't miss a word . . ." He told his mother that he had slipped up on the word *darken* when he substituted an *i* for the *e*.

"I-I-I-I knew right away it was wrong. My-my-my, you know, my heart, my heart was beating so fast," he told her, the words streaming out of his mouth.

Pharoah realized that something was terribly wrong. He didn't want to ask. No one seemed to care about his spelling bee triumph. No one wanted to hear what he had to say. Dutt was weeping. Lafeyette, while he had one ear to the conversation, stared vacantly out the window; he didn't even congratulate Pharoah. LaJoe tucked Pharoah's red ribbon into her pocketbook. (She would later display it in the living room alongside three achievement certificates earned by the triplets.) The family had just minutes earlier learned of Craig Davis's death the night before.

LaJoe turned from Pharoah to Dutt, whose daughter had been Craig's girlfriend and who felt partly responsible for Craig's death. Last night, when Craig came over to the house to visit her daughter, she had gotten into a minor spat with the boy, so he had left. If she had let him stay, she told LaJoe, maybe he wouldn't have been shot. LaJoe tried to comfort her.

"You know God, it's up to him when you going to come and it's up to him when you leave," LaJoe told her neighbor. "In what way, I ain't sure about no more, but if it's time for you to go, you're going to go and it wasn't up to you. If he had stayed and you hadn't exchanged words and you hadn't asked him to leave, it probably would of still happened."

For much of the rest of the afternoon, the three women remained at the table, sometimes talking, sometimes sitting in silence. Lafeyette huddled on the microwave still as a statue, neither crying nor talking, listening alternately to the subdued conversation and to the roar of the El. During one long pause in the conversation, Lafeyette spoke, his voice flat and tired.

"He didn't have to die like that." His stare was directed at his mother. "He had to die the way that he lived, God's way. You die the way that you live and Craig wasn't bad, so why him?" LaJoe didn't know how to respond; she felt the same way. She said nothing. Lafeyette returned to looking out the window, his face taut.

In the meantime, Pharoah had shuffled out the door, unnoticed. This was not the time or the place to celebrate his spelling victory. He went to play with Porkchop in the second-floor hallway. "I don't like to see nobody sad," he said later.

Craig's funeral was nothing like Bird Leg's. For starters, it was held at night. And it was conducted at the A. R. Leak Funeral Home, one of the city's oldest and most esteemed black-owned funeral homes, a stark contrast to the storefront church where Bird Leg was memorialized. Sam Cooke, the rhythm and blues singer, had been put to rest here, as had Flukey Stokes, a notorious gambler and suspected drug dealer. Over five thousand people had viewed Stokes's body, which lay in a coffin built in the shape of a Cadillac.

Of the funeral home's four chapels, the Mahalia Jackson Room was the smallest. The room welcomed visitors with a black-and-white photo of Jackson—"The World's Greatest Gospel Singer," the caption read—and was decorated in varying shades of green; the patterned wallpaper in emerald green, the lush carpeting the color of well-watered grass. The room seated two hundred, but at Craig's funeral an additional fifty to a hundred mourners stood along the walls, overflowing into the hallway outside.

Craig, whose head wound had been stuffed with cotton and sutured to prevent any leakage, was dressed in a fitted navy blue suit and light blue shirt and tie, all of which his mother had bought for $154. The casket's baby blue paint job contrasted sharply with the dark occasion, but the cheerful color seemed to brighten Craig, who even in death looked happy, his lips turned up slightly in a smile.

It was clear from the size of the crowd that Craig had many admirers. Six former teachers attended, one of whom had saved some of Craig's writings and now planned to have them framed. Those teachers who couldn't attend contributed $100 to the family. Children from both ABLA and Henry Horner were there, as were colleagues from work, including his boss, Percy Anderson. Flowers, almost an entire garden, it seemed, surrounded the casket. One bouquet had been sent by his teachers at Cregier, another by his co-workers at the stationery store. Two bunches had been sent by the residents of two different highrises in the public housing complex where Craig grew up. And as tradition asked, Craig's mother had contributed "a bleeding heart," a set of pink and white carnations arranged in the shape of a heart with a cluster of red roses in the center.

Lafeyette came with LaJoe, who despised funerals as much as her son did. LaJoe knew Craig only from the dances in front of the building, but she understood how much he had meant to Lafeyette, so she wanted to be here with him. Lafeyette was older now and had abandoned the corduroys and nylon jacket he wore to Bird Leg's funeral; instead, he wore a dapper blue, high-waisted silk suit that Terence, when he was making money selling drugs, had had made for himself. It no longer fit Terence, but clung to the sticklike frame of Lafeyette as if it had been tailored for him. Lafeyette also wore a white, furry Kangol cap, shaped like a golf cap, which made him look older, almost as if he were from a different era. LaJoe wore a gray dress given her by a friend who had outgrown it. Together, they made a handsome pair.

Pharoah chose not to come. He said it was because he didn't have anything to wear, but more likely he didn't want to be amid all the crying. He didn't like to be around sad people, particularly if he knew he couldn't cheer them up.

James, who wept when he first heard of Craig's death, had thought of coming, too. His mother was there; in fact, she read the obituary at the opening of the service. But James turned fifteen that day and he felt it would bring him bad luck to attend a funeral on his birthday.

In the Mahalia Jackson Room, the crowd was unusually still.

Few cried. Even fewer yelled out for Craig as they had done for Bird Leg. Few mentioned the killing, though it was referred to once in the sermon, and then only obliquely as "the tragedy." It was as if friends and family were burying an older man who had died of natural causes.

The silence, though, extended far beyond the funeral. Silence shrouded Craig's death. Neither the police nor the Bureau of Alcohol, Tobacco, and Firearms had contacted Craig's mother. No phone call of apology or explanation. No letter. No telegram. Not even, Christine thought, flowers. She spent four days after his death trying to learn what had happened. She visited the police, the state authorities, and eventually the ATF. But she learned nothing. The ATF told her they couldn't talk with her because the shooting was under investigation. We'll get back in touch with you, they said. They never did.

The ATF continued to tell reporters that Craig had been a Black Gangster Disciple. One of Craig's teachers angrily said it was a way to justify his death. Of eighteen thousand names the police had on file of people affiliated with the city's west side gangs, Craig Davis was not among them. Moreover, Craig had no criminal record as a juvenile and had been arrested only once as an adult, and that was for allegedly stealing the cookies, a crime he had insisted he hadn't done. When he died, the medical examiner found no trace of alcohol or drugs in his blood. His teachers and the principal at Cregier, all of whom thought the world of Craig, knew of no gang affiliation. Nor did his friends. And, people would point out, had he been a member of the Black Gangster Disciples he never would have been allowed to visit Lafeyette's building, which was controlled by the Gangster Stones and the Vice Lords, both rival gangs. Even a policeman who knew Craig from Horner had only good things to say about him.

It wasn't impossible that Craig had purchased a sawed-off shotgun. All the adults knew it was hard to resist the lures of the neighborhood. But no one close to Craig knew anything about any gun running by the boy. Friends said he avoided hanging out with known drug dealers and gang leaders. The police never produced any evidence. His mother just wanted to know what happened that night, why they stopped her son. Was it a case of mistaken identity? Did they have the wrong Craig?

Had he, in fact, bought a shotgun? She couldn't find out. Other than the initial press release, the police and the ATF refused to say anything about the case. They ruled it an accidental homicide.

Christine also never heard from the Chicago Housing Authority, on whose property the killing took place. The least they could have done, she thought, was to visit her and offer her condolences. But the CHA didn't learn of Craig's death until weeks later. The ATF never called them, either. Even when CHA officials tried to inquire about it, they could learn nothing.

Shortly after the shooting, a police neighborhood relations officer did visit with community leaders, but more to quash rumors—including one that Craig had been shot while handcuffed. Neighbors and friends who now worried about the safety of their own children were afraid to talk about the shooting. Cregier's principal, Ray Gerlik, who believed that "Craig was done wrong," urged Craig's friends who had been with him the night of the killing to go to the police, but he had trouble convincing them. They were afraid that they themselves might become the subject of an investigation.

"People are scared," said one friend, a student at Cregier. "Who wouldn't be? This is the FBI [sic]. They'd find out where you live. They'd get you before you even testify."

Neighbors recalled the Soto brothers' incident of twenty years earlier with a kind of wistfulness. It was not that they wanted the horrible bloodshed. Nor was it that they wanted to rise up in arms against the police again. It was just that they ached for a time when the community had a collective conscience, when neighbors trusted one another and had enough confidence in their own powers of persuasion to demand a better and more peaceful life. Everyone now seemed timid and afraid. Their whispers damning the police and the ATF fluttered weightlessly like leaves in the wind.

The community itself turned inward, sorry for Craig's family, but worried about their own well-being. The major newspapers ignored the incident. The police and the ATF simply refused to discuss it, as if by remaining mute they would somehow make people forget. Christine Davis considered filing a civil suit.

The preacher's voice reverberated among the mourners, but his protestations seemed empty at such a tragic occasion. "Craig was no gang member," he bellowed, his words barely reaching the mourners standing in the back. "There is drugs, lots of dope out there, but Craig would have none of that. Oh, he had a temper among friends, but he knew enough to walk away from trouble." His voice reached a crescendo; it was the only moment of untamed anger. "HE KNEW ENOUGH TO WALK AWAY FROM TROUBLE," he repeated. "Amen," some muttered to themselves. "Amen."

The minister continued. "But he knew his time had come. He was going home. He was going home." His gravelly, evangelical voice called for some response, some cries of sorrow and pain, some recognition of the tragedy, but the room, except for a bawling baby, remained hushed. You could hear people folding the mimeographed programs and shifting in their chairs, and through the thin walls the cries of a grieving woman in the room next door.

Lafeyette didn't stay for the service. When he had first arrived and viewed Craig's body, he pictured the summer evenings spent dancing by the porch, of a laughing and joking Craig spinning records, his body swaying in time to the music. He couldn't get out of his mind the image of Craig waving to him. Each of those evenings was a time when the present, the here-and-now, had seemed good enough to Lafeyette, one of those rare moments when he wasn't haunted by the past or worried about the future. Lafeyette couldn't get those snapshots of memory off his mind. So, early in the service, he neatly folded the funeral program, slipped it into his back pocket, and shuffled out of the chapel into the crowded hallway, where he slumped into an armchair. He bent over in the plush gold chair, his chest pulled down to his knees. His face tightened, his expression became flat and vacant. He was unwilling, perhaps unable, to cry. Only his rust-colored eyes offered any hint of his anguish. Underneath them were two puffy, dark circles. He spoke to no one. He pulled the silence in around him.

Craig's death, LaJoe believed, broke Lafeyette. From that day on, she said, he started thinking, "I ain't doing nothing, I could get killed, or if not get killed I might go to jail for something I didn't do. I could die any minute, so I ain't going to be scared of nothing."

For weeks afterward, LaJoe felt Lafeyette personally carrying the burden of Craig's death, as if there were something he might have done to help his friend. Lafeyette rarely mentioned Craig. He didn't want to talk about him. "I don't want nothing on my mind," he would say. Memories for Lafeyette became dangerous. He recalled nothing of Bird Leg's funeral. He couldn't remember the names of any of the performers at the talent show. He sometimes had trouble recounting what he had done just the day before in school. Shutting out the past was perhaps the only way he could go forward or at least manage the present. Besides, he knew, nothing could bring Craig back.

He fell into a deep depression, collapsing in bed immediately after school and sleeping long hours. And when the outward grief diminished in intensity, his distrust of others built—and his memory failed him more. He soon affected a long, jerky gait in which his upper body leaned forward as if it had been re-aligned; his eyes locked with the ground as if to block out others around him. He no longer looked thirteen; his bobbing, cocky walk made him look older.

Many weeks after the funeral, in one of the rare moments when Lafeyette talked about Craig, he asserted with a controlled anger that unnerved those around him: "He wasn't no gangbanger. They lied. If I was Craig's mama or daddy I would of walked up to that police and shot him in the head the same way he did Craig. I hope the policeman dies."

Only two days after Craig's funeral, Lafeyette lost yet another friend, Damien Russell.

Everybody called him Scooter. Scooter lived in the building across the playground from the Riverses. A couple of years older than Lafeyette, Scooter hung out with a different crowd, but Lafeyette knew him and liked him and felt sorry for him, because he'd heard that his mother was hooked on cocaine. Scooter spent a lot of his time on the streets.

Twenty minutes after midnight on March 12, Scooter and four other friends were tooling around in a stolen Oldsmobile. As the black sedan pulled down Wood Street going south from Horner, it passed a police car going in the opposite direction.

The fourteen-year-old driver slumped down in the seat. The officers were suspicious; they made a U-turn and began to follow the car with the five boys. Before they could even give chase, though, the sedan picked up speed. No one is certain how fast it was traveling, though some estimates put it at over sixty miles per hour. It ran a stop light and two traffic lights and then suddenly spun out of control. Like a top, it kept twirling until it careered into a light pole. The car hit the steel pole smack in the middle, just about where the two passenger doors met. No one, it appeared, was wearing a seat belt.

The car's interior was so mangled that it was impossible to tell where each of the boys had been sitting. The first police officer on the scene had to count the dangling arms to determine the number of passengers in the wreck. By the time the firemen were able to cut them out, two of the boys, including Scooter, were dead of massive internal injuries. Another died later in the hospital. The oldest of the three was fifteen. The driver, who had fled the accident, was later found guilty of three counts of reckless homicide.

When Lafeyette heard the news the next day, he didn't change expression. He just asked his mother not to talk about Scooter. "Let him rest," he urged her. "The [death] train done got him and he's gone. Why you gotta talk about him?"

He told his mother he didn't want to attend another funeral.

Twenty-two

THE MARBLE-SIZE HAIL crashed relentlessly off the sidewalk, the ice bouncing with the vigor of Ping-Pong balls. The children sprinted home from school on this Thursday, March 16, protecting their small heads with worn and tattered textbooks held high. They screamed in amusement and pain as the freezing rain pounded away at them. Pharoah, wearied from his short battle with the weather, straggled through the door and threw himself onto the couch, where, with his wet and dirty high-tops tucked beneath him, he sat for a moment to catch his breath. Lafeyette followed.

"Take your feet off the couch," he ordered Pharoah, who covered his mouth, sheepish at his indiscretion.

"Oh," he muttered, and sat upright.

It had been one week since Craig's funeral, and Lafeyette still had an edge about him. If he didn't fall asleep directly after school, he found some activity to busy himself with. Today, as his mother often did when she was upset, he cleaned. Sometimes he would spend an evening rearranging the living room furniture, so that during a year, the couch, chairs, and coffee table might be shuffled about nearly a dozen times.

Lafeyette hung up his jacket on the metal coat rack and then picked up a broom and began sweeping around the plastic receptacle in the kitchen, overflowing with food scraps, mostly cereal, which the children ate at all times of the day. Pharoah, the triplets, and their niece, eight-year-old Tyisha, lazily huddled on the couch to watch Popeye cartoons. With LaJoe out looking for work—she had gone to a local hospital to file a job application, Lafeyette filled in for her. He did so whenever she was away, assuming the role of parent and keeper of the house. At times he seemed like a thirteen-year-old manchild.

"Clean up that table, Timothy!" he shouted as he moved the broom back and forth in brisk strokes. "You don't clean that up, you ain't gonna watch any TV." A crumpled bag and other papers lay scattered on the heavy, wooden coffee table; Timothy, though, moved slowly, as if an invisible force were keeping him away from the table and its mess. He continued to sit on the sofa, his thumb in his mouth, his eyes riveted on Popeye; but he leaned forward, as if that position might make him seem in motion toward the clutter on the table.

Luckily for him, for Lafeyette had begun making threatening thrusts with the broom, Brian's brother, Larry, who had been staying in the apartment, walked through the door. Lafeyette liked Larry, who was good-natured, high-spirited, and easy to make laugh, but he resented that Larry's "freeloading" off his family. Larry got two feet into the living room when Lafeyette sighted him.

"Mop the kitchen," Lafeyette ordered. Larry ignored him and headed for a back room. "You gonna have to do something.

You ain't living free, punk," Lafeyette yelled at Larry's back as the guest disappeared.

"Man, you two, get them toys outta here. Put them in your closet. Come on. Get up." Tiffany and Tammie were his next targets, and, like Timothy, they tried to disregard their moody brother.

"You heard me. Get them toys outta here! OUTTA HERE! BEFORE I HIT YOU." Both girls started to cry. "MAN, JUST PICK UP THEM THINGS!"

Lafeyette turned and, like a ferocious factory foreman, began barking out orders faster than anyone could respond—and making threats if they didn't.

"Timothy, tell Tyisha to come and throw away that garbage. I'm cutting off that TV until this is clean. YOU HEAR ME? ALL OF YOUS! I'M CUTTING OFF THE TV UNTIL THIS IS CLEAN . . . COMPLETELY!"

Tyisha was a tomboy who could tussle effectively with both Lafeyette and Pharoah. When she once flexed her arm muscles for Pharoah, she tauntingly teased him, "Boys supposed to have muscles and you don't have any." She shuffled into the living room, defiantly challenging her uncle.

"Empty that garbage," Lafeyette ordered.

"I'll think about it," she retorted sassily even as she reluctantly dragged the bulging yellow plastic garbage bag through the living room and out the door.

Pharoah, to escape the wrath of his irritated and still grieving brother, had chosen to sweep the bathrooms, where he could be neither seen nor heard.

"Hurry up, Pharoah. Mop the bathrooms," Lafeyette hollered down the hallway.

"I'm doing it! I'm doing it!" Pharoah shrieked. "Stop speedballing."

Lafeyette marched to the back of the house, kicked open the bathroom door, which Pharoah had thought to shut, and examined the forever dark and dusty floor.

"Clean it up right like everybody else," he chastened Pharoah, who glared at his brother. "CLEAN IT UP!"

As Lafeyette left, Pharoah muttered under his breath, softly enough that his brother wouldn't hear, but loud enough to retain his pride, "Shut up."

The house had echoed with cacophony as the six children fought and cleaned and called each other names. Lafeyette swept a pile of garbage onto the slat of cardboard they used for a dustpan, and placed it in another full garbage bag.

"Start getting up this trash. Didn't I tell y'all?" Lafeyette barked at no one in particular. "Tyisha, take this out. You ain't taken but one." As Tyisha lugged the second bag out the door, mumbling her gripes under her breath, she took her uncle on.

"Sissy!" she shouted, running out the door, the bag bumping and clanging against the floor.

"I told you not to call me that. YOU HEAR ME? I told you not to call me that!" Tyisha was by then too far down the hall to hear or to care.

Long after the others had stopped cleaning, Lafeyette continued to arrange the chairs and coffee table so that they looked neat and orderly and to sweep the linoleum and rugs. He straightened the pendulum clock that hung in the kitchen and that permanently read 5:25, the time it read when Lelia Mae gave it to LaJoe as a present. It had stopped working on its first day. Lafeyette fidgeted with the collection of knickknacks and mementoes on the two diamond-shaped metal shelves, which were rickety and wobbly to the touch. As if playing three-card monte, he switched around the framed color photographs of each of the triplets as well as framed pictures of himself and Pharoah. He straightened a six-inch-high pair of white hands in prayer and moved forward on the shelf a green ceramic frog, which was missing its right front leg. And he picked up an iron likeness of a grazing horse. He held up the statuette and admired its grace and beauty and then put it back. It was as if he were looking for answers from the stallion.

The younger children quickly learned, in these days and weeks following Craig's death, that it was best to leave Lafeyette alone; he had become irritable and, on occasion, violent, like the time he punched Pharoah in the eye, all because Pharoah tried to finesse a seat by the window in a friend's car. "I'm gonna tell Mama," Pharoah had threatened through his tears. "When we get outta here nothing's gonna stop me from hitting you with a rock."

Lafeyette, despite his orneriness and unusually hot temper, had shrugged and laughed nervously; he had not meant to hit his brother with such force. It was a period during which Lafeyette didn't seem in touch with himself; his anger and sorrow were tangled inside him, his moods shifting wildly.

He waffled between outbursts of fury and revenge to times when he was tolerant, if not generous and mature. On a March afternoon, when Lafeyette was playing Atari with a friend in a seventh-floor apartment, they heard someone laughing. It sounded as if whoever it was was right outside. The boys opened the window. The voice was coming from above. Lafeyette twisted his head outside and looked up. There was a boy named Bubbles, his head hanging over the roof's edge.

"Bubbles," Lafeyette yelled, "I'm gonna tell your mama." He hoped that that might be reason for the boy, who was only ten, to retreat. Lafeyette worried that he might fall. But Bubbles didn't respond, so Lafeyette ran out the front door of the apartment; the gate leading to the roof had been jimmied open. Lafeyette sprinted up the flight of stairs.

"C'mon, man!" he yelled at Bubbles. "Get down." Bubbles came toward Lafeyette, who grabbed him by the collar and hauled him down the stairs. "Somebody needs to watch him," Lafeyette told his friend. He also felt that the housing authority should provide better security. The gate's padlock, he knew, could be pried open easily with a crowbar.

Lafeyette rarely spoke about Craig, though occasionally he'd go upstairs to sit by the side of Craig's girlfriend, often in silence. It was there one afternoon that he read a poem Craig had written shortly before he died and that, in its prescience, and like the death of Bird Leg, haunted Lafeyette.

> "Liven——Death"
> Dear: My BeLord
> I neel to pray
> A loose consouse leads to death any day.
> I fear no death. I fear no liven
> I fear my self for not given
> A weaken hart A helpless soul
> Strong on the out but the in ed grows old
> It took all I can stand

> All that was off'en
> Six feet down a Tombstone
> Above in the middle lays my couffen
> God bless thos I love.
> Peace to those of my honor!

Under the exclamation point, instead of a dot, Craig had drawn a heart.

LaJoe didn't know what to do with Lafeyette. He wouldn't talk about what had happened. And he looked tired and worn. His new gait no longer made him seem cocky or angry; it just made him look old, bent over like an aged man.

Pharoah hadn't been as strongly affected by Craig's death. He figured the cop was just doing his duty and had gotten the wrong guy. When tragedy struck, Pharoah didn't want to know. He continued to tell his mother he was too young to comprehend it all, as if he were trying to prolong his childhood, to keep it from passing him by as quickly as it had Lafeyette. But he too worried about his brother. " 'Cause he's getting older, they'll probably try to use him in the gangs," he would say.

One evening Lafeyette, who hadn't talked much since the funeral, told LaJoe, "Mama, I'm real tired. I could go outside and don't have to come back. Anytime I go outside, I ain't guaranteed to come back."

LaJoe felt Lafeyette had begun to recognize his own mortality, to begin to come to terms with death. Once, he asked of a friend whether he'd ever considered taking his own life, of just walking in front of a car and ending it.

"Lafeyette be telling me how tired he is, and I always ask him this because I made a mistake with Terence once," LaJoe said. "Terence used to tell me he was tired, but I used to think he was tired from just being tired and I'd say, 'go lay down.' But Terence didn't mean that. Terence meant he was just tired with what was going on. So that made me in the habit of asking now when they say they're tired, 'What you mean, you tired?' "

A month later, amid a round of semi-automatic gunfire outside the apartment's window, LaJoe shepherded the triplets and Pharoah into the hallway for safety. She couldn't, though, get

Lafeyette to join them. He continued to sit calmly and watch television on the small black-and-white set in his sister's room as the powerful percussion of the shooting forced Pharoah to cover his ears.

Twenty-three

THE SIX BOYS posed for the camera. The house music of the west side nightclub blared behind them. Like royalty, Rickey, who had got caught shoplifting videocassettes with Lafeyette, sat slumped in a broad-backed wicker chair, his legs spread wide, as if to show the others he could take up as much space as he cared to. His subjects surrounded him. Two knelt at his side. The other three stood behind him. All displayed four fingers, the sign of the Four Corner Hustlers. The camera captured one boy blowing a bubble and another smirking. They held their heads high and narrowed their eyes menacingly. All looked cocky and defiant. Except for one. Dressed like the others in jeans, starter jacket, and high-top sneakers, he had an expression of consternation. His deep-set eyes weren't a shield, as they were for the others. His stare wasn't meant to keep others away; it wasn't meant to hide his fears and insecurities. Instead, it seemed like an opening, exposing his hurt and loneliness. He looked like a wounded animal seeking help. He looked as if he didn't really want to be there. It was Lafeyette.

Rickey and Lafeyette hung together a lot now, and that didn't bode well for Lafeyette. For $5.00, they had had this photo taken at the Factory, a nightclub that catered to teenagers. The boys had begun attending the Factory on Friday and Saturday nights; it was a place to be among friends and dance and meet girls.

Rickey and his buddies formed the Four Corner Hustlers. They weren't a real gang, like Jimmie Lee's Conservative Vice Lords. They didn't run drugs; for the most part, they were young boys, only thirteen or fourteen. But they controlled their turf. They were like a training brigade for the real thing.

In huge white lettering, Rickey and his friends had declared their building their castle. They had drawn an enormous numeral 4 with a C and an H adorning it. That was followed by the word SOLID. The boys had commandeered a vacant apartment, which they used as a clubhouse. It had a couch, a television, and a VCR. They got a padlock for the door. Each boy wore an earring in his left ear. The jewelry always had four points for Four Corners. Rickey had given Lafeyette a silver earring in the shape of a cross.

LaJoe felt the distance growing between herself and Lafeyette. He had, for one thing, become interested in girls. He'd been dating a girl named Red, and he asked LaJoe whether she liked her. It doesn't matter what I feel, she had told him. What's important is whether you like her. LaJoe warned him, though, that he should use a condom when he was ready to have sex. He didn't want to be a father yet, she told him. Lafeyette said that he didn't want to have children, not for a long while, "not till I turn twenty-eight." It was to be the only time Lafeyette would talk openly with his mother about girls.

But it wasn't his interest in the opposite sex that worried her.

After all, what could be more normal for a thirteen-year-old—as long as he didn't get anyone pregnant. She fretted, instead, about his friendship with Rickey.

She had asked Lafeyette not to hang out with Rickey anymore. It wasn't that she still didn't find his friend sweet and good-natured. She, like Pharoah, was fond of him. He never lied to her, and he never misbehaved around her. Except once. And that's when she began to realize that he might not be a good influence on her son. One afternoon, she had watched from a street corner as he smashed the window of a stopped car and snatched the driver's necklace. She couldn't believe how brazen he'd been. He'd done it in broad daylight—and with neighbors watching, no less. She told Lafeyette not to hang out with him. But Lafeyette didn't listen. And LaJoe didn't persist. When Lafeyette got sent home from school for wearing his earring and the school officials tagged him as a gang member, she felt Lafeyette slipping away. It was, she began to fear, Terence all over again.

Rickey had grown more troubled. His mother had little control over him. She'd entertained the idea of sending him to a group home, a move he adamantly opposed. Rickey and his friends had begun drinking cheap red wine—"the kind," he would say, "that makes you wanna fight"—and smoking marijuana. (Very few kids experimented with the harder drugs like cocaine and heroin.) They also played with guns. One night, high on wine and reefer, Rickey's closest friend, Terrell, pulled out a gun. He turned to another boy, CeeCee. "I'm gonna shoot you."

Terrell shot twice at CeeCee's feet, hitting nothing but grass. The third time, he shot only inches from CeeCee's neck. The fourth time, he shot CeeCee in his left arm. Terrell pointed the gun a fifth time at CeeCee, but it just clicked. He had emptied the chamber. Someone called an ambulance for CeeCee, who refused to tell the authorities who had shot him.

Rickey used guns mostly to shoot at Disciples who dared venture on the Four Corners' turf. "I can get a gun anytime I want to," he once boasted. But, he added, "I don't never try to shoot them in the head. Just in the feets."

But while Rickey seemed one of the toughest brutes in the neighborhood, he was confused and torn about what he was becoming. When most thirteen-year-olds are looking forward to growing older, Rickey told Lafeyette he wished he were younger, that he were eight years old again. "Just to skip over things that I did," he told him. To make different choices. Rickey mourned for his lost childhood. The two boys enjoyed talking with each other. Rickey confided in Lafeyette that he thought about dying. "I wonder how people feel to die," he said to his friend. "Like one minute you're alive, one minute you're asleep. I'm scared to go to sleep sometime, thinking I might die sometime."

Neither Rickey nor Lafeyette knew what he wanted to be when he grew up. That seemed too far away. They spent so much energy just thinking about the present, how could they be expected to look into the future? "I can't speak on that until I get older," Lafeyette once said. What's more, Rickey could barely read. At restaurants, he couldn't decipher menus. He was too proud to admit his deficiency.

Although Lafeyette spent time with Rickey, he didn't like hanging out with Rickey's friends. He thought them too ready to fight. In fact, he warned his mother not to go over to Rickey's building; they might try to rob her. Lafeyette felt he could keep Rickey out of trouble. Maybe he could be a good influence.

A few weeks after Craig's death, Lafeyette returned to the stadium to park cars with Rickey. As the crowds walked quickly toward the stadium, the two boys strolled by a new Hyundai that had a detachable radio. "You wanna get it?" Rickey asked. "No," replied Lafeyette and kept on walking. Rickey followed. Even Rickey recognized Lafeyette's good influence. "Lafie's the best friend I have. He don't like getting in trouble. You have to con him. He tell me, 'You shouldn't do that, man. There ain't no cause for that.' "

Lafeyette denied belonging to a gang—and there was some truth in his denial. Frequently, young boys at Horner claimed allegiance to one gang or another. Children as young as four or five at a neighborhood preschool program would arrive each day with their hats turned to the left, showing allegiance to the Vice Lords, or to the right, for the Disciples. A group like the Four Corners imitated their older counterparts. But there was no real organization or discipline; moreover, they didn't sell drugs. Had it been in another community, perhaps the gang would have been just a band of friends who occasionally got into mischief. But this was Horner. Such affiliation marked children. "Oh, he's a gang member," teachers would say of a student. "He's trouble." One public elementary school asked its students to adhere to a dress code so that they could be distinguished from gang members who wore their colors. Children often believe what adults say about them. Rickey at times felt that if they expected him to be bad, he'd be bad. He'd be mean. He'd do it all. Lafeyette resisted, partly at the insistence of his mother. Yeah, he would concede, he hung out with Four Corner Hustlers, "but just 'cause I be with them that don't mean I be in the gang. The people you thinking be nice, them the ones that gonna be in the gang."

Lafeyette had grown increasingly cynical. And in a child who has not experienced enough to root his beliefs, such an attitude can create a vast emptiness. He had little to believe in. Everyone and everything was failing him. School. The Public Aid Department. His father. His older brother. The police. And now, in a sense, himself.

Pharoah had found a new interest: politics. It fascinated him. The crowds. The speeches. The promises. The power. LaJoe figured it must be in his blood. Her mother had been the precinct captain for the Democratic Party in Horner and had been in charge of getting out the vote. She handed out chickens, sausages, and pints of wine to neighbors after they voted, not an uncommon practice in Chicago in those days.

As a child, LaJoe remembers meeting aldermen, representatives, and even senators. They would visit the apartments or hold community meetings in the basement. One alderman, Ed Quigley, used to give her and other children stuffed dolls for Christmas. Quigley, who headed the city's sewer department, helped Paul Rivers get his job with the city. He had helped get her mother her job in the County Treasurer's Office. Quigley was white; his district was mostly black. His critics called it plantation politics.

Though LaJoe had grown up in a family that thrived on politics, she long ago had given up on politicians. She voted only on occasion. The alderman who succeeded Quigley, Wallace Davis, a local black man, ended his political career in 1987, when he was convicted of racketeering, extortion, attempted extortion, and lying to the FBI. His successor, twenty-eight-year-old Sheneather Butler, a former library assistant, was rarely seen in the neighborhood. Her father, who opponents claimed was the real force behind his daughter, had been a perennial candidate for office. A local magazine chided the younger Butler for not knowing who the Wirtz family was. They were the owners of the Chicago Bulls, the Blackhawks, and, of course, the stadium, a not insignificant piece of real estate in her political ward. The magazine wrote, "Such ignorance is appalling even by the standards of Chicago aldermen."

The only time in recent memory that LaJoe had gotten excited about an election was when Harold Washington first ran for mayor, in 1983. When he won, in what was considered an upset and a landmark victory for the city's blacks, she and other Horner residents went out into the streets to celebrate, cheering and whistling at the triumph. But even Washington disappointed her. Neighborhoods like Henry Horner improved little during his tenure.

But a mayor alone couldn't cure Horner's ills. The white opposition on the Chicago City Council gummed up most efforts by the administration to do much of anything. Moreover, Washington headed the city during the Reagan years, when federal funds for the nation's cities and the nation's poor were cut sharply. From 1980 to 1988, Reagan's last year in office, Community Development Block Grant expenditures were cut 28 percent; Urban Development Action Grants, 68 percent; and federally subsidized housing, 70 percent. During those years, life only worsened in neighborhoods like Horner, so LaJoe's enthusiasm and hope for change under Mayor Washington waned.

But Pharoah seemed to be picking up where LaJoe and her mother had left off. He got his first taste of politics the previous November, when he and Porkchop boarded a bus along with the Boys Club Drum and Bugle Corps to a downtown parade for presidential candidate Michael Dukakis. It was one of the Democrat's last rallies before the election. The crowd was too big and the downpour too heavy for Pharoah and Porkchop to see much, but amid all the noise and jubilation and rain, the two twirled flashlights they'd been given and hoisted a placard that read VOTE FOR DUKAKIS '88. Pharoah yanked his imitation black leather coat over his head to keep his head dry. It was Pharoah's first up-close encounter with the excitement of politics, and his adrenaline ran high.

Five months later, on March 30, just five days before the city's mayoral elections, Tim Evans, a black candidate who was running under the banner of the hastily formed Harold Washington Party, visited Henry Horner. Word of his arrival spread quickly through the high-rises. Pharoah, eager for another rally, ran from the apartment to the other side of the Boys Club. A small crowd had gathered around Evans, who was standing on the sidewalk, shaking hands and asking for votes. Suddenly a rock, the size of a baseball, fell near the crowd. Then another. And another. Evans's bodyguards pushed the candidate into his car. Pharoah covered his head and ran. A rock hit a woman in the knee and a police sergeant on the shoulder. No one was seriously hurt. No one knew who had thrown the rocks or why. It all made the evening news. Evans vowed to return, which he did the next day.

That inglorious moment didn't dent Pharoah's enthusiasm, though. The same night, he went to hear Evans and Jesse Jackson speak at the First Congregational Baptist Church. Privately, he began to fantasize about becoming a politician.

The violence never let up. Never. What's more, no one ever got used to it.

On a dreary April afternoon, LaJoe heard a group of people running from the building past her apartment windows. Often such activity meant the gangs were readying for battle. She pulled back the drapes slightly so that those outside wouldn't see her. She watched as ten teenage boys chased a man who looked to be about thirty. Two of them caught up with the stranger and wrapped him in their arms as the others flailed away at him with their fists. One boy brought a wooden cane crashing into the man's rib cage.

From her bedroom window, LaShawn yelled for them to stop. LaJoe ran outside. So did Lafeyette.

"Why'd you try to rape my cousin?" the boy with the cane hollered with each stinging blow. "Why'd you try to rape my cousin?"

The man ran, chased by the pack of teens intent on meting

out their own form of punishment. When LaJoe turned to go back to the apartment, she realized Lafeyette had joined them. LaJoe ordered Pharoah to get Tyisha and the triplets, who were playing on the second floor. Once she had the young ones inside, she told them sternly, "Don't go out of here. You don't go out of here even to buy a pop."

Apparently, the man everyone was assaulting had fondled an eight-year-old boy in a vacant fourth-floor apartment. No one thought to call the police. They chose to render justice themselves.

Lafeyette returned ten minutes later, perspiring and out of breath. He and the others had chased the man to Madison Street, where the accused sought refuge in a liquor store. Along the way, the teens had showered him with bricks and rocks.

"They all like raper mans there," he told his mother, smiling, knowing that what he was about to say had a humorous ring to it: "Maybe it's a raper mans' club." LaJoe didn't laugh.

Twenty-four

JUDGE FRANCIS MAHAN'S six-year-old courtroom in the Skokie branch of the Cook County Courts is clean and well lit, a stark contrast to the musty courtrooms in the main fifty-nine-year-old Criminal Courts building in Chicago. Handsome dark green carpeting matches the cushioned jury seats. The three rows of varnished benches shine.

For many young men at Horner, their only contact with the world outside their own immediate environs is the courts. It can be a cold and humiliating liaison. No one has enough time.

The courts are so overburdened that the county has transferred many of its Chicago cases to Skokie. Judge Mahan's court hears only such cases.

The court was late getting started this morning of March 21. The prisoners, who are bused daily from the county jail, twenty miles away, had yet to arrive. Young men and women, waiting for their relatives and loved ones to appear, sat silently on the hard benches. They listened to the friendly conversations between the public defenders and prosecutors. It seemed to an outsider as if all the attorneys—prosecutors and public defenders—were best of friends.

A young pregnant woman approached the clerk of the court. "Is my boyfriend's attorney here?" she asked. "Ma'am," shot back the clerk, "I don't know who your attorney is or who you are." The woman retreated like a chastised schoolgirl.

Nearby, a mustachioed state's attorney was asked by a fellow prosecutor what cases he had that morning. In a stage whisper loud enough for everyone in the courtroom to hear: "Bobby Rivers and Tony Oliver. We're going to stomp them into the ground." (Bobby was Terence's alias.) A young man, a courtroom spectator, overheard the exchange. He turned to his friend in disbelief. "Man, they're dealing with motherfucking lives," he said.

Judge Mahan, his hands holding up his black robe, entered the courtroom. Everyone rose. With his silver hair and thick black-rimmed glasses, he looked stern and unforgiving. His arrival made people nervous. A young man sitting in the back row began to crack his knuckles. A few feet down from him, a baby started to cry.

"The judge doesn't like babies getting noisy," a sheriff's deputy informed the uninterested-looking mother. She left the courtroom with the bawling child.

The first case the judge heard involved a Hispanic man in his twenties. He had been arrested for possession of fifty grams of cocaine and for stealing his ex-wife's car. He had already been convicted for talking to a juror in another case and for possession of marijuana. His attorney requested that the judge lower his $25,000 bond. Mahan raised it to $50,000.

Next appeared the father of the baby who had disrupted the courtroom just a few minutes earlier. The rosy-cheeked youth was tall and lanky, his shoulders hunched up to his ears; his blue jeans barely covered his ankles. He was currently on probation (his crime was never disclosed), and he wanted to move his family to Kentucky. "I understand you've been good under probation," Mahan said. "Leave granted." He then exhibited a rare smile. "Stay out of trouble."

"I will, Your Honor," the boy assured him, his attention focused on the green carpet.

A clerk came up to the judge's bench. The prisoners from the jail still hadn't arrived. Mahan called for a short recess.

It gave Audrey Natcone some time to discuss Terence's case with the prosecution. Because of the large number of cases both she and the prosecution handled, they had little if any time to talk or bargain outside the courtroom. She approached Casey Bartnik, the state's attorney who was handling Terence's charges. The two, within just a few feet of the spectators' benches, began to negotiate the terms of the plea bargain.

"What did we offer last time?" Casey asked innocently.

"Ten," replied Audrey.

"That sounds reasonable to me for two armed robberies."

"I'm *not* serving ten."

The mustachioed state's attorney overheard her remark and laughed. "*You* don't have to serve ten." Audrey smiled weakly. She knew she identified with her clients too much. She had let her guard down.

"You get paid to do the right thing," Casey needled.

"I'm doing the right thing," Audrey insisted.

"You get paid more than me."

"Rightfully so." Audrey paused. "I haven't even seen the photos. I'd like to see them before we make any decisions." Audrey was still angry that the police had not honored her request for the line-up photos. She was increasingly suspicious that something was wrong.

The state's attorney pulled from his briefcase a set of Polaroid shots the police had taken of Terence as well as two line-up photos. Ann Mitchell, the owner of the Longhorn Saloon, had identified Terence from the line-up pictures after first viewing the Polaroids. Audrey looked at the line-up photos, shaking her head. Terence stood at the end of the row of men, all of whom towered, by two to six inches, over him.

"Look at this!" Audrey said. "He's the tiny shrimp at the end. Will you look at this? That's my client. The tiny shrimp at the end. Of course she picked him out."

"I'll tell you what. I'll give you eight," Casey conceded.

"Can't you give me six?" Natcone asked.

"Go to trial."

Audrey reminded Casey that these were Terence's first offenses as an adult and that he had a supportive home life, that his mother cared about her son. She had been to all his court hearings. But the conversation ended there. Casey wouldn't come down from eight years. For three crimes, he felt, that was pretty reasonable. Besides, they had Terence's fingerprints on the most recent armed robbery. Audrey wondered where LaJoe was this day.

Terence had asked LaJoe not to come. He didn't want to put his mother through any more pain. He saw how worried she was each time she came to court.

"I let my family down," Terence said. "I promised my little brothers, my mama, my father, and all of them that I would never come back to jail again. But things didn't go my way. I just got caught up. I'm the one that's supposed to be showing an example for them. And it seem like I just failed."

On her last visit to the court, LaJoe had brought Pharoah with her. He had wanted to come. He was curious; he'd never been in a courtroom. He also was eager to see Terence. Lafeyette had wanted to come, too, but LaJoe wouldn't take him. After each visit with Terence in the county jail, Lafeyette couldn't sleep. He would daydream in school about Terence. Within a few days, he'd get bags under his eyes, not unlike his mother. He worries harder than me, LaJoe thought.

When LaJoe had entered the courthouse with Pharoah, he peppered her with questions. "How come there ain't no jurors like in *Barney Miller?* . . . Who them peoples? . . . Which room is Terence in?" It was all new for Pharoah. He had to know everything that was going on.

The two sat in the first row, listening to the proceedings. "What old boy mean he going to give him two years? What for?" he whispered. His mother shushed him. Pharoah, who was restless, had noticed the scheduling sheets outside the courtroom and wandered out to look at them. He slid them from their glass case. LaJoe followed.

"Mama," he said, reading from the sheets. "Lee Butler. Sexual. Lee Butler. Sexual. Lee Butler. Sexual. He got three cases. I know he be ashamed when he come into the courtroom." He would later describe the accused rapist who appeared in court that day: "I won't say he was dirty but he didn't know how to dress. He had holes in his pants."

That morning, Terence's case was continued—court jargon for postponed—and he was given a new court date. But LaJoe and Pharoah were able to visit with him before he was bused back to the jail. They met in a small room behind the courtroom.

When Terence greeted LaJoe and Pharoah, he took off his shirt and flexed and posed, exposing a set of rippling new muscles. In jail, Terence had been lifting weights three hours a day. He could now curl 120 pounds. His muscles bulged so that he couldn't button his gray Levi's. Pharoah would later tell Lafeyette of his visit and, in an imitation of Terence, shuffled backward, flexing his biceps and puffing up his chest. " 'I'm strong,' " he told Lafeyette, relaying what Terence had told him. " 'I got it made in here. I don't have nothing to worry about around here.' "

"You should of seen his chest," he told his brother. "He had huge muscles. They must be doing Terence all right 'cause he was skinny at home."

Pharoah had decided before his visit with Terence that he would smile through the whole encounter no matter how sad he felt. To brighten Terence's spirits. Just as he did with his father. And so, as Terence showed off his new body and talked to LaJoe, Pharoah kept up a look of good cheer, intent on making both his older brother and his mother happy. When they left, Terence gave Pharoah a thumbs-up. Pharoah signaled back in kind.

That was nearly two months ago. The visit had disturbed LaJoe. Terence had told her he wouldn't take the ten years even if that meant going to trial. It was just too many years to be away from the family.

• • • •

A deputy sheriff led Terence and the two other defendants back into the courtroom. He glanced at neither the spectators nor the attorneys; he looked straight ahead. The three stood shoulder to shoulder facing the judge, their hands clasped behind their backs, as if they were still in handcuffs. Terence's muscular body was popping out of his clothes. His blue V-neck sweater strained at the seams. His pants were so short, they exposed the red and yellow stripes on his sweat socks. He raised his head as the judge talked in a low whisper to the two attorneys, who stood before the bench. At their request, Judge Mahan agreed to a private conference. Before any plea bargain could be entered, the judge had to agree to it.

Before Audrey left the courtroom for the judge's chambers, she pulled Terence aside. "I can get you eight years," she said. Terence didn't hesitate: "I want six." Audrey told him they would talk later.

In the conference, Judge Mahan agreed to the plea bargain arrangements. If Terence pleaded guilty, he would sentence him to eight years. The prosecution could avoid a trial and Terence could eliminate the possibility of getting more time. Audrey now had to convince him.

The two met for fifteen minutes in a back room, where Audrey took out her legal pad and wrote four numbers—14, 12, 10, and 8. She circled the 14 and explained that if Terence were convicted of two armed robberies, he would in all likelihood get that many years. She then circled the 12. If he didn't get 14, she explained, the judge would, at the very least, give him 12 if he were found guilty. She then circled the 10. That's what the state's attorney had first offered. And then she drew the 8. That's what was currently being offered. She felt it was a pretty fair deal. It might, she told him, be the best she could get for him.

Terence remained silent through much of Audrey's explanation, his eyes focused on the yellow legal pad. "Why don't you try to get me seven years," he muttered.

"I don't think I can, Terence. The best deal they're offering is eight," Audrey patiently explained.

"I can't even bear with eight years. Maaan." He turned his head away from his attorney.

"What's six months extra?" she asked. Many prisoners in Illinois serve only half their sentence, since they're given one day off for each day of good behavior. "Judge Mahan, he'll punish defendants who turn down deals. He's just that kind of judge." Audrey noticed that Terence's eyes were red. She thought he was about to cry.

Audrey couldn't bring herself to urge him to take the eight years. "I can't get excited for him," she said shortly after Terence was led back to jail. "If he was being charged with murder and they were reducing it to armed robbery, that'd be something else." Audrey looked downcast. She had seen Terence change in the year she had known him. He had hardened. The weight lifting made him look older and more menacing. He seemed more defiant. "When I first saw him he was a little kid. He was soft-looking and soft-spoken," she said. She didn't think a long stint in jail would do him any good. But she wished that he were older, a little more seasoned, so that he could see that it was in his best interests to take the eight years. She suspected that a fellow inmate in the county jail had convinced him that he'd be crazy to take more than seven.

She felt that Terence believed she was trying to trick him into something. Her clients generally mistrusted "the system," even those who were intent on helping them. Audrey told Terence to talk with LaJoe about the offer. She felt his mother might give some sound advice. He agreed.

The judge granted Terence a two-week continuance so that he could talk to his mother about the eight-year offer.

LaJoe waited that day to hear from Terence, but he never called. She figured he'd taken the ten years. It demoralized her to think that her son might be locked up for so long. So it didn't surprise her that day when she spun out of control.

There was a man, perhaps in his early forties, who had been coming on to her in recent weeks. She didn't like it. She told him to stop, that she didn't want to see him around her. The man, whom she knew only as Keith, frightened her. He was often high on PCP, or happy stick, a potent hallucinogen that could cause disorientation, schizophrenia, and psychotic violence.

Later that day, Keith beckoned LaJoe over to his car. "I'm

gonna bust your head," he told her, clearly high on PCP and frustrated by LaJoe's refusal to talk with him.

"Get out and bust my head now," LaJoe goaded him. "Come on, get outta your car. Bust my head." LaJoe concealed a nail file in her coat sleeve. "I was going to stab him dead in the eye," she said later. Keith wouldn't leave the safety of his car, but he continued to taunt LaJoe, telling her that if he got her alone, he would bust her head.

LaJoe hadn't told anyone about Keith's threats, but when she got back inside the house, she couldn't contain herself. She confided in Rochelle, who was over visiting. Her son Weasel overheard her.

There are many things you can do and get away with at Horner, because people, fearful that retaliation may spiral out of control, keep their anger and fury to themselves. But when it comes to family, particularly mothers, nothing, no one, is beyond revenge. Pharoah would often say that "if I die, if someone shoots me, they'll die. Someone in my family will kill them." Such was the case with the threats against LaJoe.

Weasel, who was about to turn twenty-two, went looking for Keith. About ten minutes later, he dragged into the breezeway a man who cut a pitiful profile: sunken shoulders, unkempt hair, his eyes bloodshot and vacant. He looked too high to be scared. "Is this him?" he asked LaJoe. She nodded. Weasel began punching him with short, powerful blows to his face and body. The crushing sound of flesh against flesh echoed in the narrow hallway, giving the effect of a much fiercer fight than actually was taking place.

"No. No. Stop," Keith pleaded. His was a high-pitched, almost childlike voice. Weasel stopped, and Keith, who stood about six feet, crawled on his hands and knees to the door. Blood ran from his nose. He got up and wobbled across the trampled lawn.

LaJoe wandered back into the apartment, herself shaky and dazed. She paced between the kitchen and the living room, her face twisted. "He told me he'd bust my head. Well, bust it. I ain't going to put up with this." Her voice started to rise as she raged at no one in particular. "YOU HEAR ME? I AIN'T GOING TO PUT UP WITH THIS!"

The children filed home from school. They tried to enter unnoticed, to stay out of their mother's path. Tyisha and Pharoah set up a Monopoly game on the kitchen table and pretended to play. Lafeyette slumped down in the red lounge chair, sad and silent, his eyes focused intently on his mother.

LaJoe kept pacing, mumbling to herself. "Mama," Lafeyette asked meekly, "can we get our Easter clothes?" LaJoe whirled toward her son. "Can't you see I'm upset!" she snapped. Lafeyette sank deeper into the chair.

LaJoe continued to seethe. "What's he trying to do to me?" she muttered. "What if Weasel wasn't here? Then what? I should of hit him myself. I need a gun. I already lost two fingers trying to fight. I already lost two fingers." Tears streaked down her smooth cheeks. *"I don't need another man to ruin my life! I got my man! He ruined it!"*

Now LaJoe sobbed uncontrollably. Weasel hugged her. "It be okay," he assured her. "It be okay." He rubbed her arched back as she buried her head in his shoulder. "No one got any reason to talk to you like that. No one."

LaJoe pushed away. Her voice rose. "I GOT TO GET OUT OF THIS GHETTO LIFE. WHO DO HE THINK HE IS? PEOPLE AROUND HERE ARE CRAZY!" She caught her breath. Her posture softened. "What if Weasel wasn't here? I should of kicked him." And as she began sobbing again, those in the apartment came and hugged her. First Rochelle. Then a friend of Weasel's. Then LaShawn. Then Weasel again.

Pharoah remained fixed in his seat, the Monopoly game untouched. His buck teeth seemed to hold his lips apart even farther as his eyes darted around the room in dismay. He didn't want to hug his mother because, he explained later, "when my mama cry, sometime it make you cry. I was gonna cry." But he didn't. Nor did Lafeyette, who grabbed the broom and started sweeping.

The commotion began to subside. LaJoe sat at the kitchen table, an occasional tear running down her cheeks, apologizing to her friends and family for her outburst. Larry, Brian's brother, walked through the door. "Clean the kitchen floor," Lafeyette ordered. "Shut up, man," Larry retorted. Lafeyette turned to his mother. "Pharoah and I ain't the only people living here," he told her.

LaJoe began privately to entertain the idea of leaving, of running away with her five youngest, Lafeyette on down. But she had nowhere to go. She couldn't afford the rents outside public housing. LaJoe had once described her three oldest children as red roses whose petals had wilted and fallen off. She wished she could give new life to those flowers. But she was tired of trying. And now she worried that her younger buds might never bloom.

But LaJoe, too, was wilting like an undernourished rose. Looking for a respite from her crowded household, she spent more nights away from the family, sometimes playing cards with her women friends, other times sitting up all night talking with Rochelle and her mother, drinking soda pop and smoking cigarettes. LaJoe often leaned on Rochelle and her mother for support, usually when she felt overwhelmed by her family's problems. The card playing helped supplement her meager income, she reasoned. And being away gave her a chance to relax and pull herself together. It was her escape, the only way she knew how to recharge herself. At least, she thought, she'd be rested for her children.

The children understood, or so they said. In the mornings, if LaJoe had not yet returned, they managed without her. Weasel's girlfriend fixed oatmeal for the kids. Lafeyette ironed his clothes and did the same for the triplets, whom he walked to school. LaJoe would be there for them when they got out of school—and they knew that. But the children felt her absence on the nights she was away. They remembered how she'd been mugged and her fingers slashed. They worried that something even worse might happen to her. Their mother, after all, was all they had.

On Tuesday, April 4, Terence was sentenced, and Richard M. Daley, the son of the infamous Richard J. Daley, was elected mayor. Not that the two had anything to do with each other. But LaJoe could remember the date. Sentencing Day and Election Day. The two had absolutely nothing to do with each other, and that's what bothered LaJoe. Maybe if the politicians cared, some of the neighborhood's lost children might have been saved. The politicians' silence upset her greatly.

LaJoe had gone to the county jail a couple of weeks earlier to talk with Terence. She encouraged him to take the eight years, to get it over with. She thought it would be easier on every-body. She couldn't endure a trial and the possibility that he might be sent away for a longer time. Besides, she told Terence, with an eight-year sentence he could get out in four years, maybe three and a half years, if they counted the time already served. Terence listened to his mother. Always. He took the eight years.

Three days before his sentencing, Lafeyette and Pharoah, along with Tammie, Tiffany, Snuggles, Sir Baldheaded, and their father, visited Terence to say their good-byes. LaJoe went later in the day. Lafeyette donned Terence's suit, the same one he had worn to Craig's funeral. He wanted to show Terence that he was older, that he could take care of himself and the family, particularly their mother.

It tickled Terence to see his brother so grown. The suit made him look like a young man. He asked Lafeyette to back up against the wall so that he could view him in it. "It looks sharp, Laf," he mouthed through the thick glass. All Lafeyette could bring himself to say to Terence was "I'm straight." He sat and listened to Terence for the rest of the visit, his eyes fixed on his brother behind the glass. Pharoah told Terence, "I love you." The visit, which was filled with awkward pauses, lasted maybe half an hour.

Terence insisted that no one come to his sentencing; he didn't want them to see him sent away. He originally asked the judge if he would give him an extra two weeks in the jail so that his family might visit him once more, but then changed his mind and asked to be shipped off immediately. Other inmates had told him that had he stayed, he would have had to remain in prison two weeks longer.

LaJoe couldn't stop thinking of Terence. She tried to rational-ize his imprisonment. It would be good for him to get off the streets, to get away from the drugs and the shootings. If he were out here, he might just get in more serious trouble. He might get hurt, maybe even killed. But she knew, in her heart of hearts, that prison wasn't much of an option. It would change Terence. He would lose his softness, his gentleness. In her ef-forts to hold on to Terence, she measured Lafeyette and Pharoah against him. She had expected so much from him, and he had disappointed her. Not Pharoah or Lafeyette, she assured herself. She could see the differences.

"Terence was quiet, almost like Pharoah," she would say. "But the difference between Terence and Pharoah is that Pharoah's more open. If Pharoah do something wrong, he won't let you forget it even though you forgived him." Or, she would note, "Lafie ain't going to be like that, he ain't going to be like that. If anything Lafie do, he going to leave the projects if he has to leave on his own. I'm not worried about that. The only thing I worry about Lafie is getting hurt."

LaJoe kept her grief to herself. She had no one, except Rochelle, to share it with. She didn't talk to her husband. And she no longer wanted to burden Lafeyette with her worries. Her insides, she said, "don't be nothing but threads.

"My children are my strength. They're my love. They're what I didn't have and I had them in order to get it. And when they go away, it's like taking from me a part of me. Like, now, I'm getting real weak. You know, I don't feel good. My heart broke 'cause of what happened to Terence. It ain't too much more I could take."

Three days later, after his arrival at the Joliet Correctional Center, a maximum security facility an hour's drive south of Chicago, Terence wrote to his mother. She showed the letter to Lafeyette and Pharoah.

April 7, 1989

Dear Mom,

How are you and the family doing? Fine I hope. Well, I just made it to Joliet and I want you to no that I love you and them good things you did for me. And another thing. Don't worry about me. I'm going to be fine . . . When you send me some money, make sure it be 50 dollars money order so I can get my tv and radio . . . Be strong. I would like some pictures of the family and some pictures of my kids . . . Don't never worry about me. You got 7 other kids to worry about. I'm going to be okay.

From your truly son, Terence. I ♡ U. Write back soon.

Both Lafeyette and Pharoah missed Terence. But they both now realized he was gone for a while. They stopped asking when he was coming home, though Pharoah had a dream.

"I dreamed every time I did something like when I get married Terence'd get married. Then a monster was chasing me. My brother was the only one who controlled the monster, so he told the monster to settle down. I woke up and started to call my brother's name but remembered he was in jail and I started worrying again."

Twenty-five

PHAROAH WARNED FRIENDS of the human-headed cats in his building's basement. It didn't take much, given all that was found down there, to make that leap of imagination.

When Gwen Anderson, the newly appointed housing manager of Horner who had been entrusted to help turn the troubled complex around, ventured into the basements of Horner's high-rises, she vomited. On April 20, Ms. Anderson wrote the following memo to her superiors at the CHA:

During inspection of basements of buildings (6) in
Henry Horner Homes Project by the Manager, Assistant
Manager, and Maintenance Superintendent, the
following was found:

An estimated two thousand (2000) appliances:

Refrigerators—some new, with the insulation
pulled out, missing motors, aluminum freezer
compartments missing, electrical cords ripped out,
some standing in pool of water and rusting away.

Ranges—some stacked wall to wall—floor to ceiling
and barring entry into the storage room, parts
missing (doors, burners, grates, boiler trays,
knobs, panels, etc.), standing in the pools of water
and rusting away.

It should be noted also that these appliances were
heavily infested with roaches, fleas. Cats were
bedding and walking the rafters (pipes) and dead
rodents and animals were lying in the storage areas,
stench and putrid odor abounded. (The manager became
nauseated to the point of intensely vomiting for
relief, and could not continue the inspection until
after being revived.) Soiled female undergarments
and paraphernalia with foul odors were lying around.
No equipment presently in use by staff could be used
to withstand this odor beyond a minute! In most
storage areas, the electrical fixtures had been
ripped out and any security devices (locks, chains,
gates, etc.) had been removed or severely damaged.

Kitchen cabinets—new cabinets, with some still in
cartons—were sitting in pools of water, rusted
beyond use. These cabinets were amidst dead animals,
rodents, human and animal excrement, garbage and junk
items, and the odors were overwhelming!

According to one of the long-time employed
resident janitors, most of the aforementioned have
been in basements in Henry Horner Homes at least 15
years.

Further, that one of the areas was designated as a
fall-out shelter and it contained—besides the
aforementioned appliances and junk—hundreds of
barrels of survival items. It should be further
noted that due to the absence of security in this
development and the constant vandalism and crime

acts, in spite of our intensive efforts to secure
them, these storage areas continue to be accessible
to anyone . . .

It was anybody's worst nightmare, a basement full of scurrying rats and dead cats and dogs. For fifteen years, people had been living over this stench, and the CHA had only now discovered it. These were the basements where LaJoe and her sisters learned to sew with the Girl Scouts. As children, they had attended dances and roller-skating parties here. Politicians had visited with residents in these basements to listen to their complaints and to get their votes. Now these were the last places on earth anyone would want to spend time.

The rotting carcasses explained the putrid odor rising from the Riverses' toilet. It wasn't aborted fetuses, as LaJoe had thought. It was dead animals, the stench of rotting flesh rising through the pipes.

The pools of water in the basement explained LaJoe's backed-up kitchen sink. Sewage had risen up through the pipes and been regurgitated into the sink. A maintenance man rigged a temporary stopper for LaJoe. He wedged a three-foot-long plank of wood between a pot, which covered the drain, and the cabinets above. The secured pot kept the raw sewage from escaping into the sink. For two weeks, this ugly sculpture remained; LaJoe washed the dishes in the bathtub.

But what most infuriated LaJoe were the brand-new ranges wasting away just a floor below her. For nearly a year, her oven and broiler rarely worked. She had no toaster, so when the broiler was out, the children toasted bread in a skillet. It was a long while since she had made corn bread or cakes, since she couldn't rely on the oven. And to think, just a floor below her sat possible replacements. But they were now beyond repair. The CHA would have to throw them all out.

It wasn't just her home that was crumbling; the neighborhood was too. It all was the perfect metaphor, LaJoe thought, for what was happening to her spirit.

Henry Horner now had 699 vacancies, 188 more than last year, further fueling speculation that the city had plans to tear down the complex to make way for a new stadium. In the high-rises west of Damen, the CHA discovered it was missing heating coils in every single building. Without these small pieces of metal, none of the apartments could be heated come the cold weather. And the early spring wading pool, which was formed by an open fire hydrant immediately in front of LaJoe's building, became a bottomless gulch. A boy playing by its side waded a few feet into it to retrieve a ball. Seconds later, he disappeared from sight. He had fallen into an uncovered sewer opening that was concealed by the muddy water. Luckily, some young friends pulled him out. After the near drowning, the CHA called the city for a new manhole cover. It took three months. In the interim, the maintenance staff rolled a trash container on top of the opening.

Last July, the Miles Square Health Center, which was founded in 1967 with federal funds in response to organized community pressure, declared bankruptcy. It now appeared it would fold for good. A combination of forces had killed it. In the early 1980s, Illinois cut back its Medicaid payments to doctors, so agencies like Miles Square, which served a large Medicaid population, limped along underfunded. Also, there had been allegations of mismanagement. With both Miles Square and the Mary Thompson Hospital closed, residents were forced to use the Cook County Hospital, where waits to see a physician were so long that many people packed lunches for their visits.

Hull House considered discontinuing a first aid care team at Horner. It kept two medical technicians at Horner twenty-four hours a day to respond to emergencies. But it was becoming dangerous. There were too many shootings and robberies. Also, Ralph Garcia, who had run a corner market called Little Joe's for eleven years, just picked up and left. No one knew why, though in recent months he'd been frustrated in his efforts to protect his store from robbers. The police had confiscated two handguns, a .38 revolver and a .380 automatic, which he kept for protection. Though he monitored the small, two-aisle store with a camera and microphone, he had estimated that he lost between $25 and $50 a day in shoplifting. Ralph had been particularly friendly to LaJoe. When she had the triplets, he gave her extra boxes of Pampers free.

And the Boys Club's indoor swimming pool, which had been reopened and rededicated on February 27 after nine years of inoperation, was having troubles. The very night that Mayor

Eugene Sawyer cut the ribbon to dedicate the renovated pool, the ventilation fans on the roof were stolen. The thieves presumably sold the aluminum to a scrap yard. By the summer, the pool's underwater and overhead lighting, as well as the locks on the doors leading into the pool, needed fixing. In August, the club would have to close the pool down again, because it lacked funds for the necessary repairs. During the hot summer months, at least, the children still had the outdoor pool at nearby Union Park.

The only evident new wealth in the area were two buildings three blocks south of Horner. The structures stood out like two rose bushes in a field of weeds. The building at 1759 West Adams was a contemporary, red brick, four-story apartment complex with a three-car garage. Just across the street was the one building, though, that caught everyone's eye: a two-story, recently renovated single-family home with a garage large enough to house eight cars; it also had a solarium and a $20,000 television satellite dish on the roof. There had been talk about what might be inside, but even the most vivid imaginations couldn't do it justice. The house was magnificently furnished. Gold faucets in the bathrooms. A marble staircase and Persian rugs. A wood-trimmed fireplace. A Steinway piano. And a finished basement with sunken tub and Jacuzzi. The owners, Jonathan and Clara Penney, allegedly ran a vast drug network in Illinois, Michigan, and Iowa. They purportedly sold cocaine and heroin. On April 5, federal authorities seized the Penneys' property, which included seven other pieces of real estate and ten cars. They did so under a law that permits such seizures if there is evidence that the property and goods were used in, or acquired through, criminal activity. Few at Horner knew the Penneys, though they had envied their lavish digs from afar. It was here, in fact, that a year earlier LaJoe, at the insistence of Lafeyette, had inquired about renting one of the Penneys' new apartments. She didn't even bother to view one after she learned the rent. It was more than her entire monthly payment from Public Aid.

Pharoah and Porkchop ran up the three flights of stairs. Out of breath, they banged on Dawn's door.

"Who is it?" Dawn hollered.

"Pharoah and Porkchop," Pharoah hollered back.

She let in her cousin and brother. The two boys often came to visit Dawn, who since graduation had continued to live illegally in the building. In recent weeks, though, Dawn had been so depressed that she occasionally pretended she wasn't home. So the boys were glad when she came to the door.

"You got any quarters, D'won?" Pharoah asked, hoping she might be able to provide him and Porkchop with some change to play video games. Dawn shook her head. Pharoah and Porkchop lingered.

Pharoah admired and respected Dawn, but he couldn't understand why she still lived at Horner. Why she hadn't left? After all, it was nearly a year since she had graduated from high school and now she was attending a two-year college. Why was she still hanging around the projects? "That don't make sense," Pharoah would tell his mother. "When you moving?" he'd ask his cousin. Lafeyette, too, was puzzled. "She should move," he'd urge. Dawn had placed her name on the housing authority's lengthy waiting list. Public housing was all she could afford, with her four children. It bothered Lafeyette and Pharoah. Here was their family's one success story—hell, they used to brag about her to friends—and she was still living in the projects. Dawn began to feel that she was failing her family.

Since her graduation from Crane and the party at LaJoe's, it had been a struggle. She still lived with her boyfriend, Demetrius, but they had postponed getting married. Neither had a job, so they couldn't afford the money for rings or for a wedding. Dawn had been unable to find work. She hoped to find a retail job and had filled out applications at numerous clothing stores, including the Gap, the Limited, the Foot Locker, and Marshall Field. She also applied for a job with the county. But nothing materialized. She remained on public aid, receiving each month $452 in financial assistance plus $277 in food stamps.

Dawn's apartment was sparsely furnished. The living room was bare except for a battered stereo. She and Demetrius shared a mattress on the floor with a color television at one end. They were saving up for the box spring. Their four children shared two beds.

Despite these difficult times, Dawn continued to maintain a close-knit family. To Patricia Johnson, a former Horner resident herself and now a counselor with a YMCA-sponsored group called West Side Future, which provided guidance and aid to young mothers, Dawn seemed an unusually responsible mother. Patricia had first met Dawn two years earlier, when Dawn was having trouble at home and had considered dropping out of school. Like LaJoe, Patricia encouraged her to continue. Dawn sought Patricia's advice often. Over half the young mothers Patricia worked with were on drugs. They had, Patricia would say, given up on themselves. Their children's fathers had deserted them. Some of these women, in fact, had turned to other women for support and love. It made perfect sense to her. Whom else could they turn to?

But Demetrius was an attentive and loyal dad. Patricia would often see him in the playground with one child in each hand and another on his shoulder. He baby-sat for the kids while Dawn took classes in business administration at nearby Malcolm X Community College. His friends kidded him about being such an upstanding father. They jokingly called him "the nanny." This was a big turnabout for him. As a teenager, he had been a member of the Disciples and had spent a short time in the county jail. He had stolen cars, shoplifted clothes, and had occasionally wielded a pistol against rival gang members. He still has the gang's insignia, a pitchfork, tattooed on his left biceps. Now, though, he took care of the children and repaired cars to help supplement Dawn's income. Having children had slowed him down. He no longer hung out with the gangs.

Dawn and Demetrius never let their children out of their sight. Dawn read to them in the evenings or, when she could afford to, bought them Mother Goose tapes to listen to. Patricia bought her books when she could. Now, she was trying to help Dawn get an apartment outside Horner. Patricia, like Pharoah and the others, wanted desperately to see Dawn make it.

Pharoah and Porkchop glanced at the cartoons on TV. Dawn's four children were gathered at the end of the mattress, entranced by the animation.

"What you do at college?" Pharoah asked his cousin.

"You pick your own days to go to school and pick your own credit hours," Dawn told him.

"What are credit hours?" Pharoah asked.

"Each class is three credits."

"What if you pick four classes?"

"You get twelve credits," Dawn patiently explained.

Pharoah pondered that for a moment, then beckoned to Porkchop. "Let's go," he said. The two waved to Dawn as they walked to the front door. It made Pharoah sad that Dawn hadn't gotten very far. It worried him to think that even if he made it through high school, he'd still be stuck in the projects. It worried him a lot.

"When you gonna get a job?" Pharoah asked.

"I'm trying," Dawn replied.

As Pharoah walked out the door and down the long dark hallway, he turned around as if he'd forgotten to tell Dawn something. "Have a nice day," he called out. It had become one of his favorite expressions. "Have a nice day."

Summer 1989

Twenty-six

ON FRIDAY, May 19, LaJoe and Rochelle taped the last of the streamers to the walls; the narrow strips of crepe paper crisscrossed the living room like tangled vines. Balloons hung from the ceiling and bounced unfettered on the floor. Party hats and party favors lay on the table, which was covered with a paper cloth adorned with Disney cartoon characters. A gold crown, also made of paper, sat to the side for the birthday boy. Eleven candles circled the strawberry shortcake, which read: I LOVE YOU. FROM MAMA AND ROCHELLE.

"LaJoe, here, put it up here," Rochelle urged. LaJoe pulled the last of the banners from the package. They read, "It's a Boy." LaJoe and Rochelle laughed. They hoped Pharoah wouldn't notice.

A few weeks earlier, after Pharoah had attended a birthday celebration for a friend, he mentioned to his mother that he'd never had a party. So she decided to throw him one—and to keep it a surprise. Rochelle had helped her buy the decorations and the cake. She seemed nearly as excited as LaJoe.

Since the incident the month before in which she lost control of herself, LaJoe had slowed down and tried to pull herself and her family together. With summer fast approaching, she wanted to be prepared. She did what she could to lift her spirits and her children's. She had finally made the last of the down payments on the five bunk beds, so Lafeyette, Pharoah, and the triplets now each had one. The wooden bunks were used but in good condition. LaJoe had paid $479 for them. Lafeyette and Pharoah kept the plastic covering on their mattresses. "It keeps them clean," Pharoah explained. They dreamed about what they would do now to decorate their room. Lafeyette wanted to paint it black " 'cause then it won't get dirty so easy." He had taken a steel door off a vacant apartment to replace their broken wooden one, and he had installed a new lock so that only he and Pharoah could enter. They had hung a torn venetian blind over the windows, which kept the room dark but private.

LaJoe also bought a handsome wooden table and chairs from the same used-furniture dealer who had sold her the beds. The storekeeper liked LaJoe and gave her a good buy—$80 for the table and chairs—and even delivered the goods, though he refused to carry the items into the building, because he feared for his safety. Neighbors helped haul the furniture from the truck into the apartment. Pharoah particularly loved the new wooden table; he told his mother that it was the kind they had in mansions.

The triplets and Lafeyette traipsed home from school, wet from the spring downpour. Other youngsters soon arrived, mostly children the triplets' age. They awaited the birthday boy. Someone knocked on the door. The children, giggling, put their fingers to their lips. "Shh. Shh. Shh." The knocking got louder and more forceful. Lafeyette moved to the side of the door and undid its lock.

"SURPRISE!" Lafeyette slapped the back of Pharoah's head with his open palm. In all the excitement, he didn't quite know how to greet his brother. Pharoah shuffled into the living room, surprised and embarrassed by the attention. Just as he had done during the first spelling bee, he balled his hands up under the fold of his shimmery green raincoat, where he nervously played with the plastic. The children, about ten in all, quickly scattered, many running into the kitchen for hot dogs. Pharoah stood by the door, his toothy smile lighting his face. He didn't say anything. Instead, he walked back to his room and sat on the plastic-covered mattress, trying to take it all in. Lafeyette sat with him.

"I thought you forgot it," he told his mother, who poked her head through the door. She rubbed the back of his head and gave him his present, a green shorts set. Pharoah put it on. With the suspenders and knee-length shorts, he looked quite handsome. He silently readied himself for the party: he found a new pair of white socks, and scrubbed his face and hands; he ran jell through his long, curly hair and then secured the gold paper crown on his head. And as he did almost everything, he did it all slowly and with great deliberation. The dressing and preening took him half an hour—and when he was done he wasn't fully satisfied. "I should have greased my legs," he told his brother.

"You look proper," Lafeyette told his brother. Rickey, who had been invited to the party by Lafeyette, wandered into the bedroom. With his hands in his pocket, he looked uncomfortable. He often did. "You look straight, Pharoah," he assured him. "Happy birthday."

"Thanks," Pharoah said. He didn't say much that afternoon. He mostly grinned and giggled. In Polaroid photos of the day, his smile seems to cover his face; his big grin forces his cheeks into plump balls and squeezes his eyes neatly shut. In one photo, he stands behind his seated grandmother, who has come over for the party, with his arm affectionately around her neck. In another, he sits behind the cake in one of the new chairs, his paper crown sliding off his head, looking pleased with the festivities. In yet another, LaJoe steadies Pharoah's small hands as he cuts the cake with a big kitchen knife.

Once Pharoah was dressed and had made his entrance into the party amid the screaming gaggle of kids, Lafeyette and Rickey sneaked out the door. Lafeyette told his mother he didn't want to hang around "no children's party." It was LaJoe's one disappointment. All the guests were much younger than Pharoah; no one Pharoah's age came. He didn't have many good friends, except for his cousin Porkchop. But even he wasn't there. Throughout the festivities, Pharoah asked, "Where's Porkchop?" or could be heard muttering, "I hope Porkchop comes." Porkchop showed up two hours after the party began; he'd forgotten all about it. The two, as usual, embraced. "Happy Birthday," Porkchop mumbled through his soft giggles.

The children, with half-eaten hot dogs squirting out of their hands, danced to the rap music of L. L. Cool J. Pharoah, who sat with his mother and grandmother and his Aunt LaVerne as they admired his new outfit, mouthed the words to one of his favorite songs.

When I'm alone in my room sometimes I stare at the walls
And in the back of my mind I hear my conscience call
Telling me I need a girl that's as sweet as a dove
For the first time in my life—I see I need love
I need love.

"Keep the kids inside," a panicky voice hollered to LaJoe, distracting Pharoah from the rap music. "Keep them here. Someone's figuring to get killed at four trey." Dawn had come by with her four kids. Four trey was how everyone referred to the building next door, whose address was 1943 West Lake. LaJoe locked the door.

"Y'all stay inside, you hear," she told the children, who had momentarily stopped their dancing, knowing that something was wrong. Apparently there had been an altercation between drug dealers in the building, and Dawn was worried it might erupt into something more. Nothing, though, happened. The children resumed dancing. Dawn gave Pharoah a hug.

Just as Pharoah blew out the candles—after an off-key, half-shouted rendition of "Happy Birthday"—something heavy fell in the living room. The crash startled everyone. A relative of LaJoe's, who had passed out on the couch and had been there throughout the noisy party, had tried to get up to go to the bathroom. He didn't make it. He lay face down, urine seeping through his blue jeans onto the linoleum floor.

Pharoah took Porkchop's hand and the two went outside to get away from their drunken relative and the screaming kids. As they walked out the building's back door, they stopped. A teenage girl stood there vomiting. The two boys quietly walked around her. Pharoah hadn't stopped smiling.

It was a good few weeks for Pharoah. Not only did he celebrate his birthday, but he had been picked to recite a short poem at Suder's year-end assembly. Pharoah had gotten his stammer under control. It wasn't gone entirely, but he managed it better, having learned, when necessary, to slow down before he spoke. And so this was a big honor for him; it was as if his teachers were recognizing Pharoah for conquering his stutter.

As soon as Pharoah got a copy of the rhyme he was to recite, he set it to memory. He felt so confident that he eventually threw away the crumpled piece of paper he'd been carrying around in his back pocket for weeks. He wouldn't forget it.

He wanted to look tidy for the assembly, so he had his hair shorn. He also cleaned and ironed a black-striped sport coat that his mother had bought for him two Easters ago. He didn't have many occasions to wear it. With his neatly pressed white pants and olive-green shirt buttoned at the collar, LaJoe thought, he looked very handsome.

LaJoe got to the school's gymnasium early. She was as excited as Pharoah. When she saw her son on stage, she couldn't help thinking, There's the one. There's the one. I'm going to get it back.

Lafeyette sat with his class. He too was "happy for my little brother." Ms. Barone was so proud of her former student that she took a snapshot of him in his new clothes and haircut.

Pharoah had been on this platform before for the spelling bees, so he knew what to expect. He knew that he had to speak loud and clear, and that he needed to speak deliberately so as not to stumble. But in his excitement, as he stretched to reach the microphone, he realized that he had to go to the bathroom something awful. His bladder felt ready to burst. Not here, he told himself. He locked his knees together, tensing his bladder muscles. He wasn't going to pee on himself, not in front of all these people. He tried to look relaxed.

He spotted his mother in the crowd, with her full and open grin. But he tried to avoid her eyes and fixed his stare at the back of the auditorium. That way, he'd been told, it would look as if he were talking to everyone.

"Uh-uh-uh . . . uh." Pharoah paused. He wasn't going to stutter. Not here. Not now. Slow down, he told himself. Take your time.

"Try, try, try, try, that's what special effort means." His soft, amplified voice rang through the auditorium; once he got through the first line, his confidence returned. His heart was in it. He indeed believed hard work could overcome all.

And when you put your best foot forward, it really
    isn't hard as it seems.
Success comes to those who when given a chance
Do their very best and work hard to advance.
The special effort award is what they've earned.
Though it can't begin to match the things they've learned.

The applause rang in Pharoah's ears. He looked over to his mother. She winked. Lafeyette clapped so hard and long that his teacher had to ask him to stop. "Nice job," Ms. Daigre, the principal, whispered to Pharoah. He thanked her, stepped off the stage, and then sprinted for the bathroom.

That morning Pharoah received two certificates: one for placing second in the school's spelling bee, the other for special effort in math and reading. His brother Timothy got three, including the much coveted principal's list as well as one for scholastic achievement and another for excellent conduct. Tammie received one for outstanding student, another for excellent conduct. Tiffany got one for special effort in handwriting. "The only person who didn't get a ribbon was Lafie," Pharoah said later. "That made me feel bad." Along with the certificates came ribbons. LaJoe was so proud of her children's accomplishments that she pinned all eight of them to her white sweatshirt.

She paraded around the neighborhood all day with a rainbow of green, purple, white, and red ribbons hanging from her chest; she looked like a decorated war hero.

After the assembly, Pharoah and his mother attended a meeting at which it was announced that Pharoah was one of twenty-five Suder students chosen for Project Upward Bound, a summer school designed to assist minority students in bringing up their math and reading scores. Primarily a program for high school students, this Upward Bound, which operated at the University of Illinois, had in recent years begun to focus some of its efforts on sixth-, seventh-, and eighth-graders with the hope of following them through their four years of high school, working with them on Saturdays and during the summers.

The Upward Bound staff described the Summer Scholars program and then asked the assembled children what they wanted to be when they grew up. Pharoah knew. A congressman.

"I want to change a lot of rules," he told the others. "I want to change them and everybody move out of the projects. I'll pay people to build housing. Let the people who live in the projects live in other houses. Any gang member who has their hat turned, they'd go directly to jail. Stop stealing and stuff. A little kid got to come into a store with their parent or guardian or they can't come in. They'd probably steal."

He paused, then added, "If you be a congressman, there be people guarding me so you won't get hurt. I like that."

LaJoe and the children got caught up in the warmth and beauty of those first few days of summer. The children shot baskets on the jungle gym. At night, they wandered over to the stadium to watch cars and make a few dollars. Pharoah's and the triplets' awards at school had brightened the family's outlook. LaJoe displayed them on the wobbly shelves in the living room. They offered some promise of a better tomorrow. And everyone was thrilled with Pharoah for being picked to participate in the summer program. Pharoah would come back with tales of the University of Illinois campus that delighted LaJoe. He talked of the footbridges and the big glass buildings and of the students who seemed to be everywhere, always carrying books. Pharoah would tell LaJoe that he planned to attend college there. But it wasn't long before LaJoe was rudely reminded of summer's true character at Horner.

One afternoon, she and Rochelle were walking down Washington Boulevard to a corner store. She waved to two teenage boys she knew who were walking on the other side of the street; both wore red, the Vice Lords' color, in Disciples' territory. LaJoe noticed that two children, one no bigger than Pharoah, and a young man were tailing the two teens. They'd duck into alleys and behind the porches of the two-family homes on Washington. LaJoe yelled to the two teens that they were being followed. Then she watched in horror as the man handed a pistol to the little boy who reminded LaJoe of Pharoah in his small size and bobbing gait.

"Go kill the motherfucker," LaJoe overheard him say. The boy aimed the pistol, his entire body straining just to hold it straight, and opened fire on the two teens. POW. POW. LaJoe and Rochelle ducked into the corner store for cover. The two teens ran. They escaped unharmed.

The incident angered and frightened LaJoe. How did that little boy even know whom he was shooting at? All he saw was a couple of people wearing red and their hats turned to the left. From the back, they could have been girls. Later that day, LaJoe ripped the red Louisville cap off Lafeyette's head and told him he couldn't wear any hats. No earrings, either, she told him. That was that. She was putting her foot down. That could have been Lafeyette the boy was shooting at.

Twenty-seven

HAD LAJOE KNOWN about the July 13 meeting held by the Chicago Housing Authority's new chairman, Vincent Lane, she would have attended. But Lane wanted to keep it small. A large meeting, he feared, would lead to shouting and complaints. He wanted to meet with the neighborhood's leaders, to reassure them that the housing agency was going to clean up the basements.

Twenty residents, most of them women, packed the first-floor apartment at 1900 West Washington that had been converted into an office for Horner's tenants' association. It had been many years since the group had been a real force in the neighborhood, but it was the only organized group of residents in the complex, and its leader, Mamie Bone, could, when she wanted, make lots of noise and force a swift response.

The women found seats on the folding metal chairs as they fanned themselves with their hands to push away the still and heavy heat. They bristled with anger. It had taken them weeks to get an accurate and full account of the mess in their basements. They'd heard rumors, all right. When the tales began to circulate, the tenants whispered among themselves about radioactive material beneath their buildings. Then they heard talk of brand-new stoves and cabinets, thousands of them, sitting below them, unused. Finally, though, when they couldn't get answers from the bureaucrats at the housing authority, Ms. Bone went down to see Lane personally. She told him what she'd heard, and he began to ask around. He had heard nothing about the problem with the basements.

Gwen Anderson's April 20 memo had never reached him. Those who had received the memo held on to it; they were afraid they would get fired if Lane found out about the two thousand rusted ranges and refrigerators. When Lane learned of all this, he was outraged. And when he finally got hold of the memo, six weeks after it was written, he got sick to his stomach. Nobody ever thought of the tenants, he fumed. Having been director for one year, he had come to understand that many of his employees had only one thing on their mind: preserving their jobs. And if that meant covering up mismanagement, even if it wasn't their own, so be it. Now he'd have to explain to Horner's residents why everything had been so hush-hush and why nothing had been done.

Vincent Lane provided some hope to LaJoe and the others at Horner, though he seemed an unlikely candidate to head the troubled housing agency. The eighth head in five years, he was a political unknown. When his name first surfaced in the spring of 1988 as a possible director, local reporters scrambled to find out all they could about the nominee. What they learned initially was somewhat disconcerting. He had never managed more than thirty-six employees; the CHA employed thirty-two hundred. And what's more, Lane, who at forty-five had become one of the city's premier black developers of residential housing, had shown only a passing interest in social issues. He eschewed New Deal politics, considered himself more a Republican than a Democrat, and cited Robert Moses, the deceased New York builder of public works, as his hero.

Baby-faced and broad-shouldered, Lane was occasionally mistaken for Jesse Jackson. Besides a passing resemblance, he possessed a similar personal magnetism. People flocked to him and developed loyalty and reverence. Friends boasted of their closeness to him.

Despite a temper that sometimes vented itself in lofty explosions, Lane could be gentle and warm. And when he spoke with people whose allegiance he wanted—tenants, employees, federal officials, the press—he placed his arm around their shoulders or rested it on their back, physically drawing them closer as if they were the oldest of friends. Women found him extraordinarily handsome, and in later months, after he became a kind of folk hero to the residents of public housing, some women greeted him with kisses and hugs and then dreamed with their friends about how magical it would be if they could manage to get a date with him.

Lane came to the job with few illusions. As early as 1965, *The Chicago Daily News* ran an extensive series on "the misery, bungling and a hellish way of life" at the Robert Taylor Homes, the city's largest development. It detailed regular shootings and rapes, broken elevators, and apartments so overheated that children got nosebleeds. A steady stream of reports and investigations followed. In one five-year period, 1978 through 1982, the CHA was the subject of half a dozen highly critical studies.

In 1968, a presidential commission on urban problems wrote of Chicago's public housing that "the sheer scale of such projects . . . is stultifying to the human spirit. Administration is heavy-handed. The . . . child caught in such a social environment is living almost in a concentration camp from which he has little chance of escape."

A 1975 *Chicago Sun-Times* series uncovered dubious, and possibly corrupt, practices on the part of Charles Swibel, then the CHA head. It alleged that Swibel's private management firm had received $79,000 a year in fees from a bank that handled lucrative CHA accounts, that Swibel turned CHA business over to politically connected firms, and that he waived waiting-list procedures for persons seeking to get relatives into the coveted elderly housing apartments. Swibel, who for nineteen years was boss of the CHA, became symbolic of all that had gone wrong with the authority. Under Swibel's tenure, Chicago's public housing had gone from bad to worse.

Then, as if all that weren't enough, a 1982 Department of Housing and Urban Development audit uncovered a roster of problems that eventually led to Swibel's dismissal. The 227-page report, which was unusually frank and blunt in its observations, concluded that only five of the agency's nineteen project managers were "competent or knowledgeable enough to be managing projects." It found that because of extensive patronage, the CHA never laid off or fired any of its 2288 employees, and that over a third of CHA elevators were out of commission at any one time.

The CHA, the report concluded, "is operating in a state of profound confusion and disarray. No one seems to be minding the store; what's more, no one seems to genuinely care."

Lane knew about all this. The exposés had all been widely known. Nonetheless, he was in for some startling surprises. It was even worse than had been reported.

Events in just his first few months on the job had eaten away at his optimism. He had come in knowing he had to win back the confidence of tenants and employees. He thought he could do so gradually, with gestures of good will. He organized town meetings at each of the developments. He met regularly with his staff. He built a new bridge to the Department of Housing and Urban Development, which provided most of the authority's funding and which only a year ago had threatened to take it over.

But Lane quickly learned the depth of the chasm. The CHA had been so poorly run that the staff didn't even have an accurate count of the number of tenants in its complexes or, for that matter, the total number of apartments. At town meetings, he heard stories that made him shake with anger. One woman testified that her refrigerator hadn't worked in two months. She stored her food at her daughter's. Others told of a front door that had swollen in the heat and wouldn't close, a bathtub and bathroom sink that periodically spewed out human waste, and plumbing leaks that went unrepaired for weeks.

But the most horrific stories were of the gangs and their virtual control of public housing's high-rises. Lane, in a move that in later months he conceded was the result of frustration and pique, decided to reclaim some buildings. The first one he raided was in Rockwell Gardens, a few blocks to the west of Henry Horner. With the help of sixty Chicago policemen, housing authority officials went from apartment to apartment, looking for weapons and drugs. They secured the building by constructing a makeshift lobby, placing doors at the entrance to the breezeway, and assigning full-time security guards. The one disappointment was that the police confiscated only one gun and made no arrests. Lane learned later that someone in the CHA had tipped off the gangs the night before. Overnight, they had moved their drugs and guns. The problem, Lane realized then, was more insidious than he had been led to believe.

In later months, Lane got word from a drug dealer that if he wanted to take back the high-rises at Rockwell Gardens, he could have them. The dealers would just move their operations to the low-rises at ABLA and other complexes. The low-rises would be harder for the housing authority to secure, since, unlike the high-rises, they didn't have only a single entrance that could be enclosed and guarded. Lane heard about threats on his life. He was assigned two bodyguards. The CHA received a bomb threat. During one of the raids, which came to be known as sweeps, the police found two pounds of C-4 explosives and two electrical detonaters, enough to blow up a considerable section of a high-rise. This summer of 1989, Lane vowed to sweep all eight buildings at Rockwell and reclaim the entire complex from the gangs. Then came Henry Horner.

Lane arrived at the meeting twenty minutes late. The women might have been angry, but they wanted so badly to hear what was going on with their homes that they waited. They'd been stood up before by other CHA officials.

Lane, dressed immaculately in a gray suit, wasted no time getting to their concerns. He immediately began talking about the basements and the vacant apartments.

"The reason it was brought to my attention was because of

Mamie Bone," Lane told those assembled. "When I got the full scope of what we were dealing with, apartments that have been sealed with dead cats and dogs, it's just unbelievable. Unfortunately, our own staff tried to deal with it internally, but that didn't work."

Lane told the women it would cost as much as $500,000 to clean the basements and vacant apartments. But that wasn't all the money Horner would need, he told them. It would cost upward of $400,000 to replace the stolen heating coils. Moreover, the vacancy rate at Horner had soared because the CHA didn't have the money to fix up the apartments as tenants left; in some buildings, 85 percent of the units sat empty. Sinks and toilets had been stolen, as had window frames, 249 in all, which addicts sold for scrap.

"It's never been like this before," a tenant, James Mayes, yelled at Lane.

"It's been deteriorating for thirty years," Lane countered.

"Vince, I'm telling you, it's never been this bad."

Lane jumped up from his chair and, as happened when he got upset, his voice rose an octave. "Now, I'll tell you, I can't wave no wands or anything, but we're going to make a difference. Regardless of what Mayes says. But it doesn't happen overnight. We've got problems in CHA. Now, I feel as bad about the situation at Horner as anyone else. But it's not going to change overnight. We don't have the same resources."

A few *amens* rose from the seated women.

"The gangbangers and drug dealers are eating this development alive. We've got to make these buildings manageable . . . I have the faith and belief that people in public housing are no different than anyone else."

Lane told the gathered tenants he had to go; he had another meeting. They came up to shake his hand. One gave him a kiss on the cheek. He'd get the basements cleaned up, he assured them. He'd fix the heating coils. He'd get the money. But what he couldn't tell the tenants is that he wasn't sure what he'd do about the gangs and drugs.

Jimmie Lee may have been gone but as the residents knew all too well, there were many people waiting to fill in for him. No one stepped forward with the power and authority Lee had, but the drug trafficking continued and the gangs battled for retail turf. Standing in their way was a new and determined CHA led by Lane, so the gangs sent a message to him.

In one week's time, in late June, the local management staff at Horner came under attack. The assistant manager had to fend off two teenagers with a camera he was carrying. Three days later, the manager's 1989 Hyundai was vandalized while parked in front of the management office; the windows were smashed and the seats ripped. The office's key-cutting machine was taken. An elevator repairman had an $800 gold chain ripped from his neck. Then the offices were broken into and only files were taken. In later weeks, two female maintenance employees were badly beaten by a group of teenage girls, and a bricklayer had a gun put to his head when he mistakenly bricked over a bag of cocaine.

What's more, the local manager, Gwen Anderson, was shot at while escorting a group of U.S. Census workers through the development. During their tour, she discovered on the eleventh floor of 111 North Wood a gaping hole in a wall, which led to another building, 120 North Hermitage. The passageway was six feet high and six feet wide, big enough for people to pass through. The gangs had punched it out for easy escape from the police—and the tenants hadn't reported it because it gave them access to the other building's elevators if theirs weren't working. On seeing this makeshift tunnel, Anderson wept. No one had ever reported it to the office.

The main drug-dealing operations were now carried on at the building immediately to the west of Lafeyette and Pharoah's building, 1943 West Lake. The CHA had boarded over the windows of a first-floor vacant apartment there, but the gangs ripped out the wooden planks so that they had an escape route. In what became a war of nerves, the gangs ripped out the wooden boards and the CHA replaced them as often as four times a week.

Anderson wrote in a memo to her boss, Lane, that "these acts are deliberate messages being sent to us to back off. We cannot emphasize the urgency of this situation with regards to our safety, and coping with this level of stress, fears, and pressure; not to mention the sounds of gunfire which can be heard throughout the day in the Management Office." Anderson now wore gym shoes so that she could run if need be. She also carried a weapon in her purse and, though she wouldn't admit to it, didn't deny that it was a gun. The residents, had they known, certainly would have understood.

The shooting continued. Pharoah told his mother he hoped Lane would sweep their building. It would be good, he told her, if people had to have identification cards to get in. LaJoe thought it would help make life safer, but Lane had had dozens of requests from tenants to secure their buildings. He didn't have enough money to sweep them all. LaJoe's building was one of 125 Lane felt needed to be swept. But to do all of them, Lane needed $30 million, money the CHA didn't have.

One night in July, amid the *rat-a-tat-tat* of a semi-automatic weapon, LaJoe heard a noise in the hallway. She turned to see what it was. In his sleep, Pharoah was crawling in the hallway to escape the gunfire.

A few days later, Pharoah, now eleven, told a friend: "I worry about dying, dying at a young age, while you're little. I'll be thinking about I want to get out of the jects. I want to get out. It ain't no joke when you die."

Twenty-eight

LAFEYETTE sat on the edge of his bed as he quietly folded his shirts and his slacks and stuffed them into a cardboard box. His whole wardrobe fit without much fuss. Pharoah lay in bed and watched. The only sound was the water splashing against the bathtub and the occasional roar of the El outside. LaJoe poked her head through the door.

"Come on, Laf, we got to get going," she said. She looked at the box next to Lafeyette and realized how scared he must be.

Four weeks earlier, on June 2, Lafeyette had been arrested,

along with four other boys, for allegedly breaking into a small Toyota truck parked by the stadium. Taken from the truck were two speakers, a radar detector, twenty music tapes, and a box of shotgun shells. Lafeyette had insisted to his mother that he hadn't done it, that he happened to be passing by when a boy he knew only slightly smashed the window of the truck. Lafeyette told his mother he ran for fear of getting blamed. The police caught him and four others racing toward the safety of Horner. Today was their first date in court. It was Lafeyette's first arrest.

"They're not going to keep you locked up," she assured Lafeyette. "They're just going to hear the case."

"No, they kept Terence. I ain't coming back. Remember that day you told Terence to come and go to court and he didn't come back?" Lafeyette was referring to the time Terence had been falsely accused of shooting Maggie Atlas.

"Yeah, I remember that day." LaJoe didn't know what else to say. Though she knew better, LaJoe got to worrying too. What if they did keep Lafeyette? If they locked him up? What would she do? Could she last through another child's going off to jail? LaJoe gathered herself before her fears overran her.

"Take that stuff out of that box, Laf. You ain't going nowhere. Now come on; I'll meet you outside." LaJoe walked out of the room.

Lafeyette didn't take his clothes from the box. Instead, he placed the box on the highest shelf in the open closet.

"Don't you go wearing none of these," he instructed Pharoah, who remained tucked beneath the covers. "You hear me?"

"See you," Pharoah said softly. "Good luck." He too wasn't sure that Lafeyette was coming back.

Since the shoplifting incident and the altercation at the stadium last December, Lafeyette hadn't been in any trouble with the police. LaJoe had watched him closely. As she had requested, he no longer wore a baseball cap or his earring. He stopped going to the other side of Damen Avenue to the Four Corners' building. Lafeyette had been hanging out with a fast crowd, but he excused himself when it looked as if things might get out of hand. Just a couple of weeks ago, Rickey had asked Lafeyette if he wanted to go outside, but Lafeyette had had a bad feeling. Rickey seemed nervous and antsy, as if he were ready to do something. Lafeyette told him to go on without him. Later that day, Rickey was arrested for snatching a chain off a motorist stopped at the traffic light.

If anything, Lafeyette seemed to be spending more time in the house. He didn't trust going outside. Too much going on, he'd say. Too many wrongheaded people. But cooped up inside the sweaty, noisy apartment wasn't without its tensions. LaShawn often left in the mornings and didn't return until nightfall. "I'm going to the store," she'd tell Lafeyette or their mother. "I'll be back in five minutes." "Shawnie, you better be back. I ain't watching after your Baldheaded and DeShaun," Lafeyette or LaJoe would warn her. LaShawn wouldn't come back until evening. This scene repeated itself with such regularity that whenever LaShawn left home, it was assumed that LaJoe or Lafeyette or Tyisha would baby-sit for her kids. Lafeyette let her know how he felt. He'd yell at her for leaving her children behind. He'd tell friends of hers who came over that she wasn't home even if she was. He spoke his mind when it came to family and drugs. Though LaShawn denied taking anything since she'd gone cold turkey shortly before the birth of DeShaun four months earlier, Lafeyette suspected her of still dabbling, and like his mother, he'd have none of it.

Late in the afternoon of June 2, Lafeyette went to the stadium to watch the Chicago Bulls go in early for a playoff game. The kids often stood by the entranceway to catch a glimpse of their heroes, particularly Michael Jordan. Lafeyette was with a boy named Curtis. They craned their necks to see players Scottie Pippen and Horace Grant. No Michael Jordan.

At the same time, Michael Berger, who worked for a catering service, pulled up to the stadium in his white Toyota four-wheel drive. His company had been hired to cater a party for the Bulls and CBS. When he arrived, a young boy, no older than fourteen, asked Berger whether he couldn't watch his vehicle. Berger told him no. "I'd sure hate for something to happen to your truck, mister," the boy said. It was a not uncommon ploy: scare them into paying you to watch their car. But Berger refused. He locked the doors and pretended to set a burglar alarm.

Forty-five minutes later Berger came out of the stadium to find police surrounding the truck and the right passenger window smashed. The dash had been ripped apart. Whoever had broken in couldn't get the radio out, but had ripped it apart in trying. A few minutes later, a police officer spotted five black teens running toward Horner. They started dropping things from their pockets: a screwdriver, a pair of pliers, and five of Berger's tapes. Though he didn't know who dropped what, the officer arrested all five boys, including Lafeyette.

The Juvenile Temporary Detention Center, a five-story building, takes up an entire block. Only a mile and a half south of Horner, it was built in 1973, though it looks much newer. Everyone calls it the Audy Home, the name of the building it had replaced. Any child seventeen and under who has committed a crime is tried here unless the violation is heinous and violent, like murder or rape, in which case he or she can be tried in the adult courts.

Illinois's juvenile court system, founded in 1899, is the oldest in the country. It had once been staffed mostly by social workers. The lawyers have begun to take over. There are 250 probation officers and 137 state's attorneys, public guardians, and public defenders operating in the juvenile court. For many lawyers and judges, it's a training ground, a place where they can prove their mettle and move on to the real thing, adult court. Some attorneys derisively refer to it as "the kiddie court." It is not a friendly place. The attorneys and judges are overworked. Public defenders frequently have only a few minutes to prepare for a case. Judges handle seventy-five to eighty cases a day, twice the load of a judge in adult criminal court. Each probation officer keeps watch over thirty-eight to forty children.

The number of cases had jumped 40 percent in the three years since 1986. No one is quite sure why; speculation varies. It could be the rampant use of drugs or the unwillingness of the police to let juveniles go with just a warning, or the greater effort, for political reasons, to prosecute even the most minor of offenses.

The fourteen courtrooms line both sides of the first floor. The juvenile jail occupies the other four floors. The jail—or detention center, as it's called—houses up to five hundred children at a time. Some children have been sent here as many as fourteen or fifteen times. Many kids like it here. They're guaranteed three square meals a day, and the school is among the best in the city because of the low teacher-student ratio. Nonetheless, imprisonment can drive children crazy. Since the center's staff doesn't practice corporal punishment, misbehaving children are locked in their cells, narrow brick rooms six feet by thirteen. Some restrained children have, for lack of anything better to do, used their fingers to scrape away the mortar that holds the bricks in place. Some have dug deep enough to remove a brick and then urinate into the cell next to theirs. On the day Lafeyette went to court, Rickey was just completing a two-week stay here for the smash and grab he had committed on Damen Avenue.

LaJoe pushed her way through the revolving doors. A quiet and despondent Lafeyette followed. All LaJoe could think about was Terence. How often she had walked through these doors with Terence straggling behind her. Often, she didn't know if they'd leave together. Sometimes, they locked him up. Theft. Shoplifting. The shooting of which he was eventually exonerated. It exhausted LaJoe. But she always came with her son. She never let him come alone, as other mothers did. She waited with Terence on the hard-backed benches for their case to be called. Sometimes it took hours. She knew the building well by now. All cases involving children from Horner were heard in the same courtroom, Calendar 14. She could get tea from the vending machines in the basement, or, if they had to wait an especially long time, she could go across the street to Lu-Lu's for a hamburger or a pork chop sandwich. It was all so familiar. But it had been a while since she'd been here; Terence last had a case tried as a juvenile over two years ago. Now, she thought, here we go all over again.

The hearing was set for one-thirty. They had gotten there fifteen minutes early. It was to be a long, anxiety-ridden day.

After they walked through the metal detectors, LaJoe and Lafeyette went to the information desk.

"My son has a court date today. Can you tell me what courtroom he's in?" LaJoe asked the gray-haired lady behind the desk.

"What's his name?" the woman asked.

"Lafeyette Rivers."

The woman leisurely flipped through a pile of papers on her desk to the R's. "Is his name Derrick?" she asked.

"No. Lafeyette," LaJoe said patiently.

She flipped through another pile on her desk. "There's no Lafeyette."

"We were told to be in court today," LaJoe insisted. The gray-haired lady told LaJoe to go to the clerk's office. They, too, had nothing. So they sent LaJoe and Lafeyette to yet a third person who, like the others, flipped through a pile of papers. Nothing. LaJoe went back to the gray-haired lady.

"I know we got a court date today," LaJoe insisted. "I know it."

The woman sifted through her piles of paper again. "Lafeyette Rivers?" she asked, her finger resting on Lafeyette's name. "I'm sorry," she mumbled. "It was my fault. Just have a seat over there until Mr. Smith gets back from lunch."

LaJoe and Lafeyette joined the four other accused boys and their mothers on a marble bench in the lobby. Lafeyette took some ribbing for his T-shirt, which hailed the Detroit Pistons as the NBA champions. He had let his hair grow long and combed it straight back, so that now it almost reached his shoulders. Usually well groomed, he looked a bit ragged, though he had pressed his black Levi's and the T-shirt for the occasion. LaJoe wished she had gotten his hair trimmed.

Two of the boys were called into a nearby office. A few minutes later, the woman who was interviewing them peered out the door. "Were both those boys with you?" she asked of the remaining three children sitting nervously on the marble bench. Nobody answered. LaJoe was about to tell Lafeyette and the others not to respond. If they did, they might incriminate themselves, she thought. But before she could say anything one of the boys spoke up. "Yeah," Curtis told the woman. A bit ashamed at having put his friends at the scene of the crime, Curtis bowed his head. "They're only kids," LaJoe muttered to one of the other mothers. "She shouldn't do them like that." Though nobody explained it to the parents, such statements couldn't be used in court.

Lafeyette was called next. Each child who comes to juvenile court goes through an initial screening process in which a court official interviews the child to ascertain whether there is a real case. No statements made in the interview can be used in court. It is a way to weed out cases that do not have to go to trial. Children who have been arrested for stealing candy or toilet paper, for example, may just get a lecture and be sent home.

Lafeyette sat next to LaJoe across the desk from Mr. Smith, the court official. Lafeyette's eyes focused on the wall behind his inquisitor. He had admitted to LaJoe just before they walked into the room that he was scared.

"What's your name?" Mr. Smith asked.

"Lafeyette." His voice was barely audible.

"Where do you live?"

"Nineteen-twenty West Washington."

"What's your mother's name?"

"LaJoe Rivers."

"Your father's?"

"Paul Rivers."

"Where do you go to school?"

"Suder."

The questions were quick and impersonal. Lafeyette responded in kind. His hollow voice didn't carry. He refused to look at Mr. Smith.

Mr. Smith straightened a piece of paper in front of him and read it through quickly before reading it to Lafeyette and LaJoe. It was the allegation that he, with four others, had broken into a car and stolen over $300 worth of goods. "Did you do it?" Mr. Smith asked.

"No," Lafeyette replied and then proceeded to tell his version of the story. It was what he had told his mother. He and Curtis had been at the stadium to view the players after getting something to eat at a nearby store. When they were leaving, they saw a boy smash the window of the Toyota. Worried that the police might show up and blame them, they ran toward home. Lafeyette told it without any trace of emotion. He had insisted from the start that he was innocent.

Mr. Smith paused. It was clear that he didn't believe Lafeyette. He didn't seem even to have listened to his explanation. "You know better," Mr. Smith proceeded to lecture. "If one of your buddies is breaking into a car, leave."

"We did," insisted Lafeyette, his eyes still focused on the wall.

Mr. Smith continued, talking as much to himself as to LaJoe and Lafeyette.

"It's called extortion. They ask to watch your car. If you don't let them, they'll break into it. That's extortion. I'm smart. When I go to the stadium I give the kids a couple of bucks. Nothing will happen to it. If you don't give them any money, you know you better watch out. You just might have a window smashed. I'm smarter than that." And on he went, lecturing LaJoe and Lafeyette about all that he took into consideration when parking by the stadium. LaJoe shifted restlessly in her chair. Lafeyette continued to stare, his thoughts far away from Mr. Smith's reproof.

Finished, Mr. Smith handed LaJoe a copy of the complaint. He told her that the man whose car the boys had robbed had identified some of them. "It could be a problem," he said. He directed them to Calendar 7. Calendar 14, where the cases from Horner were usually heard, was closed down for the afternoon.

The waiting rooms are the size of racquetball courts. On each side are five rows of wooden benches. The courtroom is sealed off. Outsiders aren't allowed to view the proceedings, as they are in adult courts. People may wait hours for their cases to be called. Women have given birth in these waiting rooms, and gangs have brawled.

LaJoe gave her name to the deputy sheriff in charge of this courtroom. He told her he'd call them when their name came up. That was at two-thirty. Lafeyette and LaJoe sat. Occasionally, LaJoe would go out into the hallway for a smoke or would strike up a conversation with another mother. Lafeyette remained silent. He slumped on a bench next to Curtis. Curtis's name was called around three-thirty, and he left with his mother. Lafeyette sat and waited. He ran his fingers along the carvings on the bench. A dollar sign. A six-pointed star. The numeral four with a C and an H, for Four Corner Hustlers. He wondered what they'd been carved with. A screwdriver? A knife? A key? How did they get a tool through the metal detectors? His mind wandered. He wanted to go home.

A woman sitting next to LaJoe was close to tears. She'd been late to court that morning, so they had taken her son into custody. If a child missed his case when it was called, a warrant was issued, and when he arrived, he was placed in lock-up for the day. She worried that they might keep him overnight. LaJoe panicked. She didn't want them to take Lafeyette. She wondered if because of the switch in courtrooms she had somehow missed Lafeyette's case. She beckoned to Lafeyette, and half walked, half ran to the front desk to make sure. She was okay. The case hadn't been called. They returned to the waiting room.

At five-thirty, four cases remained to be heard. The deputy sheriff asked LaJoe her name again. "Rivers," she replied, holding back her exasperation. He flipped through his pile of papers.

"What's the name again?" he asked.

Without waiting for an answer, he said, "I'll take care of it." It was clear to LaJoe that somewhere along the way they'd misplaced Lafeyette's name. She and Lafeyette had been here for over four hours.

Twenty minutes later, the deputy sheriff called the last case. "Walter Helgo. Walter Helgo." LaJoe and Lafeyette were the only ones left on the benches. There was no Walter Helgo. "What's your name?" the deputy sheriff asked Lafeyette for the fourth time that afternoon. "Rivers. Lafeyette Rivers." The deputy sheriff disappeared into the courtroom.

Finally, at six o'clock, Lafeyette's case was called.

The courtroom held only the judge, the court reporter, the state's attorney, the public defender, and the deputy sheriff. Judge Robert E. Woolridge, a gray-haired man, had his head buried in papers. He never looked up. He never so much as glanced at Lafeyette. The questions started coming faster than Lafeyette could think, faster than even Mr. Smith could manage. "What's your name? When were you born? What's your address? Where does your father live? When did you last see him?" By the last question, Lafeyette was so flustered that LaJoe had to answer. "Three days ago," she said. The judge handed out the trial date: September 8.

As LaJoe and Lafeyette left the courtroom, LaJoe realized that the judge had given them a different court date from that of the other four boys, all of whom had since gone home. Had he made a mistake? Should she say something? She told the deputy sheriff. He told them to go back into the courtroom. They did. LaJoe explained the situation to the judge. She didn't want to cause him any problem, but she worried that he might have given them the wrong court date. Judge Woolridge looked up from his papers. "What's the name again?" he asked of Lafeyette, who had been before him only minutes earlier. "Lafeyette Rivers."

The judge looked bewildered. "Did we have a case by that name?" Someone in the courtroom stifled a giggle. Three minutes had passed and he didn't even remember Lafeyette. LaJoe felt as if no one cared. It was as if they were invisible. No one saw them or heard them or cared enough to treat them like human beings.

Lafeyette, though, was relieved. At least, he thought, he was going home. He could take his clothes out of the box. His case wouldn't be heard until the fall.

August 9

Dear Mom,
How are you and the family doing? Fine I hope. Well I'm fine, but I could be better if I was at home taking care of you, but it just got to be this way for now. You no what I'm saying but I no it's just a momentary thing so I don't let it get to me because only the strong shell survive. I no this a bad situation I'm in but I can handle myself because I'm only me. You understand. I'm just letting you no, mom, because your son is cooling . . . So mom how are my grandmother. Is she feeling better or what. Send me the address so I can write her because I haven't heard from her in 11 month and I'm worry about her. So mom when you write me send me the address okay. Mom tell cameo [Weasel's other nickname] and lashawn I said hi and dad, okay. Well mom I really don't got to much to say but tell everyone to take of they self . . .

So mom I guess I'm going to end this short brief but not never my love for you. From your son, Terence R. Rivers for sho!!
P.S. When are you coming out here to see me. Write back soon.

LaJoe read the letter to Lafeyette and Pharoah. Both boys liked to hear their brother's letters. But they didn't ask about him as they used to. They knew he would be away for a while. Their visits to him at the county jail had reassured them that he was okay. He always seemed happy then. "I can tell," Pharoah told LaJoe. "I know he okay. I can see it in his face."

"I don't like to see him in that predicament," Lafeyette said. "But now he can get his time over with. Then he'll be home with us again." LaJoe had told both boys that she was going to try to move so that Terence wouldn't have to come back to Horner.

Twenty-nine

EARLIER IN THE SUMMER, Weasel had brought home two pit bull puppies for Pharoah and Lafeyette. The boys kept them locked up in one of the bathrooms. Pharoah lost interest in his and eventually gave it away. But Lafeyette took a liking to his dog. Ever since his time with Bird Leg, he relished the thought of owning his own. He called his Blondie.

One July afternoon, Lafeyette came inside after hanging out on the porch with some friends. He went straight to the bathroom to say hi to Blondie and to take her out for a walk. The

puppy wasn't there. "Anybody seen my dog? Where she at?" Lafeyette yelled out to no one in particular. He walked up and down the apartment's long, narrow hallway, poking his head into each of the four bedrooms, calling, "Blondie, Blondie, Blondie." He whistled for her, too, but got no response. "If my dog don't show up, I'm gonna snap," he muttered to himself, loud enough for his mother and father to hear. His father was sitting on the couch, watching a show on public television; his mother was sitting at the kitchen table. "Somebody took my dog."

"Laf, there's nobody in here but me and and your father. Who you talking to?" LaJoe asked.

"Mama, I ain't talking to you," Lafeyette said, politely.

Paul knew what was going through his son's mind. Lafeyette, Paul thought, suspected him of selling the puppy for drug money. He got up from the couch.

"Son, if you continue to talk like that, to suspect me, I'm going to put you in your place." Lafeyette sat down at the kitchen table and gulped down a glass of milk. He ignored his father's protestations. It was a familiar scene. Lafeyette just pretended his father wasn't there.

"Who you going to snap on, son?" Paul asked.

"Anybody that be selling my dog."

"Your dog is here in the house somewhere. You have to look for it."

"You probably got it and sold it," Lafeyette accused.

"If I had got it and sold it, ain't nothing you could do about it," Paul challenged.

"I wish you'd stay out of our house. I don't know what you be coming back for. You be on the corner with all those dope fiends, embarrassing us."

"What'd you call me?" Paul walked over to Lafeyette, placed a firm grip on his shoulder, and shook him. "What'd you say?"

Lafeyette jumped up from his chair and, as Paul reached for him, backed up against the living room window. Paul reached for him again. "What'd you call me?"

Lafeyette's right fist came smashing into the side of his father's temple. Paul, once the amateur boxer, reeled back as much out of shock as pain, and then assumed the fighter's stance, his fists moving, circling his son.

"You're fourteen. You're of age. You want to be a man, okay, you got a chance to be a man," Paul told his son. Lafeyette could hold his own, but certainly not with his dad. The jabs hit Lafeyette sharply. In the shoulder. The chest. The armpit. The open-palmed slaps got Lafeyette across the head. Lafeyette didn't try to fight. He just tried to soften the blows. His eyes glared menacingly at his father, never losing contact. His body rocked from his father's stinging blows.

"Y'all stop that," LaJoe screamed as she jumped up from the couch to try to break up the fracas. "Y'all stop it." She restrained Paul for a moment, enough time for Lafeyette to grab his coat and run for the door. LaJoe and Paul said nothing to each other. LaJoe shared her son's anger. Paul was hurt by such an affront from his son. Minutes later, Lafeyette appeared at the front door. He held a steel chain in his right hand.

"C'mon outside. C'mon outside," he yelled at his father. "I'm gonna kick your ass."

Paul, whose nerves got the better of him in such tense situations, jumped up from the couch and headed toward his son.

"No, Paul!" LaJoe screamed. "Don't go out there. Y'all cut that out."

Paul hesitated. So did Lafeyette. "Boy, you don't know what you're up against." Paul pointed his finger at Lafeyette, who looked more scared than anything else. The last thing he wants is for me to come out there, Paul thought. He realized then that he had made a big mistake. He felt ashamed as much for how he had reacted as for putting Lafeyette in such a squeeze. Of course Lafeyette didn't respect him. For good reason. He sometimes didn't respect himself.

"LaJoe, talk to your son 'cause I'm having problems getting anything across to him. He don't want to, he at the point right now where he's not going to listen to me." Paul shrugged and sat back down. Lafeyette took a step into the apartment.

"You dope fiend," Lafeyette muttered. "That's the reason why you ain't working now, because you're a dope fiend." Paul's shoulders shrank. He knew no son would hit his father over a lost dog. It was the drugs. They had destroyed his relationship with LaJoe and now with his son. He had never hit Lafeyette before except for occasional spankings when he was younger. It wasn't his nature. Now, his own children were

turning on him. The only reason he came around was to see his children. He loved them but knew that he was failing them. Lafeyette's last remarks sapped what spirit and fight he had left. He sank onto the couch and didn't say a thing. Nor did Lafeyette, who continued to look for Blondie. He found her hiding under the stove.

Every morning, Pharoah went off to summer school at the University of Illinois. He awoke each morning with energy and verve and anticipation. He liked getting away from the neighborhood and the idea of being on a college campus. He also liked being considered a scholar. But his brother was tired. The long summer days dragged, and Lafeyette talked a lot about getting out of Horner. LaJoe told him again they'd move when Terence got out of prison. He and his father, who came around even less now, ignored each other. He kept to himself. He told his mother he'd stop hanging out with "the wrong people." But he seemed on edge. Ever since Craig's death in March he'd become more withdrawn. He stopped confiding in his mother. He stopped confiding in anybody.

One early July evening, under a cool drizzle, a group of teenagers on Damen Avenue surrounded a fourteen-year-old boy. LaJoe happened to walk by and could hear the taunts and then the sound of fists smacking. Then she heard a familiar voice. It was Lafeyette's. "Stop. Don't hit him. Stop." Lafeyette sounded frantic. He was in the middle of the fracas, trying to keep the others from beating his friend.

LaJoe ran to the circle and started making her way through. "Mama, make them stop," Lafeyette pleaded. His friend was doubled over, gripping his stomach.

LaJoe was furious. She turned to the group of kids. "What y'all doing? What y'all doing? Get off of him. What do you accomplish by this? Ain't you tired? What you beating on him for?" One boy said the surrounded youth had been fighting them. "How he beat on all of you?" LaJoe screamed. The teenagers seemed to listen to her only momentarily. One took a plank of wood and smacked the boy across the back. He doubled over again. It looked as if they might take on her and Lafeyette next.

A familiar voice rang out. "Don't hit my mama. Now y'all

don't hit my mama." It was a friend of Weasel's, a boy who, like others here, LaJoe had nurtured as a child. "Let 'em go. Ya hear me. They're straight." The other boys listened. They dispersed. LaJoe sent the beaten boy home. She and Lafeyette walked back to their building.

LaJoe wiped Lafeyette's forehead where he'd been nicked with a broken bottle. His face was without emotion: the eyes stared straight ahead, the head never bowed to one side or the other. He never cried. LaJoe would say, "When he laugh, you caught him off guard." His face seemed incapable of expression.

This evening, as they neared the porch, Lafeyette dropped to his knees. LaJoe wasn't sure whether he had slipped or whether his legs had just given out. "I'm tired, Mama," he said. She helped him to his feet. She wondered what he meant by tired. She remembered what Terence had once told her. She believed he was just tired of being.

Dawn answered the knocks on her front door. There stood two housing authority security guards. They told her she was being evicted from her apartment. The CHA had discovered that she'd been living there on someone else's lease. Dawn had known this would happen eventually, but nevertheless it caught her off guard. She spent the next two days moving what furniture she had back to her mother's, just across the street. There, she and her four children packed into one room. Demetrius slept where he could, occasionally bedding down in the back seat of his car.

Pharoah worried about growing up. "Maybe when I get a little older, I'll understand," he told a friend. "But," he added after a short pause, "I feel good not understanding."

LaJoe just noticed it one day. Lafeyette hadn't said anything about it. On his bedroom wall, he had hung the program from Craig's funeral. On its cover was a picture of Craig in his mortarboard and graduation gown. LaJoe thought it a good sign. Other than a few asides here and there, he never talked about Craig. This was the first indication she had that he was still grieving for him, four months after his death. Maybe, she thought, it would help him get over the sudden loss of his friend.

But two weeks later, LaJoe took the picture down. It had given Lafeyette nightmares. One in particular recurred a number of times, startling him awake, sometimes drenching him in sweat. It unnerved him just to talk about it. In the dream, someone—he didn't know who—was chasing him. But because of a strong wind, he couldn't run away. And when he tried to call for help, nothing came out of his mouth.

Thirty

THE RAINDROPS appeared incandescent in the midafternoon sun, like crystals falling from a chandelier. They looked as if they might shatter on hitting the ground. Pharoah stood by his bedroom window, mesmerized by them.

"Pharoah, let's get us some fries," Lafeyette said. Pharoah didn't hear. As was often the case, he was daydreaming, a prisoner of his thoughts. "Pharoah!" Lafeyette yelled, his adolescent voice rising. "Maaaan, Pharoah. You hear me? Let's get us some fries."

In order to get Pharoah's attention, Lafeyette started to reach across his bed to smack him. But Pharoah heard Lafeyette move up on him and turned around before any blow could be struck.

"It be raining," he said.

Lafeyette stuck his hand out the open window. "It ain't raining. Maan, you lying." Pharoah looked back outside. The rain, indeed, had let up. Bright rays of sunlight tore through the clouds like powerful spotlights. The effect was an eerie one; even the muddiest of puddles seemed to sparkle.

"Come on, you going?" Lafeyette asked.

"Yeah," Pharoah replied.

The two boys told LaJoe they were going to get some food; they'd be back shortly. They began the two-block walk to a take-out hot dog stand on the corner of Damen and Madison called Main Street. On the way, they ran into Rickey, who asked whether he could join them. They hadn't seen much of Rickey in recent weeks, especially after he had been arrested and then released a couple of weeks later. They'd heard rumors that Rickey was running drugs for the older boys, making as much as $600 a week. Nonetheless, both Lafeyette and Pharoah were fond of Rickey, as he was of the two brothers. They invited Rickey along.

At Main Street, Rickey bought Pharoah a bag of cheese-coated french fries. Lafeyette bought his own. They stood in the parking lot in front of the hot dog stand, relishing the cool, crisp summer air. Suddenly, Pharoah got excited. He couldn't quite get the words out. His neck strained; his mouth worked hard. Finally, he just pointed. Arching over the downtown skyscrapers was a rainbow. Its colors were brilliant, as if they'd been painted on the sky's canvas. Yellow. Green. Blue. Purple. Red. It seemed to emerge out of Lake Michigan and arc over the Sears Tower, setting down again just a mile or so south of Horner. It was the first rainbow the boys had ever seen.

All three—Pharoah, Rickey, and Lafeyette—stood in the middle of the parking lot, munching on their cheese fries, admiring the arc of colors.

"Daaag," Lafeyette muttered. "I thought it wasn't any real rainbow."

"L-l-l . . ." Pharoah tried again. "Let's-let's-let's . . ."

Rickey and Lafeyette were too taken by the sky's colors to notice Pharoah's stutter. That made it easier for him to slow down, to take his time. If they didn't see him or hear him or acknowledge his presence, they wouldn't make fun of his stammer.

"Letsgochaseit." He spat the words out so that they wouldn't get caught in his throat. "Letsgochasetherainbow."

"Maaan, I ain't gonna chase no rainbow," Lafeyette said, deriding his brother's loony scheme. "That's kiddie stuff."

"It-it-it . . . pro-pro-probbably be some gold there," Pharoah said. He was getting excited again. He tried to slow down. Maybe they could touch it. "Maybe," he told Lafeyette and Rickey, "there be leprechauns."

"Shut up," Lafeyette said. "Ain't nothing there." Rickey laughed heartily at Pharoah's imagination. He too thought there might be something there, but he didn't dare say so out loud. Lafeyette might think him foolish. He'd heard if you got to the end of such a thing you could dig and find some treasure. He'd been told that when he was younger. At thirteen he held on, however tenuously, to that hope.

"I'll go, Pharoah. C'mon," Rickey said curtly. Lafeyette shook his head.

"Go if you want. Don't make no sense," he scoffed.

Pharoah and Rickey trotted south on Damen, their eyes following the rainbow's arc. It looked as if it might come down right around Cook County Hospital, about a half mile away. They passed Damen Courts, where Pharoah used to go for peace and quiet. It had since been plagued by gangs, so he no longer visited its manicured lawns. They alternately ran and walked still farther south, their heads bobbing up and down from fatigue. As they approached Crane High School, from which Dawn had graduated last summer, Pharoah noticed that thick, milky clouds had begun to hide part of the rainbow. Then he realized it was beginning to fade.

"The rainbow's leaving," he said to Rickey, who was a few feet behind Pharoah, keeping an eye on his younger friend.

"Sure is," Rickey said. Pharoah ran faster. He hoped to get there before it disappeared altogether.

"Let's-let's-let's hurry," Pharoah urged.

"I ain't chasing it no more, Pharoah. It's going," Rickey said. Pharoah kept racing, ten, twenty, then thirty yards in front of

Rickey, who was shaking his head, smiling at Pharoah's excitement, not letting his little friend get out of his sight. The rainbow vanished, its colors melting back into the sky. Pharoah craned his neck. Nothing. Dejected and exhausted, he walked slowly back to Rickey.

"Man, we could of seen what was there. We could of seen what was there," he insisted. Rickey was too out of breath to argue. They walked the three blocks back to the Main Street hot dog stand in silence.

Lafeyette was still in the parking lot, eating his fries, the setting sun warm on his back. He too had watched their treasure fade. "You was psyched out," he needled Pharoah and Rickey. "I told you so. Man, it stupid. Chasing rainbows." Rickey laughed.

Eleven-year-old Pharoah said nothing. He couldn't believe how close they'd come. He knew there might not be anything at the rainbow's end, but he wanted the chance to find out for himself. What if they'd gotten there and there'd been all this gold? That would have shown Lafeyette. At the least, he figured, he could have made a wish. He had turned it over in his mind as he was running. Not until weeks later did he disclose what his request to the heavens would have been.

"I was gonna make a wish," he said. "Hope for our family, like get Terence out of jail, get a new house, get out of the projects." When he disclosed his appeal, he had to stop talking momentarily to keep himself from crying. It hurt to think of all that could have been.

Lafeyette too conceded that he'd wondered about what they would have found at the rainbow's end. He had pooh-poohed the chase as kid stuff. But maybe Pharoah was right. Maybe they could have found something there. Heaped with disappointments, fourteen-year-old Lafeyette wanted to believe. He wanted to be allowed to dream, to reach, to imagine. He wanted another chance to chase a rainbow.

Maybe, he said later, "there be some little peoples, not more than an inch, just about this little." He held apart his skinny index finger and thumb. "I wish I could of found some real little peoples and they'd of been my friends, went home with me. I wouldn't of told nobody."

_____ September 29, 1989 _____

Thirty-one

LAJOE grabbed Lafeyette's hand before they walked through the revolving doors of the Juvenile Temporary Detention Center. She could see the fear in his tightly wound face. Last night, Lafeyette had asked her, "Mama, what you think's gonna happen?" "They're gonna let you go," she had told him, only half believing it herself. As she caressed her son's thin hand this morning, she assured him that "everything's gonna be all right. You hear me? Everything's gonna be all right." Lafeyette looked away.

The two slowly pushed through the revolving doors. Lafeyette, dressed in gray corduroys and a gray T-shirt, hobbled along on crutches. The previous week, he'd taken a fall on the stairwell in a friend's building. The metal stripping had come loose on one of the steps, and Lafeyette tripped over it, stumbled down a full flight of stairs, and tore a ligament.

In the waiting room at Calendar 14, LaJoe and Lafeyette met up with the four other accused boys. Accompanying two of them were their mothers; another had his father there; another stood by his uncle, who couldn't have been more than seventeen.

Pharoah had said he didn't want to come and, besides, he had school. He'd come with LaJoe and Lafeyette for a court date in August, but the case had been postponed then. Pharoah had barely said anything during the visit. He mostly worried about his brother. This morning before he left for school, he told his mother that he had prayed for Lafeyette the night before. He thought the judge might send his brother to the detention center. Of the triplets, only Tammie expressed any interest in coming. "His leg's hurting and if they keep him they might not take care of him right," she told her mother. LaJoe assured her that Lafeyette would be all right, and sent her to school with the others.

In the waiting room, the five boys barely spoke to one another. With the exception of two who were cousins, they didn't know each other well. Lafeyette had spent time only with Curtis—and even that had been on rare occasions. The boys all lived in the same neighborhood but hung out with different crowds. Lafeyette sat on the wooden bench next to Curtis. The cousins sat on another bench. The fifth boy, Derrick, who Lafeyette said had broken into the car, sat by himself.

After a short wait, their public defender, Anne Rhodes, called the five boys, the three mothers, the father, and the uncle into a small room by the courtroom. She wanted to explain their options. Anne Rhodes on first encounter appeared hard-boiled and curt, almost as if she didn't care. A tall woman, nearly six feet, she sometimes forgot that her size intimidated the youngsters, most of whom barely came up to her shoulder. She spoke forcefully and quickly and took little guff. And because her caseload was so large—over four hundred active cases at a time—she had little time to befriend or comfort her clients. LaJoe found her

unfriendly. Lafeyette so disliked her, he thought she was prejudiced against blacks. He felt she'd already made up her mind
that they were all guilty.

But Anne Rhodes's appearance and demeanor were deceiv-
ing. Unlike many of the public defenders who were assigned to
juvenile court and viewed it as a training ground, Anne Rhodes,
thirty-two, chose to work here. She wanted the trial experience,
but, more important, she wanted to feel that she was doing
something useful. What could be more redeeming, she thought,
than defending troubled children from impoverished neighborhoods? She'd been here two years, and it had been a difficult and
tiring period. She started out in Abuse and Neglect, where she
saw children taken from their parents in trials that lasted no
more than five minutes. Before the year was out, she was transferred to Calendar 14, where she represented children from numerous housing projects, including Henry Horner. Half the
time, the children's parents didn't show up. And when they did,
they often created problems themselves. She once saw a
drunken mother slash a deputy sheriff across his face with her
fingernails. The children could be brash and unnerving. One
time in the courtroom a youngster flashed gang signs at the
complaining witness's brother. All this horrified her: the over-
load of cases, the absence of parents, the hastiness and confusion
of the trials, and ultimately the inattention to the children.
"We're supposed to be helping them and we just don't have
time," she lamented. "It's scary." Nonetheless, she stuck with it.
There were moments—like the time a fifteen-year-old boy who
was on trial for mugging people with a fake gun burst into tears
in his mother's arms—when Anne was reminded that whatever
their misdeeds, they were still just children.

The adults stood against the room's white walls as the five
boys huddled around the circular table. Lafeyette, because of
his injured leg, sat down in one of the room's two chairs. Anne
began with her usual lecture. "There's going to be a trial," she
told the boys and adults. "The person making a complaint
against you will testify. Then you will. Just tell the truth. If you
don't remember, don't be afraid to say you don't remember."

Curtis, the largest and oldest of the accused, spoke up. "If I
didn't do it, how come I have to sit up here with them?" he
asked indignantly, nodding at his codefendants.

"Shut up," Anne shot back. She then chastised herself for her impatience. In the rush to get things done, she could become short-tempered and abrasive. She never had enough time. She knew that the children rarely felt they were getting adequate attention. But what could she do, she thought, when she had as many as fifteen cases to handle each day? And the irony in this instance was that she believed most of the five boys were innocent.

The meeting lasted another ten minutes, during which Anne continued to explain the procedure. On the way out, Curtis turned to Lafeyette. "I hate her," he said. Lafeyette nodded in agreement. They returned to the wooden benches in the waiting room.

About a half hour later, Anne Rhodes approached the boys and their parents. She explained that the man whose car had been broken into, Michael Berger, was willing to make a deal. If each boy's family would pay him $100 in restitution, she told them, they wouldn't go to trial. Instead, the boys would be placed on supervision, which is essentially probation without a finding of guilt. The boys and their parents had stopped listening. After hearing the amount $100, they had begun shaking their heads. For LaJoe that would be one fifth of her monthly income. "We're gonna go to trial," one mother said. The others agreed. "Where am I gonna get that kind of money?" another asked rhetorically. The boys remained silent. Anne had expected this response. It happened all the time. The victim comes to court figuring he might get reimbursed for his losses, but the families can't afford it. They almost always turned down any deal involving restitution. They'd be going to trial later this morning—and Anne still had to prepare for it. She hadn't yet talked to the kids about what had happened that day. She hadn't had the time. In the best of all worlds, she thought, each of these kids would have his own lawyer and she would have been able to prepare for trial days in advance. What if one of the children witnessed who did it—and was willing to testify? There was nothing she could do. The Public Defender's office had the resources and time to assign only one lawyer to all five boys.

Lafeyette slouched on the bench. He said nothing. His crutches rested at his side. He didn't like Anne Rhodes; her brusqueness upset him. Lafeyette had told his mother again that it was Derrick who had broken into the truck. Though Lafeyette had resolved not to snitch on him, he was afraid the judge might trick him into telling. All he wanted to tell the judge was that he didn't do it, that he didn't break into the truck.

Anne asked to meet with the five boys—without the adults. She had five minutes to prepare for trial. She needed to hear their stories—quickly. She asked them what happened. She needed to figure out who should testify, who would be the most articulate. It was clear from listening to them and seeing them together that they weren't all friends. That made it seem unlikely to her that they had all broken into this truck as an organized gang of kids. Moreover, they all seemed to have credible alibis—except for Derrick, who conceded that he had asked the man whether he wanted his car watched. The two cousins said they were on their way to the stadium to work in one of the parking lots for the game that night. Curtis and Lafeyette explained that they were returning from a store on Madison Street.

Even with adequate time, trial preparation was difficult with children, Anne thought. They could rarely remember where they were on a particular day. Every day seemed like the next to them. And they didn't know which direction was north or south or east or west, so that when the prosecution asked them which way they were headed, they often got flustered. In the end, she felt, children just wanted to please adults, so they would do what they could to that end.

As Anne scribbled notes on her legal pad, she began to believe more firmly in the innocence of at least most of these boys. She thought they might have a good chance of acquittal in front of Calendar 14's judge, Julia Dempsey. Judge Dempsey, a middle-aged former attorney for the Illinois Board of Education, heard all the cases from Horner. She was noted for her compassion toward the children. She went out of her way to make sure they got good counseling or adequate care from their probation officers or in the detention center. Most public defenders liked her because they thought her fair when it came to sentencing. The police thought her too soft. In one station house, they hung her picture on a wall and peppered it with darts. Anne chose the three most verbal of the boys to testify. Lafeyette was not one of them. He'd barely said anything in the short meeting. He rarely did.

Soon after Anne met with the boys, the deputy sheriff called the case. The five boys and the adults walked into the spacious courtroom. Its high ceiling and sparse furniture made it look unusually large. To the left hung the American flag. Judge Dempsey sat behind a raised desk. The public defender and the prosecutor each had a metal table on opposite sides of the room. In the back were two rows of wooden benches where the adults all sat.

The five youngsters nervously lined up in front of the judge. Lafeyette leaned lazily on his crutches. "Lafie, Lafie," LaJoe whispered loudly across the courtroom, "stand up straight." He pushed his thin body up on the crutches, perched on one leg. Anne handed one of the boys a small piece of paper, pointing to his mouth. He spat a wad of gum into the paper, crumpled it up, and shoved it in his pocket. Another fidgeted with his hands. As the judge determined the identity of each child, the boys stood erect, almost automatically placing their arms behind their back. All LaJoe could think was that it looked as if they were handcuffed. Her stomach churned with anxiety. The judge told the boys to raise their right hands as a court officer asked them if they swore to tell the truth. In unison, they muttered, "I do."

The trial lasted about twenty minutes. Michael Berger testified as to what happened and what he had lost. He pointed out Derrick in the courtroom as the boy who had asked if he could watch the truck.

"He approached the vehicle," Berger said under questioning from Andrea Muchin, the state's attorney. "I couldn't get out of the vehicle. He was in the open area where the door was and he asked if I wanted my truck watched and I told him no. And he told me he sure would hate for something to happen to my truck."

Andrea looked to another prosecuting attorney for help. This was her first trial. She was nervous, unsure as to what to ask the witnesses. She identified with the victim, whose catering service was located in the suburb where she'd grown up. She believed his story. But she wasn't sure that all five boys had broken into his truck. She thought she'd be lucky if the judge found just

Derrick guilty. Her partner assured that she had asked the right questions.

After Berger, two police officers testified. The first, Bill Freeman, was stationed at the Boys Club and knew the neighborhood children well.

"What happened when you arrived in the area?" Andrea asked Freeman.

"I observed five male black teens running northbound," Freeman replied.

"Did you see the five male black teens that you observe in court today?"

Freeman turned and pointed to the five boys, describing for the court reporter what each was wearing.

"What happened after you saw the minor respondents?" Andrea continued.

"I ordered them to stop and at that time they began dropping stuff from their pockets."

"When you say dropping stuff, could you describe what stuff that was?"

"Screwdrivers, pliers. I couldn't tell you which one dropped what, but they were dropping."

"Did you recover any of this stuff?"

"Yes." Freeman said he also found five tape cassettes.

The next officer who testified had arrived on the scene after Freeman apprehended the five boys. He testified that he found part of the truck's radio on Derrick and, contrary to Freeman's testimony, that he had recovered the screwdriver and pliers from Curtis. In cross-examination, Anne Rhodes tried to establish that the officer couldn't remember whether Curtis was wearing sweatpants or shorts. In later testimony, Curtis said he was wearing shorts without pockets.

Anne called Derrick, Curtis, and one of the cousins to testify. Their alibis, filled with gaps and pauses, seemed unconvincing in the courtroom. When the state's attorney asked Curtis what store he was coming from, he replied that he didn't know the name of it.

"What did you buy at the store?" Andrea asked the youngster.

"I can't recall that either. We just going up there," Curtis answered.

"And so you don't recall what you had bought?" she shot back.

"No," he muttered.

Anne knew they'd have trouble remembering such specifics. It had been four months since the crime occurred. What kid could remember what kind of junk food he'd bought that long ago? Anne argued that the evidence was "purely circumstantial." She also tried to point out apparent contradictions in the testimony from the police.

"One of the minors stated in court that he had two tapes," Anne told the judge in her closing remarks. "The officer testified that he found three tapes on him and the other officer said he found five. The inventory said five tapes, and none of them were listed." She also pointed out that the radio part allegedly found on Derrick had never been inventoried by the police.

"Further, Your Honor," Anne continued, "there has been no eyewitness testimony as to anyone actually seeing these minors breaking into the truck. There was a conversation between one of the minors and the complaining witness. The complaining witness did not give any testimony that he saw any of the other four minors here in the area of the automobile . . . We believe that the evidence put in the testimony today falls woefully short of proof beyond a reasonable doubt. And we ask for a finding of no delinquency."

Judge Dempsey, though, felt differently. She had seen many cases like this. Cars by the stadium got broken into all the time. The kids always denied they were involved.

"I have no doubt whatsoever but that these minors broke into the car and took all of those things," she told the two attorneys in front of her. The faces of the five boys, who sat in the first row of benches, remained blank. No smiles or smirks. No anger or tears. Expressionless. Judge Dempsey continued, "And just because some of the things were not found does not place any doubt on the guilt of these minors . . . I am going to enter a finding of delinquency that is against all five of them on the case. Do any of them have any background?"

"No," Andrea replied.

"No background? This is the first?"

"Yes."

"If they had background I would have taken them into custody," the judge said. "I think they are really a big threat to the public . . . out there breaking into cars that are parked. The disposition [sentencing] date on all five is October eighteen."

Both Anne Rhodes and Andrea Muchin were surprised by the verdict. Anne truly believed that at least four of them were innocent. She'd done what she could—but that, she conceded, was limited. Five minutes to prepare for trial. One attorney for all five boys. "We're looking at our future [in these kids] and we're not doing our job," she would say later. The rookie prosecutor, Andrea, hadn't thought she'd be victorious in her first trial. She felt certain that the judge would find one of them guilty. But not all five. In later months, she, like Anne, would become perplexed and saddened by the huge volume of cases and the little time she had to prepare for them. For her and for Anne it made no sense—such little attention paid to the defendants, all of them children, who most needed it.

Lafeyette thought the judge would lock them up, and when she didn't, his immediate reaction was relief. His face didn't show it, though. It looked angry. Angry that Derrick had not confessed his crime. Angry that he didn't have a chance to say he hadn't broken into the truck. Angry that the judge said he had done something he adamantly denied doing. Angry that even his public defender didn't seem to believe him. The five boys walked out of the courtroom without exchanging a word. Though on crutches, Lafeyette was the first one out the door. He didn't linger. He hobbled ten feet in front of his mother until he left the building through the revolving doors. There, he waited for his mother and muttered something unintelligible under his breath.

"What'd you say?" she asked.

"Mama, I got a case, don't I?" he repeated.

"You don't have a case. You have a record," she explained.

"For what?"

"For breaking into a truck."

"But I didn't do it," he insisted.

"They found everybody guilty."

"Ain't nothing you can do?" he pleaded.

"No."

Lafeyette raced ahead on his crutches.

• • • •

Once home, Lafeyette went straight to his room. He hadn't said anything since the short conversation outside the court-house. An hour later, Pharoah came home from school, his heavy bookbag slung over his shoulder.

"Where's Lafie?" he anxiously asked his mother.

"He's in the back," LaJoe said.

Pharoah ran to his bedroom. LaJoe could see he was happy that his brother hadn't been locked up. He had been worried. The two brothers looked out for each other. Pharoah, in partic-ular, now worried about Lafeyette.

As LaJoe sat on the couch braiding the hair of one of the triplets, she heard shouts from one of the back bedrooms. It was Lafeyette and Pharoah arguing over a shirt. Lafeyette had lent Pharoah's Bulls T-shirt to Tyisha without asking.

"You better get it back!" Pharoah shrieked.

"I ain't gonna get nothing," Lafeyette huffed.

"Yes, you is!"

"No, I ain't!"

As LaJoe walked toward the back to break up the fight, she smiled. At least, she thought, I still have both of them. At least they're still mine. She never thought it could be such a comfort to hear her sons arguing.

Epilogue

IT HAS BEEN nearly a year since Lafeyette was found guilty of breaking into a truck. He was given a year's probation and was required to perform a hundred hours of community service at the Boys Club. After school, he worked with small children. He taught them how to catch a ball and played games with them. He said he tried not to be too mean with the younger children and that if they cursed he told them to stop rather than kicking them out of the club, as he was supposed to do. Lafeyette loved being a big brother to small children. But his troubles didn't end with probation.

I helped get both boys into a private school a couple of miles west of Horner. Providence—St. Mel had been a parochial school until 1978, when the city's archdiocese threatened to shut it down. The school's principal, Paul Adams, kept it open as a private institution. All of the five hundred students there are black; three quarters of them are from the surrounding neighborhood. Paul Adams runs a strict school. No gangs. No drugs. No excessive absences or tardinesses. The children are financially rewarded if they make the honor roll. Over 90 percent of each graduating class goes on to college. Funding is a constant struggle, though. Half of the school's annual $2 million budget comes from private sources, mostly individuals, foundations, and corporations.

Pharoah is thriving there. He likes being challenged and being given two hours of homework every night. It hasn't all been easy for him, though. Behind in his reading and math scores before he entered, he hasn't completely caught up. His one consistently good subject is not surprisingly, spelling, in which he gets mostly A's. His daydreaming and forgetfulness have sometimes interfered with school. There were times, for instance, when he forgot to complete assignments. Now he writes down upcoming events in a small notepad that he calls his "memo." He also had a problem getting to school on time. His teachers suggested that he repeat sixth grade to buttress his basic skills, but Pharoah insisted on going on to seventh. The school agreed to promote him on the condition that in the first month of the next school year he reduce his tardy days, get his assignments in, and maintain good grades. If he didn't live up to the terms of the contract, they would place him back a year. Pharoah willingly signed the contract. He also, through the school, was awarded a full scholarship to a six-week summer camp in Indiana.

For Lafeyette, Providence–St. Mel was more of a struggle. He was unable to keep up with the work, and returned to public school with two months left in the year. The year wasn't by any means a waste, however. Lafeyette discovered what it meant to be a serious student. He occasionally went to school for five to six hours on a Sunday to try to catch up on his assignments.

And despite his poor grades, he learned a lot. He talked with great enthusiasm about the Aztecs and Madeleine L'Engle's book *A Wrinkle in Time*. He also learned to ask for help, something that is extraordinarily difficult for him.

But after just two months back in public school, Lafeyette was wrestling again with the lures of the neighborhood. He was caught smoking marijuana one morning before school with boys considerably older than he—and on occasion he played hookey. After his mother was called to the school, Lafeyette admitted he had made some mistakes, and promised his mother he would straighten up. LaJoe knows that it's not a neighborhood that allows adolescents room for mistakes, so she has kept a close eye on her son.

On June 19, 1990, Lafeyette, who had just turned fifteen, graduated from eighth grade. It was one of the few times he seemed truly happy and at ease. He laughed and smiled and embraced his mother and friends with such warmth and spirit that everyone around him was filled with pride and hope for him. It was a small but important victory for Lafeyette.

He plans to enter a parochial school next year that won't be as academically rigorous as Providence–St. Mel and that offers special assistance to children who have learning problems.

It has been well over a year since Craig Davis was shot and killed by the Bureau of Alcohol, Tobacco, and Firearms agent, and Lafeyette still will not talk about his friend. The ATF and the police also have remained mum, refusing to discuss the case. One police official, however, who said he couldn't talk about the incident, challenged the contention that Craig was not a gang member, despite the considerable evidence to the contrary. "Al Capone didn't have a criminal record either," he asserted in our brief phone conversation.

Craig's mother, Christine, plans to file a lawsuit against the ATF. Twice a year, she visits her son's grave at the Restvale Cemetery, placing on it a wheel of roses and a small American flag. The site is unmarked; it can be found by locating Section A3, Lot 7, Grave 140. She has been unable to afford a tombstone.

Rickey began running drugs for one of the local gangs, though he insists that he has since stopped. The Four Corner Hustlers slowly evolved into a gang that sold drugs, rivaling the Conservative Vice Lords and the Disciples. A man in his early twenties, fresh out of prison, became the group's leader. Rickey and his friends continued to belong to the Four Corner Hustlers.

Last February, the police caught Rickey with a long butcher knife. Since he was on probation for breaking into a car, they put him back in the Juvenile Temporary Detention Center for six weeks. He's been to numerous court psychiatrists, all of whom have told his mother that he's mad at the world and feels it owes him something. His mother checks Rickey's room every couple of days to make sure he isn't storing any guns there. Rickey rarely attends school and spends many nights away from home. "I feel someone's gonna hurt him or he's gonna hurt someone if he doesn't get out of here," his mother says.

Lafeyette doesn't hang out with Rickey anymore, though they run into each other all the time. Lafeyette still likes his friend and worries about him. Rickey turned fourteen in December 1989.

If there is one constant at Henry Horner, it is the violence. Gwen Anderson, the CHA's manager at Horner, was transferred to a less stressful job. In one two-week period in the spring, six people were shot, including a plainclothes detective who was returning from a hockey game at the stadium. He was robbed and shot with his own revolver. Luckily, the bullet only grazed his head. The proprietor of the Main Street restaurant, where the boys first saw the rainbow, was also shot. Pharoah and Lafeyette had both gone there to buy a sandwich for their mother and saw his body wheeled out on a stretcher. They presumed him dead. I happened to stop by the apartment the next morning to run an errand with LaJoe. Pharoah was late for school. He said he didn't have any clean socks—and then started crying. He told me about his friend at the restaurant being shot. He recounted how he and Porkchop would go there to buy french fries or a hamburger and how the man would joke with them. "Ya wanna hamburger?" the man would ask. "Thirty-seven dollars. Ya hear me? Thirty-seven dollars." Pharoah said he and Porkchop would laugh at their friend's jokes. A few days later, Pharoah, much to his relief, learned that his friend had survived.

Weeks later, Lafeyette saw a friend run out of a building, clutching his stomach and hollering, "I've been shot! I've been shot!" Lafeyette thought he was joking until the friend moved his hand, revealing a circle of blood. Lafeyette ran to the corner store to call an ambulance. None of these shootings made the newspapers.

Both Lafeyette and Pharoah want to move to a safer and quieter neighborhood. Lafeyette talks about it on occasion. So does Pharoah, who sat on his bed one day and cried because he worried that he might never get out of the projects.

In the spring, shortly after the spate of shootings, LaJoe tried to move—and for two months it seemed as if she'd found a way. Through friends, she contacted a man named Robert Curry, who told her that for $80 he could get her name on the top of a waiting list for subsidized housing. She gave him the money and over an eight-week period met with him regularly at a local McDonald's. Lafeyette and Pharoah told all their friends. Lafeyette began packing his clothes. For two weeks, LaJoe vigorously cleaned her apartment in anticipation of a housekeeping inspection. Curry took her to the city's north side one Saturday to look at apartments and gave her the address of a building that might have apartments large enough for her family. She planned to take with her Lafeyette, Pharoah, the triplets, and possibly LaShawn's three children. But it wasn't to be. As the promises flowed and the time dragged, LaJoe became suspicious. Finally, she went to check out the address of the building where she was promised an apartment. It didn't exist. That same day, Curry was arrested on charges of theft by deception, having allegedly sold false promises to a group of residents in another neighborhood. His was the second housing scam uncovered that year. Pharoah asked why someone would do such a thing. LaJoe had no answer. She had suspended her disbelief for a while—and now felt humiliated and depressed. It was yet one more disappointment. She planned to testify at Curry's trial.

Some things have improved. Chicago Housing Authority employees, wearing moon suits and gas masks, cleaned the basements at Henry Horner, removing the animal carcasses and rusted appliances. The CHA has also repaired leaking roofs and replaced the missing heating coils at Horner. In the Riverses' apartment, the CHA fixed the bathtub faucet so that it no longer runs day and night. Also, LaJoe got a new stove as well as paint, which she and Lafeyette used to put a fresh coat on the walls in the kitchen and in two bedrooms.

Vincent Lane, the CHA's director, raided and reclaimed all eight buildings at Rockwell Gardens. Each high-rise now has round-the-clock security guards. Lane provided nine hundred new bedroom doors for families who had long gone without them. The complex has new playground equipment, and in the spring the area is awash in bright colors: pink and red begonias, pink and white spider ladies, and seven hundred white and pink rosebushes. CHA employees there wear buttons that read I'M PART OF THE SOLUTION.

On one of his frequent visits to Rockwell, Lane met an elderly tenant who was standing outside her first-floor apartment. She took Lane's hand and pressed it between both of hers. "I'm very pleased with what you're doing," she said, looking him directly in the eye. "I'm so happy." Her face lit up with a big smile. Lane told her he hoped to do more to spruce up the complex and to put a stop to the shooting and the drug dealing. Already, the sweeps had had some effect. Violent crime, though it by no means disappeared, was down. The gangs had moved some of their drug operations elsewhere. Lane was about to leave when the woman, still smiling, hollered after him, "I opened my bedroom window for the first time in about seven years last night and got some air. I slept good last night." Lane turned and smiled. "I'm so happy," she repeated. "Any way I can help you, I'll be here."

Lane would still like to sweep Henry Horner and all the buildings in the other nineteen complexes, but money from the Department of Housing and Urban Development has not been forthcoming.

Chicago Commons has expanded its Better Days for Youth program, which saw Lafeyette as one of its first participants. A new $750,000 grant from the Department of Health and Human Services will allow Chicago Commons to launch a major gang- and drug-prevention program for children up to seventeen in Horner and nearby neighborhoods. It has also expanded its literacy program and is making an effort to put together its own library for the neighborhood children. A drug rehabilitation center for young mothers plans to open at the boarded-up Mary Thompson Hospital, just a couple of blocks from Horner. And the juvenile court is doubling the number of courtrooms to accommodate the overload of cases.

Dawn and Demetrius finally got an apartment in another housing complex, the ABLA Homes, where Craig had lived. They are now on the fourteenth floor of a sixteen-story high-rise. Their apartment is sparsely furnished, but they're doing everything they can to get by. Dawn got pregnant again and tried to have an abortion, but it cost too much. She now has five kids. Her new son is named Demone. Although she hasn't found permanent work, she spent six weeks, while pregnant, going door to door for the U.S. Census. Demetrius continues to watch the kids and lands an occasional job repairing cars. They rarely visit Horner.

Terence expects to get out of prison sometime in 1991. He has earned his high school equivalency and continues to write regularly to his family. LaShawn, Brian, and their three children live with LaJoe. Paul, the boys' oldest brother, moved out of the apartment with his girlfriend. They got their own apartment elsewhere in Horner. Paul, the boys' father, found a part-time job with a moving company. After his first few days on the job, he was able to give LaJoe money to buy Tammie and Tiffany sandals for the July Fourth holiday.

A Note on Reporting Methods

IN REPORTING this book, I spent a good deal of time just hanging out with Pharoah and Lafeyette, sometimes as much as four to five days a week. We watched TV together, played basketball, and sat in their room talking. We ate at nearby restaurants, where I would conduct interviews, some of them tape-recorded. LaJoe was like a second pair of eyes and ears for me. She relayed incidents involving her children that I would talk about with them at a later date. LaJoe and I met regularly over a three-year period.

In addition to my time spent with Lafeyette, Pharoah, and their family, I interviewed over a hundred other people, including the boys' friends and neighbors, police, schoolteachers, judges, attorneys, Chicago Housing Authority officials, and local politicians. Almost everybody offered cooperation, though there were a few people who declined to be interviewed.

Of the numerous scenes in the book, I witnessed nearly half. I usually took notes at the time—and frequently went back later to question participants about the episode. Those events at which I wasn't present I re-created from interviews with people who were. Where possible, I talked to at least two participants, especially if one of them was a child. When only children were involved, like the afternoon on the railroad tracks, I returned to the location with one or more of the boys so that they could help me envision what had taken place. In those instances where dialogue was re-created, it was based on the memory of at least one of the participants, and often on the memory of two or three.

Because this book involves children, I made an extra effort to review thoughts and episodes many times not only to ensure their accuracy but also to make certain that the child felt comfortable at my including the material in the book. There were times when Lafeyette or Pharoah asked me not to write about something that had happened in his life. I obliged both boys in all cases. It was my feeling that none of those events would have altered the shape of the story. In fact, such requests usually had to do with kids' concerns, things they felt embarrassed about. Often, they didn't want to get friends into trouble. In the case of the adults, there is some material I have chosen not to write about, in almost all instances to afford those people a measure of privacy.

In the matter of the accidental shooting of Craig Davis, I relied on separate investigations conducted by the Chicago Police Department and the Bureau of Alcohol, Tobacco, and Firearms. I received the two reports as well as Craig's arrest record under the Freedom of Information Act. Both the police department and the ATF refused to discuss the case. I wrote to and called the two officers involved. Neither replied to my inquiries, except once, when Richard Marianos of the ATF returned a phone call, only to hang up when he realized why I had phoned. I talked with friends of Craig's, some of whom were with him the night he was killed, as well as family members, teachers, and his employer. With permission from the family, the Medical Examiner's Office provided me with a copy of the autopsy report.

For the chapters on Jimmie Lee, I interviewed numerous police officers, residents of Henry Horner (all of whom asked for anonymity when talking about the gangs), former gang members, and officials of the Chicago Housing Authority and the Cook County State's Attorneys' Office. I also examined extensive court records involving Lee and members of his gang. Some documents dated as far back as 1969. Jimmie Lee, on advice of counsel, declined to be interviewed for the book. At the time of this writing, his attorney was filing a postconviction appeal, claiming ineffective assistance of counsel. The Rivers family provided me with no information on the gangs.

Certain books, articles, and reports gave me historical background on Henry Horner, the neighborhood, and the Chicago Housing Authority. They have been included in the Selective

Bibliography. The Chicago Housing Authority gave me complete access to its historical files.

One final note. As I mentioned in the Preface, over the course of reporting and writing the book I became good friends with Lafeyette, Pharoah, and their family. While the family agreed to cooperate fully with the writing of this book, they did so without the promise of receiving any remuneration. There were times, however, when I helped the family financially, particularly the children, in small ways. For instance, I bought Lafeyette and Pharoah new jeans or sneakers when they needed them and their mother didn't have the money. There is one exception. When Terence was first arrested, I used $2000 I had received for the Robert F. Kennedy Journalism Award (for *The Wall Street Journal* story on Lafeyette) to bail him out.

With proceeds from the book, I intend to set up a trust fund for Lafeyette, Pharoah, and a couple of their friends. The money will be available to them when they graduate from high school. And, as I mentioned in the Epilogue, I have used money from the book to help send both boys to private school. I know there are people who will say that I became too involved with the family, that I broke my pact as a journalist to remain detached and objective. But, in the end, I had to remind myself that I was dealing with children. For them—and for me—our friendship was foremost. Anything I could do to assist them I did—and will continue to do.

Acknowledgments

THERE WERE MANY who contributed to this book, but it was the cooperation of LaJoe and her family that made it possible. They opened their hearts and their home to me. Always willing to sit down for interviews, even during the most trying of times, they were unflaggingly frank and candid in their discussions with me. They never questioned what at times must have seemed my constant presence in their home. Their decision to let me, and subsequently all the readers, into their lives was a courageous act, and it was done with the hope that it might make a difference for their children as well as for future generations.

Residents of Henry Horner, too numerous to name, guided me through the neighborhood and its history—and, as did the Riverses, opened their hearts and homes to me. Others also gave generously of their time, including James (Major) Adams of the Henry Horner Boys Club, Audrey Natcone of the Public Defender's Office, Diane Barone of the Suder school, Patricia Johnson of the YMCA's West Side Future, and Excie Seifer and Frank Seever of Chicago Commons. Lieutenant William Guswiler and the other officers of the police department's Thirteenth District tactical unit met with me periodically and offered their perspectives on the neighborhood—as did the officers of the west side's gang crimes unit.

Vincent Lane, the director of the Chicago Housing Authority, met with me regularly over a one-year period and encouraged his staff to do the same. Particular thanks to Katie Kelly, Gwen Anderson, Lillian Russell, Velma Butler, Chris Maerz, Carol Adams, James Kirby, Doug Guthrie, and Greg Burns, all, currently or formerly, of the CHA.

Two people deserve particular mention, especially since, to my regret, I could not find room for them in the book. Mildred Wortham and Brenda Stephenson, both residents of Rockwell Gardens as well as staff members of West Side Future, were my guides to the west side. These two untiring women brought me to parties and political functions, and lunched with me regularly, recounting stories of the resilience and fragility of the neighborhood's children, including their own. They were a constant source of inspiration and companionship.

I was blessed with an editor, Nan A. Talese, who was all that an author could hope for: patient, critical, and wise. My agent, David Black, spurred me on to do this book, and though I resisted initially, I'm grateful for his persistence.

Frances Apt's merciless but sensitive copy editing made it a better read. Kathy Trager of Doubleday and David Sanders of Jenner & Block gave me legal advice, guiding me through the filing of numerous Freedom of Information Act requests. Betsy Rice and Dale Eastman researched the history of the Henry Horner Homes, the Chicago Housing Authority, and the public schools. Both spent days and sometimes weeks chasing down obscure reports and studies. *The Chicago Sun-Times* graciously gave me access to their clip library. Kathy Nerat transcribed over fifty hours of taped interviews—and did so with exactness. The photographer Stephen Shames first introduced me to the Rivers family in 1985. The staff of the Erikson Institute shared with me their research on children exposed to violence. And my friends at the Ragdale Foundation gave me a place to stay and the time to write without distraction.

Norman Pearlstine, managing editor of *The Wall Street Journal*, granted me a leave from the paper and has been unflinching in his support of my reporting on the inner city. John Koten, the *Journal*'s Chicago bureau chief, has been a close friend throughout this entire project. His editorial insights helped me sculpt early drafts of the manuscript into a story with a beginning, a middle, and an end.

I am also indebted to Nancy Drew, Kevin Horan, John Houston, and Beverly Donofrio, all of whom provided suggestions and criticisms on various permutations of the manuscript. Nancy, in particular, helped fine-tune my prose. My appreciation also to John Conroy, Andrew Patner, Frank James, David

Halberstam, Sue Shellenbarger, Robert Johnson, Michael Yales, Jonathan Kaufman, Mary Decker, Jimmy Adler, and my brother Dan Kotlowitz.

Barbara Nell Hunt, a woman of unusually strong conviction, helped me in more ways than she may be aware. Her gentleness and generosity of spirit gave me comfort along the sometimes rugged journey of writing this book.

Finally, there are Horner's children. Adlous Huxley once wrote that "children are remarkable for their intelligence and ardour, for their curiosity, their intolerance of shams, the clarity and ruthlessness of their vision." So it was with Lafeyette, Pharoah, James, Rickey, and the other children of the neighborhood. Their resilience, resourcefulness, and vision have been an inspiration to me. Their friendship has enriched my life. This book is for them.

Selective Bibliography

I RELIED ON ARTICLES, some dating back over thirty years, from *The Chicago Tribune*, *The Chicago Sun-Times*, *The Chicago Defender*, *The Chicago Reporter*, *The Chicago Reader*, the former *Chicago Daily News*, and various local and national news magazines, including *Chicago Times*, *Chicago* magazine, *Newsweek*, *Time*, *The New Republic*, *Look*, and *The New Yorker*. What follows is a list of the books and reports that I found particularly useful.

ANSON, ROBERT SAM. *Best Intentions: The Education and Killing of Edmund Perry.* New York: Random House, 1987.

ARLEN, MICHAEL. *An American Verdict.* New York: Doubleday, 1973.

AULETTA, KEN. *The Underclass.* New York: Random House, 1983.

BALDWIN, JAMES. *The Fire Next Time.* New York: Dial Press, 1963.

BOWLY, JR., DEVEREUX. *The Poorhouse: Subsidized Housing in Chicago, 1895–1976.* Carbondale: Southern Illinois University Press, 1978.

Chicago Bar Association report. "Special Committee to Study the Juvenile Justice System in Cook County," May 1989.

The Chicago Tribune staff. "Chicago Schools: 'Worst in America,' " May 1988.

FREMON, DAVID K. *Chicago Politics Ward by Ward.* Bloomington: Indiana University Press, 1988.

GITTENS, JOAN. "The Children of the State: Delinquent Children in Illinois, 1818–1980s." The Chapin Hall Center for Children at the University of Chicago, 1986.

GOLD, MARTIN, et al. "Experiment in the Streets: The Chicago Youth Development Project." Institute for Social Research, c. 1968.

HAGEDORN, JOHN M., with MACON, PERRY. *People and Folks: Gangs, Crime and the Underclass in a Rustbelt City.* Chicago: Lake View Press, 1988.

HARRIS, FRED R., and WILKINS, ROGER W., editors. *Quiet Riots: Race and Poverty in the United States.* New York: Pantheon, 1988.

HIRSCH, ARNOLD R. *Making of the Second Ghetto: Race and Housing in Chicago, 1940–1960.* New York: Cambridge University Press, 1983.

Institute for Community Design Analysis report. "Review and Analysis of the Chicago Housing Authority and Implementation of Recommended Changes." January 31, 1982.

KEISER, R. LINCOLN. *The Vice Lords: Warriors of the Streets.* New York: Holt, Rinehart and Winston, 1969.

MEYERSON, MARTIN, and BANFIELD, EDWARD C. *Politics, Planning and the Public Interest: The Case of Public Housing in Chicago.* New York: The Free Press, 1955.

National Commission on Urban Problems, "More Than Shelters: Social Needs in Low- and Moderate-Income Housing," 1968.

ROSENBLATT, ROGER. *Children of War.* New York: Doubleday, 1983.

SILBERMAN, CHARLES E., *Criminal Violence, Criminal Justice.* Random House, 1978.

SLAYTON, ROBERT A. "Chicago's Public Housing Crisis: Causes and Solutions." Chicago Urban League, June 1988.

SPEAR, ALLAN H. BLACK. *Chicago: The Making of a Negro Ghetto, 1890–1920.* Chicago: The University of Chicago Press, 1967.

U.S. Department of Housing and Urban Development, "Management Review of the Chicago Housing Authority," November 5, 1986–April 17, 1987.

U.S. General Accounting Office. "Chicago Housing Authority Taking Steps to Address Longstanding Problems," June 1989.

U.S. Riot Commission, "Report of the National Advisory Commission on Civil Disorders." New York: Bantam Books, 1968.

WILSON, WILLIAM JULIUS. "The Truly Disadvantaged: the Inner City, the Underclass and Public Policy." Chicago: The University of Chicago Press, 1987.

WOOD, ELIZABETH. "Housing Design: A Social Theory." Citizens Housing and Planning Council, May 1961.

——. "Public Housing and Mrs. McGee." Citizens Housing and Planning Council, October 24, 1956.

Index